Essentials of Online Teaching

Teachers' active online participation and engagement with students are critical factors to the success of online courses. *Essentials of Online Teaching* is a standards-based, straightforward guide to teaching online in higher education, high school and vocational training, or corporate learning environments. This brief but powerful book encourages immediate application of concepts with the help of real-world examples, technical insights, and professional advice.

The guide includes:

- a practical approach informed by, but not about, relevant learning theories;
- clear models and examples from a wide variety of online courses;
- teachers' reflections about their online practice;
- a checklist of standards to help guide teaching decisions; and
- an accompanying website (www.essentialsonlineteaching. com) with additional resources.

Essentials of Online Teaching addresses key instructional challenges in online teaching and presents the reader with practical solutions for each phase of a course—preparation, beginning, middle, and end.

Margaret Foley McCabe works with universities and other institutions to provide quality online programs through her consulting company, GoodTeachingOnline.com. She launched her first online faculty development program for The New School, in 1994.

Patricia González-Flores promotes teaching innovation at the Department of Educational Development and Curriculum Innovation of the National Autonomous University of Mexico. For more than 25 years, she has participated in distance education initiatives in both corporate and academic contexts.

Essentials of Online Learning Series

Series Editor: Marjorie Vai

Essentials of Online Course Design: A Standards-Based Guide, Second Edition
Marjorie Vai and Kristen Sosulski

Essentials for Blended Learning: A Standards-Based Guide
Jared Stein and Charles Graham

Essentials of Online Teaching: A Standards-Based Guide
Margaret Foley McCabe and Patricia González-Flores

Essentials of Online Teaching

A Standards-Based Guide

Margaret Foley McCabe and
Patricia González-Flores

Routledge
Taylor & Francis Group

NEW YORK AND LONDON

First published 2017
by Routledge
711 Third Avenue, New York, NY 10017

and by Routledge
2 Park Square, Milton Park, Abingdon, Oxon, OX14 4RN

Routledge is an imprint of the Taylor & Francis Group, an informa business

Library of Congress Cataloging in Publication Data
A catalog record for this book has been requested

ISBN: 978-1-138-92053-8 (hbk)
ISBN: 978-1-138-92054-5 (pbk)
ISBN: 978-1-315-68690-5 (ebk)

Typeset in Helvetica
by Florence Production Ltd, Stoodleigh, Devon, UK

We dedicate this book to the memory of Stephen Anspacher, a visionary in distance education who brought us together.

Stephen knew that true progress in online learning comes from teachers' innovative use of technologies. It is their willingness to reach students in new ways that propels discovery in this field.

Contents

Acknowledgments   xi
About the Authors   xiii

Introduction to This Guide   1

i.1   The Distinction Between Course Design
       and Teaching   1
i.2   A Unique Guide for Online Teaching   2
i.3   Who Will Benefit from This Guide?   3
i.4   A Standards-Based Approach   4
i.5   Organization of the Book   6
i.6   Chapter Features   8
i.7   Terminology   8

1. Orientation to Online Teaching   10

1.1   Evolution of Online Education   11
1.2   A Spectrum of Online Course Models   12
1.3   The Online Environment   20
1.4   Attributes of Online Teaching and Learning   23
1.5   Online Teaching Responsibilities   24
1.6   Example: Overview of a Week Online   26
1.7   Time Expectation for Teachers   30
1.8   Summary and Standards   32
       References and Further Reading   33

2. Factors That Influence Online Teaching   35

2.1   Online Teaching   36
2.2   Online Learners   39
2.3   Course Content and Learning Objectives   40
2.4   The Online Environment and the Tools
       Used   42

2.5 The Mission and Priorities of the Host
     Institution   45
2.6 Influences in Action: Sample Course   46
2.7 Summary and Standards   52
    References and Further Reading   53

3. Teaching with Digital Tools and Resources   56

3.1 Supporting Learning with Digital Resources
    and Tools   57
3.2 Communicating with Students   60
3.3 Sharing Resources with Students   70
3.4 Assessing and Grading Student Learning   81
3.5 Creating Collaborative Resources   88
3.6 Beyond the LMS   92
3.7 Summary and Standards   96
    References and Further Reading   98

4. Preparing to Teach Online   99

4.1 Planning Your Teaching   101
4.2 Defining the Course's Time Frame   108
4.3 Setting the Stage for Interaction   114
4.4 Preparing Course Materials   121
4.5 Establishing Procedures for Technical
    Failures   122
4.6 Summary and Standards   123
    References and Further Reading   125

5. The Beginning Weeks: Launching an Online Course   126

5.1 Helping Students to Work in the
    Environment   127
5.2 Encouraging Communication   134
5.3 Building Self-Directed Learning Skills   148
5.4 Reflective Teaching: Learning as You Go   152
5.5 Summary and Standards   153
    References and Further Reading   155

6. The Middle Weeks: Facilitating Online Learning   156

6.1	Guiding Students Through the Plan	157
6.2	Humanizing the Online Environment	162
6.3	Gathering Information About Your Students' Progress	165
6.4	Improving Your Course	172
6.5	Example of the Course Improvement Strategy in Action	176
6.6	Summary and Standards	183
	References and Further Reading	184

7. The Ending Weeks: Synthesizing and Extending Learning   186

7.1	Helping Students to Reach the Finish Line	187
7.2	Promoting Self-Directed Learning	190
7.3	Reviewing and Synthesizing Learning	193
7.4	Concluding the Course	197
7.5	Summary and Standards	201
	References and Further Reading	202

8. Online Collaboration   204

8.1	Weighing the Benefits and Drawbacks of Collaboration	205
8.2	What Makes a Good Collaborative Discussion?	210
8.3	What Makes Successful Group Work?	221
8.4	Summary and Standards	234
	References and Further Reading	236

9. Online Assessment   238

9.1	Communicating a Clear Assessment Plan	239
9.2	Gathering a Variety of Information About Students' Learning	247
9.3	Providing Ongoing Feedback	254
9.4	Sharing Responsibilities for Providing Feedback	258
9.5	Guarding Against Cheating and Plagiarism	262
9.6	Summary and Standards	264
	References and Further Reading	266

10. Pulling It All Together: An Online Teacher in Action   268

10.1   The Teacher and the Course   269

10.2   Factors That Influence Online Teaching   271

10.3   Digital Tools and Resources   276

10.4   Preparing to Teach Online   279

10.5   The Beginning Weeks   281

10.6   The Middle Weeks   285

10.7   The Ending Weeks   288

10.8   The Essentials of Online Teaching   291

10.9   Summary and Standards   292

      References and Further Reading   292

Appendix A: Using the Standards Checklist   293

Index   299

Acknowledgments

We are grateful to all the online teachers with whom we have worked over the past 25 years. Your creativity inspires us. We are indebted to the following teachers for sharing their experience and expertise with us for this book:

Joyce Anderson, Instructor of English at Millersville University, Millersville, PA.

William Archibald, Assistant Professor of English at Millersville University, Millersville, PA.

Tisha Bender, Assistant Professor in the English Writing Program, Online Teacher Trainer and Hybrid Coordinator at Rutgers University, New Brunswick, NJ.

Carmen Coronado, Educational Design Coordinator and Professor at the Virtual University System of Universidad de Guadalajara, Guadalajara, Mexico.

Robert Dunn, Associate Teaching Professor in the Writing Program at The New School for Social Research, New York, NY.

Daniel Eastmond, Evaluation Manager and IRB Chair at Western Governors University, Salt Lake City, UT.

Benjamín Mayer-Foulkes, Professor, Founder and Director of 17, Instituto de Estudios Críticos, Mexico City, Mexico.

Rosario Freixas, Professor of Social Research at the Universidad Nacional Autónoma de México, Mexico City, Mexico.

Thomas M. Geary, Associate Professor of English at Tidewater Community College, Virginia Beach, VA.

Damien Mansell, Senior Lecturer in Geography at the University of Exeter, Exeter, United Kingdom.

María Pescina, Accounting and Finances Professor at the Universidad Virtual Liverpool in Mexico City, Mexico.

Allen Stairs, Professor of Philosophy at the University of Maryland, College Park, MD.

Scott Thornbury, Associate Professor of English Language Studies at The New School for Social Research, New York, NY.

Adrienne Wheeler, Professor in the Computer Information Systems Department at Baruch College, New York, NY.

Sepi Yalda, Professor of Meteorology at Millersville University, Millersville, PA.

Our sincere thanks to: **Dr. Yolanda Gayol** and **Joan Marlow Foley** for their close reading of the text; **María León González** for the cartoon in Chapter 3; **Lorenzo Ceballos Caballero** and **Samantha Fernández González** for the book illustrations; **Emma Martínez Yanes** for her meticulous help in preparing the manuscript; **Mois Cherem**, **Raúl Maldonado**, and **Jorge Camil** for the generous accommodations they made to support this project; and the **Enova Contents Team** for their help with the graphic requirements. We are grateful for **Marjorie Vai's** invitation to contribute to this series and her commitment to its quality.

Our love and thanks to our families for their patience and support throughout this undertaking: **Kevin**, **Liam**, **Kerrigan**, **Ronan**, and **Ted McCabe**, and **José Luis**, **María**, and **Ana Sofía León**.

About the Authors

Margaret Foley McCabe has been at the forefront of online course design and teaching since 1994, when she launched the first faculty development program for the Distance Instruction for Adult Learners (DIAL) program at The New School in New York City. She holds a Doctorate of Education from Teachers College Columbia University, specializing in Curriculum and Teaching. Margaret has a diverse background in education, teaching and leading programs in: interdisciplinary curriculum design (Teachers College Columbia University); online learning (The New School for Social Research, University of Reading in the United Kingdom, Millersville University in PA, University of North Carolina, Charlotte, and University of Maryland); and arts and dance education (New York City Ballet and Lincoln Center Institute). She currently works with universities and other institutions to provide quality online programs through her consulting company, GoodTeachingOnline.com.

Patricia González-Flores has 25 years of experience designing, planning, and implementing educational systems that use technology to promote learning. She has worked launching distance education and online learning initiatives in the public and private sector (National Autonomous University of Mexico, *UNAM*); The New School in NY; the Matías Romero Diplomat Academy of the Mexican Foreign Affairs Ministry; the Mexican Ministry of Education; and the Universidad Virtual Liverpool, a corporate university in Mexico). As a consultant, Patricia has designed corporate online training courses for organizations such as IBM, Coca-Cola Export, Banco Santander, the Mexican Ministry of Health, and the University for International Cooperation (Costa Rica). She served as the Education Director at Enova, an organization that aims to reduce the digital divide in Mexico and has recently joined the Department of Educational Development and Curriculum Innovation at UNAM. Patricia holds a master's degree in Media Studies from The New School in New York.

Introduction to This Guide

> The real value [of online education] will continue to come from learning opportunities that involve an educator working directly with a student.
>
> (Joshua Kim, 2014)

Teaching is—and has always been—about making authentic connections with students. Whether online or in the classroom, teaching requires presence and actions that respond to students' needs in order to promote learning. **Essentials of Online Teaching: A Standards-Based Guide focuses on the online teacher as a decision-maker on the frontlines of engagement with students.** The information and standards of best practice offered will help teachers make informed decisions as they teach an online course.

i.1 The Distinction Between Course Design and Teaching

Developing and teaching an online course is a process that evolves along a continuum.

First, an **online course is designed**. During this phase:

- Learning outcomes are named.

- Learning activities are designed and sequenced.

- Learning resources (books, articles, videos, podcasts, data, experts, etc.) are identified or produced.

- The whole plan for the course is laid out in the online course syllabus that shows how all the elements of the course fit together.

Next comes a **preparation phase** in which the teacher readies the online course for students. Whether the teacher or someone else has designed the course, he or she has to decide how to put the course design into action. This involves careful consideration of the intent behind the design, as well as the context in which it will be taught.

Once the semester begins, the course takes on a life of its own. **The beginning, middle, and ending weeks of the semester can be seen as different phases, each with its own set of dynamics and instructional challenges.**

Figure i.1 A Diagram of the Continuum from Online Course Design Through Instruction

This book walks you through a teacher's process from the design phase through instruction. We look at what a teacher needs to do to prepare to teach online and ready the online learning environment for the students. We describe instructional challenges and solutions from the beginning weeks of an online semester, through the middle weeks, to the end of the course. Explanations and examples from online courses are offered to help you understand the factors involved in online instructional decisions.

i.2 A Unique Guide for Online Teaching

This book features:

- **Voices of online teachers.** We draw from our work with hundreds of online teachers over the past 25 years. Sixteen of these teachers from around the United States, Mexico, England, and Spain share their experience and advice about online teaching in these pages. Their courses range in subject matter from the sciences to liberal arts and represent a range of instructional approaches as well.

- **Standards of practice.** The standards describe best practices based on research, learning theory, and experience. They identify specific situations that require teachers to make decisions and highlight principles to guide instruction.

- **Clear explanations and examples.** The book combines text, illustrations, and examples from online courses to clarify the concepts explored. The concise and jargon-free language makes the text easy to understand.

- **Practical information.** This book provides guidance to prepare, launch, and teach a successful online course. We do not assume that the reader is an expert in the technologies used in online teaching and learning. The basic tools, resources, and functions of the online teaching and learning tools are described in simple terms. However, teachers new to technology may require additional technical support and training.

- **Sound pedagogy.** The educational rationale for the recommendations and standards of practice offered throughout this guide is thoroughly explained.

- **An accompanying website.** Excerpts from the interviews with online teachers, examples of online teaching materials, technical resources, research on online learning, and other related information are available on this book's website: **www.essentialsofonlineteaching.com**

WEB

i.3 Who Will Benefit from This Guide?

Teachers who are new to online teaching or those who want to improve their practice will benefit from the analysis and suggestions offered in *Essentials of Online Teaching*. The book draws primarily from examples from higher education and college courses.

Trainers in corporate and other educational contexts can also apply the suggestions and standards cited because the underlying theory and base research pertain to a wider range of online learning situations.

Faculty development professionals who support online teachers will find this book useful as a resource for their training efforts. The structure of the book outlines critical issues they will need to address. The checklist of standards provides a focus for mentoring faculty. The standards-based models and examples reduce the burden on these instructors to provide such resources on their own.

Academic administrators, department heads, and decision-makers, such as managers, chief learning officers, and board members, can use this book to understand the characteristics and qualities that make an effective online course. The descriptions, examples, and analysis offered in this guide provide a nuanced look inside the online classroom that will help them make decisions as the demands for online programs intensify.

Students and teachers of education will be interested in the discussion of online pedagogy offered. Many schools of education are adding courses and even departments to address the changing demands of teaching in the twenty-first century. They recognize the importance of preparing teachers for classes that are no longer bound to traditional curriculum rules.

Entrepreneurs and individuals that work with online course development and training can use this book to understand the challenges online instructors and trainers face and design products to serve their needs.

Anyone interested in education will find that this guide offers a fresh look at online teaching, including how it differs from online course design. It also clarifies the different online course models that are popular today.

i.4 A Standards-Based Approach

The standards offered throughout this guide describe best practices of online teaching. They serve as a checklist to help teachers make and evaluate instructional decisions as they plan and teach a course over a semester.

We present the standards in three stages:

1. In each chapter as they are covered. At this stage, they look like this:

   ☑ **Learning activities and ease of use determine the best technologies to use.**

2. Next, all standards covered in a chapter are listed at the end of the chapter. Use this summary to review the points covered in the chapter.

   ☐ **Learning activities and ease of use determine the best technologies to use.**

3. Finally, "Appendix A: Using the Standards Checklist" organizes the standards topically for easy reference and use. To simplify the review of each standard, it is here followed by the page(s) and chapter(s) it appears on.

   ☐ **Learning activities and ease of use determine the best technologies to use. (C2, p. 45) (C3, p. 60)**

Underlying Principles

The standards cited take into account the definitions of quality online teaching generally accepted in the field today. We draw from the following resources and our own experiences with online education to present and reinforce the standards in a straightforward and constructive way:

Chao, T., Saj, T., & Tessier, F. (2006). *Establishing a Quality Review for Online Courses*. Retrieved from http://net.educause.edu

Council for the Advancement of Standards in Higher Education. (2014). *CAS Professional Standards for Higher Education*. Retrieved from www.cas.edu

Hanover Research Council. (2004). *Best Practices in Online Teaching Strategies*. Retrieved from www.uwec.edu

International Association for K-12 Online Learning. (2011). *National Standards for Quality Online Teaching*. Retrieved from www.inacol.org

Online Learning Consortium. (2016). *The Five Pillars of Quality Framework*. Retrieved from www.onlinelearningconsortium.org

Quality Matters. (2014). *Standards from the QM Higher Education Rubric* (5th ed.). Retrieved from www.qualitymatters.org

The analysis of online courses and the recommendations made throughout this book are influenced by the foundational theorists in distance education, including: Börge Holmberg, Michael G. Moore, and Desmond Keegan, as well as many researchers in the online environment such as Tony Bates, Linda Harasim, Robin Mason, Daniel Eastmond, D. Randy Garrison, Terry Anderson, Elizabeth Burge, and Morten Flate Paulsen.

Note: A full list of sources and references is provided at the end of each chapter.

i.5 Organization of the Book

The first three chapters provide an introduction to online teaching.

- **Chapter 1: Orientation to Online Teaching** presents a brief overview of online education from its roots in distance learning to the wide range of online course models popular today.

- **Chapter 2: Factors That Influence Online Teaching** looks at how context affects instruction. We focus on the importance of the teacher, the students, the online learning environment, and the host institution as factors that influence best practices.

- **Chapter 3: Teaching with Digital Tools and Resources** describes the basic technologies needed to teach online.

Chapters 4–7 walk you through the process of preparing and teaching an online course throughout a semester.

- **Chapter 4: Preparing to Teach Online** focuses on what a teacher needs to do **before** the semester begins. We examine what teachers do to ready themselves and the course to support their online learners.

- **Chapter 5: The Beginning Weeks** gives suggestions on how to launch a successful online course. We highlight procedural, social, and academic needs that teachers address in the first weeks of the semester to get students on board and comfortable in the online learning routines.

- **Chapter 6: The Middle Weeks** looks at how teachers monitor and support students' learning once the course has begun. This chapter also addresses ways teachers evaluate the effectiveness of the course design and make improvements as necessary.

- **Chapter 7: The Ending Weeks** discusses how to end a course in a satisfying way. Many students need help fulfilling end-of-course requirements and reaching learning outcomes. We offer suggestions and standards that point to ways teachers can help.

Chapters 8 and 9 provide an in-depth look at two critical areas of online teaching and learning: collaboration and assessment.

- **Chapter 8: Online Collaboration** provides explanations and examples of how discussions and small group work can be carried out online. We offer practical advice on discussion prompts, grouping, and facilitating collaboration.

- **Chapter 9: Online Assessment** addresses how teachers evaluate students' progress online and use the information to promote learning and improve instruction.

Finally, in Chapter 10, we close with an example of how the standards are put into practice.

- **Chapter 10: Pulling It All Together** focuses on one teacher's experience of teaching an online course as a case study to illustrate the standards in practice.

i.6 Chapter Features

We incorporate information in boxes throughout the book. These boxes enrich the narrative and can be read independently.

- **Personal Reflections** offer teacher reflections about different aspects of online instruction.

- **Descriptions of digital tools and resources** follow a consistent format, addressing:
  - **what** the tool is;
  - **why** to use it; and
  - **how** it functions.

- **Real-world examples** include screenshots (reproduced for clarity) from online courses and excerpts from teacher/student communications.

- **Teaching Dilemmas** highlight decisions or controversies that teachers may face as they teach online and do not have clear-cut answers.

- **Teaching Tips** are suggestions that apply to many, but not all, situations.

i.7 Terminology

For the sake of consistency and simplicity, we have used the following words and phrases as follows:

Course designer: the person or team of people who plan, write, and lay out the online course before it is taught. Teachers, instructional designers, information technologists, and administrators may be involved in the course design process. Or it may just be the course teacher who creates it.

Course design: the strategic plan for an online course that is laid out in the syllabus, the course outline, and the online course materials. It includes:

- a description of the course purpose, content, and objectives;

- the learning outcomes;

- an outline of weekly study units;

- the sequence of learning activities;

- the core learning resources; and

- the means of assessing students' progress towards the learning outcomes.

Online course: any course in which the content is taught through digital devices and networks (see Chapter 1, p. 12, for an in-depth discussion of the term).

On-site course: a course that is taught in a physical location where teachers and learners are present in a face-to-face setting.

Learning Management System (LMS): the technical platform that serves as the "virtual classroom" to facilitate online course activity. It is used to design, develop, teach, and manage online courses. (Note: Other technical terms are defined within the text as they appear and cross-referenced throughout the book. They can also be found in the index.)

Teacher: the course instructor, professor, facilitator, tutor, or trainer. This book is directed towards teachers and often uses the second person "you" to refer directly to the reader as a teacher.

Student/learner: the individual who is taking the online course. While we recognize that these terms can have different emphasis, we use them interchangeably throughout the book.

Chapter 1 Orientation to Online Teaching

What's the first image that comes to mind when you hear the term "online course?" If you ask 10 people this question, you may get 10 different answers. To some, the term describes a self-paced online tutorial. Others think of a collaborative experience in which teachers and students interact online over a semester. Still others will describe courses in which 100,000 people engage with free learning resources online. There are so many different models and variations of online courses that it can be difficult to have a meaningful discussion about best practices within this growing industry. But that's just what we intend to do.

This book is designed to help teachers teach effectively online. So we begin by defining the terrain to help us establish a shared context. A brief overview of the evolution of online education is provided to situate our discussion. We then describe some of the basic features of online learning environments and draw distinctions among different models of online courses commonly offered today. Finally, we look at the variety of roles an online teacher fulfills to support students' learning and present an example of a teacher's online routine.

Online education is evolving at a mind-boggling pace. As we seek to take advantage of new technologies to reach students, it is important that we keep in mind what generations of research and practice have taught us about learning. After all, technology simply provides a means to transfer ideas, but learning is still a very human activity. The principles of sound educational practice continue to be as relevant online as anywhere.

The suggestions and standards offered throughout this guide are based on three assumptions:

1. Teaching is important to the learning process.

2. Online education is a viable context for learning.

3. Effective online teaching requires sound pedagogy and knowledge about the online environment.

We encourage teachers to find ways to actively engage with their students online and make informed instructional decisions as they do.

1.1 Evolution of Online Education

For more than a century, distance educators have created alternative formats to offer education based on the principle that media can be used to perform some of the teaching functions. For example, in early correspondence courses, content was presented through printed materials developed to enable a "guided didactic conversation" (Holmberg, 1989). Tutors—who communicated with students through the telephone or correspondence—offered individualized support, answered students' questions, and graded students' assignments. Instruction relied on carefully designed materials, while teachers advised and graded.

Online learning stems from the same principle and represents a new generation of distance education (Moore & Kearsley, 2005). In the course design phase, content delivery and learning activities are carefully planned, and multimedia resources are produced. A syllabus is strategically crafted and provides detailed instructions. When the course is taught, teachers support students as they work through the activities. Direct instruction from teachers may be required, but less intensely than in on-site courses. Assessing students' progress and offering feedback continue to be important in order to help students master the learning outcomes.

For students, the experience can be disjointed. They are responsible for making sense of the pieces. Here is where the teacher's intervention becomes critical. Independent learners might be able to achieve the learning outcomes by themselves, but many others will need the help of an expert who knows the content and understands the course structure, progression, and potential trouble spots.

Institutions of higher education began offering courses online in the late 1980s and early 1990s, as computer networks became available. Early efforts used text-based computer conferencing to connect teachers and learners. Faster connectivity and new technologies allowed for better graphical interfaces and wider communication options for teaching and learning. The global expansion of the Internet over the past 20 years has helped online learning become an emerging frontier of education. The sheer number of online students today (estimated at 7.1 million just in the United States in 2013) is evidence of the excitement and promise of this educational platform (Allen & Seaman, 2013).

Online learning is an important alternative for the growth of an educational institution. It can serve students unable to participate in traditional programs, and it reduces the pressure on physical facilities. The Internet provides global access to resources. Communication networks and tools enable ever-more sophisticated ways to share information. Students can put together their own educational paths by selecting online offerings that address their personal interests and needs.

1.2 A Spectrum of Online Course Models

An **online course**, according to the Babson Survey Research Group, is a course in which "80% or more of the content is delivered through digital devices and networks" (Allen & Seaman, 2016). This means that the teaching and learning in an online course happens mainly through the Internet. This is a useful definition that distinguishes online courses from those that use the technology to augment classroom learning. Table 1.1 presents different content delivery modes popular in courses today.

Table 1.1 Types of Courses by Delivery Mode

Type of Course	Percentage of Content Delivered Online	Description
Traditional or face-to-face	0%	Content is delivered on-site in oral or printed format.
Web-facilitated or technology-enhanced	1–29%	Web-based technologies are used to support a face-to-face course.
Blended/hybrid	30–79%	Online and face-to-face instruction are combined, so that the number of on-site sessions are reduced.
Online	80% or more	All or most of the content is delivered through digital devices and networks.

Source: Adapted from Allen & Seaman (2016)

If you are interested in finding effective ways of weaving online and on-site learning, refer to *Essentials for Blended Learning: A Standards-Bases Guide* (Stein & Graham, 2014).

The "80% rule" does little to clarify the practical definition of an online course. What does it mean to take an online course? Participating in an online course can mean anything, from watching a series of video lectures to completing a semester's workload for an accredited online course. The vagueness of terminology adds confusion and lessens credibility for more intensive online courses.

A competency is the capacity to perform tasks or face situations successfully in a specific context, applying knowledge, skills, and attitudes in an integrated and interrelated way (Zabala & Arnau, 2010).

There is a wide variety of online courses that differ in their instructional orientation, format, and methods. Some common models include online seminars/workshops, competency-based programs, webinars/webcasts and Massive Open Online Courses (MOOCs). Table 1.2 summarizes basic characteristics of each of these models. These categories are intended to be descriptive rather than definitive of any particular model and illustrate popular online practices. Many online courses combine components from various models to serve different purposes and students' needs.

We present examples to illustrate how each of these online course models work in practice on pages 14–17, after Table 1.2.

Table 1.2 Common Online Instructional Models

Model	Description	Group Size
Seminar/ workshop	Learning is promoted through structured discussion and activities where students build knowledge with the support of teachers. Digital resources may be used to deliver content. Students complete assignments, often work collaboratively, and may take quizzes and tests.	Small (i.e. 5–25)
Competency-based/tutorials	Learning focuses on the mastery of discrete knowledge or skill sets. Students use resources, work individually through sequenced activities, and complete assessments to demonstrate proficiency.	Individual study
Webinars/ webcasts	Teachers and students log on at designated times to participate in live sessions. Teachers present information, and coordinate discussion and activities. Instant messaging, screen sharing, and classroom management tools allow students to participate.	Small for webinars (i.e. 5–25) Large for webcasts (i.e. 100+)
Massive Open Online Course (MOOC)	Students view lectures recorded by instructors, complete activities or quizzes, and participate in large-scale open discussion forums.	Unlimited

Online Seminar
Introduction to Logic (20 students)

Allen Stairs teaches a philosophy seminar online for the University of Maryland College of Arts and Humanities in the United States. Over the 15 weeks of the semester, Allen's students watch mini-lectures that he creates to introduce the weeks' topics. Students also read chapters from books and selected articles. Allen participates actively in the online discussion with his students. He provides feedback, adds relevant information, and poses questions to nudge students' thinking into new territory. He encourages students to support their contributions to the discussion with information gained from the learning resources and to interact with their classmates. The students write weekly essays, two research papers, and take an open-book midterm and final exam. Allen grades and gives instructional feedback on all of the students' work. The learning outcomes are the same as those for the on-site course taught on campus (4 credits).

Online Workshop
Creative Writing (15 students)

Robert Dunn teaches a writing workshop online for The New School for Social Research in New York City. This course is intended to help students develop their own writing projects. His students read published short stories, articles about writing, and their classmates' writing projects as the basis for their online discussion. The discussion focuses on the craft of writing and the skills of critical review. Students use the discussion forum to learn about successful writing conventions and how they can apply these techniques to their own writing. The students share their original stories by posting them as blogs. Classmates review each other's work and provide constructive feedback. The peer-review process gives Robert information about the students' works and about students' ability to analyze and critique writing. Robert participates actively in the discussions, reads and responds to students' writing projects, and oversees the peer-review process. Grades are based on participation, peer review, and effort and quality of written work. The online workshop shares the same learning outcomes as the campus-based creative writing workshop (3 credits).

Competency-Based Online Course
Western Governors University (individualized study)

Western Governors University (WGU) is an online, competency-based, not-for-profit university that allows students to progress toward a degree by demonstrating what  they know and can do rather than credit hours. Each degree program WGU offers is developed in collaboration with a council of experts who define the competencies students need to master to graduate.

WGU's learning model is guided independent study, allowing students to move through courses as rapidly as their prior knowledge and current effort allow. For many courses, students can take a pre-assessment to understand their starting level of competence associated with course subject matter. If the student and his or her course mentor agree that the student is fully competent through prior learning from academic or work experience, the student can proceed directly to the final assessment. If the student passes (with a minimum score of the equivalent of a B grade or better), the student passes the course. However, in most cases, students will lack some competencies and will need to develop those by using the learning resources (usually online, interactive, multimedia, self-paced material) and individualized instruction if needed. Once the student has successfully completed the required assessments for a course, he or she moves on to the next course.

This model allows students to study and learn on schedules that fit their lives, moving quickly through material they already know so they can focus on what they still need to learn. WGU's competency-based learning model allows many students to accelerate their progress to a degree—the average time to complete a bachelor's degree at WGU is about two and a half years.

WGU faculty are called mentors because they work with students individually to help them progress through courses and their degree programs. Student mentors serve as coaches and guides to students from the day they enroll until the day they graduate. Course mentors are experts in subject matter (for each course) who are available to provide individualized instruction via phone or email. These mentors also work with groups of students in asynchronous learning communities, in cohorts using synchronous or recorded webinars to help them accelerate in mastering the target competencies. A separate group of WGU faculty members are responsible for evaluating performance assessment. Progress is marked by mastery of competencies, not a credit based system.

Webinar Course
Accounting (10 students)

María Pescina teaches a webinar-based course in accounting for Universidad Virtual Liverpool, a corporate university in Mexico. Every Monday and Wednesday for 13 weeks, Maria meets her students online for one hour. She begins the videoconferencing session by introducing the topic and explaining some core accounting concepts and formulas. The screen-sharing tools let her illustrate concepts and show examples of accounting documents, such as financial statements. She can also open a spreadsheet and share her screen with students to allow them to manipulate the data. Students can ask questions and contribute to the discussion by using their microphone or chat (see Figure 1.1 for an illustration of a videoconferencing screen). Between sessions, learners work independently on readings and assignments. As a culminating activity, students present projects during the live sessions and take tests during a webinar session. While the tests are graded automatically, María provides personalized feedback on the assignments, projects, and participation (3 credits).

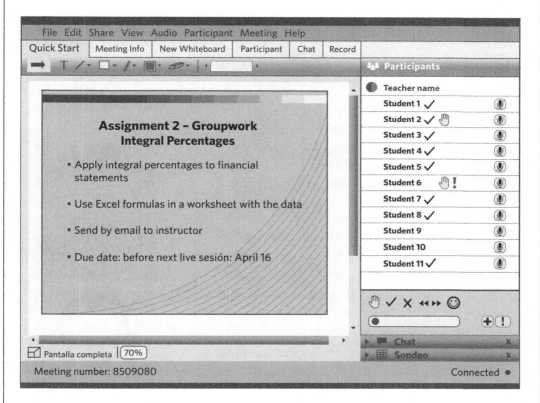

Figure 1.1 A Typical Layout of Videoconferencing Software Used for Webinars

Webinar Course
Example: ATD Watch and Learn Series (over 100 students)

The Association for Talent Development hosts a series of webcasts for professional development. During these live sessions, experts in the field share their knowledge with members. Participants from all over the world join in the ATD series to watch

and post questions. Topics such as "Building a Talent Development Structure Without Borders" or "The Five Behaviors of a Cohesive Team: Transforming Organizations with Teamwork" are covered in short stand-alone conferences broadcast through the Internet (no credit).

Massive Open Online Course (MOOC)
Climate Change: Challenges and Solutions (16,000 students)

Climate Change: Challenge and Solutions is offered by a team of eight academics led by Tim Lenton and Damien Mansell from the University of Exeter in the United Kingdom. It is distributed through FutureLearn, a platform developed by the British Open University, over an eight-week period. Students can join at any time and the material stays online after the end of the course.

This MOOC features a series of high-quality video lectures about different aspects of climate change. Several articles on the course topics are also included

in the learning resources. Students are invited to watch the lectures, read the articles, take a short automated quiz to self-test comprehension of the material covered, and bring their questions to an open discussion board. All students enrolled in the course receive automated emails, letting them know when new material is available and what to expect in the upcoming week. A team of teaching assistants monitor the discussion forums and

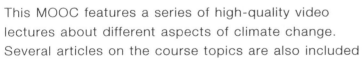

identify common or key student questions, which are shared with Tim Lenton and Damien Mansell. The questions are answered in a videotaped feedback session that serves as the wrap-up to the week's lessons. The MOOC is offered for free as a non-credit course. Students can also "buy a certificate of completion."

The instructional course models shown above differ in significant ways:

- **Focus.** Some course models serve as learning resources available to anyone interested in finding out more about a subject (MOOCs and some webinars). Others develop proficiency in discrete skills and recall of knowledge (competency-based). And some models are centered on discussion and collaborative learning (online seminars/workshops, some webinars).

- **Timing of interaction among participants.** Most models rely on asynchronous communications (not at the same time). This provides flexibility of scheduling and allows people in different time zones to participate. Webinars and webcasts use synchronous sessions (also known as live or real-time communication) as the main venue for learning for a number of reasons, including immediacy of communication and live connection.

"Asynchronous" is a term used for online interactions that do not happen at the same time; "synchronous" identifies simultaneous or real-time communication. Today, both kinds of communication are possible through the Internet.

- **Number of students served.** Seminars, workshops, and webinars serve small numbers of students (5–35). Competency-based courses, webcasts, and MOOCs serve large or unlimited numbers of students.

- **Level of teacher-student interaction.** The level of support teachers provide to individual students within each model is related to the teacher-student ratio. MOOCs use automated feedback, peer-to-peer interaction, and limited teacher-student interaction to respond to very large numbers of students. In seminars, workshops, and webinars, teachers interact directly with students and attend to their personal needs as they arise throughout the course. Competency-based courses have varied levels of support.

It's important to recognize different instructional online course models to help us establish standards of quality within them. This guide is designed for teaching that uses asynchronous communication for interaction among a limited number of participants, which is most common in the seminar/workshop model. **The strategies offered are also applicable to other models as long as they involve interaction between teachers and students.**

1.3 The Online Environment

Online courses are offered across the Internet. They are part of an interconnected global network that offers a vast array of information and services. As an online teacher, you can draw from this web of information to gather resources for your course. You can use communication networks and digital tools to share information and interact with your students in ever-more sophisticated ways.

An online course is usually offered through an institution's Learning Management System (LMS). The LMS is a technological platform that serves as the "classroom" to facilitate course activity. There are many popular LMSs with different looks and functionalities. Host institutions usually go through lengthy evaluation processes to decide on which LMS to use for all their courses and provide technical training to help teachers and students understand basic procedures for use. Table 1.3 describes common features of LMSs.

WEB

Refer to the book's website for examples of LMSs (i.e. Moodle, Canvas, Blackboard, Desire2Learn, Edmodo): www.essentialsofonlineteaching.com.

Table 1.3 Sample Learning Management System Features List

LMS Feature	Definition
Syllabus	An overview of the course in outline form; it includes objectives, requirements, etc.
Calendar	Schedule of deadlines and course events.
Teacher announcements	Teacher updates and reminders. In an online course, they usually appear upon entering the LMS.
Course email	Correspondence between course members.
Lessons	Content sections usually organized by units.
Discussion forums	Ongoing online discussions. They may include text, audio, video, and images.
Wiki	An online environment that can be shared and edited by all members of a collaborative team.
Blog	An online space where one author creates a posting (e.g. article, critique, some type of narrative) and others comment.
Testing/quizzing	Assessments that determine how successfully outcomes have been achieved. Ungraded self-assessments help learners adjust their pace and reflect on their learning.
Assignments and dropboxes	Students' products such as papers, worksheets, and multimedia projects. Students upload assignments to the LMS and the instructor grades, comments, and returns work to students. Some LMSs use a tool called dropbox for submission of work.
Portfolios	Collections of student work from current and, possibly, past courses.
Chat	An online exchange of text comments and remarks between two or more participants **in real time**.
Live classroom/live meeting	Online class sessions in which the teacher and all members are there **at the same time** and communicate using voice and video.

Source: Adapted from Vai and Sosulski (2016)

The Language of Technology

The emergence of technologies in education has introduced a new use of language that influences the way we think and talk about learning. When used in a learning context, words such as "interaction," for example, used to mean the exchange of ideas between human beings. Now, this term is used to describe the exchange of information—with or without human involvement. As innovations in technology open up new avenues of communication, the very language we use to do so reflects a shift toward automation.

"Online teaching" as concept and term sprang onto the educational landscape in the late 1980s as computer conferencing software began to support interaction between teachers and students. Suddenly, educational marketing, researchers, and program developers began talking about online teaching and e-teaching as a new category of instruction.

The language used by researchers, program developers, and marketers to describe how online courses are taught suggests an instructional shift toward automation. The word "teach" is often replaced by passive verbs. Online course are said to be "released," "disseminated," "delivered," and "installed." For example:

- "17 courses *were released* on the edX platform over a period of rapid development" (Ho et al., 2015).

- "Online courses are those in which the content is *delivered* online" (Allen & Seaman, 2016).

The passive language used in such descriptions de-emphasizes the personal action involved in teaching. The choice of language implies that the course is a product to be distributed rather than a process of human interaction. A shift toward automated instruction is not a necessary by-product of online teaching and learning. You will notice that **teaching is always described in active terms throughout this book to reinforce the notion that teaching and learning are active and interactive processes**.

1.4 # Attributes of Online Teaching and Learning

Let's look at some of the distinctive characteristics of the online environment and how they affect teaching and learning.

Asynchronous Communication

In many online courses, communication happens asynchronously. This means that **everyone in the course participates at times convenient to him or her and may not be online at the same time**. Each person works alone, even as he or she contributes to group activities. Busy people may find it easier to participate because the schedule is flexible, and students from different time zones can work together. In asynchronous discussions, participants can take their time to contribute; they can look things up and reflect before they post. This added time can add depth to students' comments. An online discussion usually happens over the course of a week or more, so every student has the opportunity to contribute.

Asynchronous communication has some drawbacks too. The wait time between posts can sometimes make the conversation feel disjointed. It can be hard to build momentum in a discussion that happens over days. Coordinating group work can also be challenging if students are participating at very different times.

Remote Access

Participants in online courses log on from anywhere they have access to the Internet. So an online course can have students, teachers, and guest speakers from different places around the world. Remote access allows people to participate in a course whose schedules, circumstances, or physical limitations may prohibit them from coming to a classroom.

Remote access also means that people are not physically present at the same place. All students work alone from their own environments, so they don't share the same immediate references. Facial expression, voice inflection, and other nonverbal cues that support face-to-face communication are omitted from text-based interaction. Differences in local connectivity can affect the students' experience.

Networked Learning

An online course exists as part of the Internet and is seamlessly connected to resources available on the global data network. So participants have immediate access to a wide range of learning resources and tools. Virtual libraries with catalogued references, e-books, and media can be linked to a course. Online communication helps students become part of a community that expands beyond the boundaries of the campus.

The amount of information available on the Internet can be overwhelming and uneven in its reliability. Networks also provide increased opportunities for plagiarism and other unethical use of material.

The characteristics of the online environment are neither good nor bad. They simply add dimensions that need to be taken into consideration as you plan and teach an online course. The goal is to find teaching strategies that capitalize on the benefits while minimizing or alleviating potential difficulties that come with the territory. The teaching suggestions, examples, and standards identified throughout this book are offered to help you understand the online context and find strategies that allow you to work effectively within the online environment.

1.5 Online Teaching Responsibilities

If there is any one secret to good teaching, it is summed up in the word "activity."

(Moore and Kearsley, 1996)

The real challenge of teaching online is to encourage students to become active participants in learning.

Most online students need the same kind of reassurance, personalized instruction, responsive feedback, and targeted challenges as students everywhere do. Depending on the instructional model of the institution, some of these teaching functions have been integrated in the course design and the teacher will perform others.

Typically, online teachers will be actively involved:

- **Guiding students.** Teachers help students navigate the online environment and the learning activities.

- **Instructing.** Teachers share information, explain concepts, make connections, and offer insight and expertise.

- **Moderating discussions.** Teachers facilitate online discussion. They prompt and respond to students' questions and encourage thoughtful dialogue.

- **Managing the group.** Teachers coordinate participation and learning events to work effectively throughout the course. They troubleshoot problems and revise plans as needed.

- **Evaluating progress.** Teachers gather, analyze, and evaluate evidence about students' learning and the course throughout the semester.

- **Providing feedback.** Teachers respond to students' contributions by offering them counsel, support, and encouragement.

- **Modeling learning.** A teacher's contributions, tone, level of participation, inquisitive responses, and shared learning demonstrate expectations for students.

While these tasks are similar to teaching activities in an on-site course, they play out differently online. Once you understand the specific features of the environment, you will be able to take advantage of the available resources and tools to support your students in new and effective ways. In the remaining chapters of this book, we focus on specific strategies to handle different kinds of learning needs, and give you suggestions for an efficient and enjoyable online teaching practice.

Online teachers can and should hold the same accountability for students' learning as classroom-based instructors.

☑ Teachers and students are active participants in the learning process.

1.6 Example: Overview of a Week Online

In online courses, students learn by working with digital content, interacting with their teacher and peers, and completing activities. A typical online teaching week might look like this:

Monday

Teacher:

- At 9 a.m., the teacher posts an announcement with instructions for the week: (1) view a video and read two articles; (2) write an essay based on the learning resources; and (3) participate in the online discussion forum.

- The teacher opens a new thread in the discussion forum with the topic to be discussed, and posts an initial response to get the ball rolling.

- He sends an email to two students (John and Mary) who did not turn in last week's assignments. He asks them if they need help and encourages them to catch up.

Students:

- Some students start logging on throughout the day, some from work, others from home or public places.

- They read the teacher's announcement, and start viewing the video and reading the assigned texts. A couple of them download the resources to their devices, but others review them online.

- Kim sends an email to the teacher to ask about the assigned essay.

- John emails the teacher to explain the technical problems he faced uploading last week's assignment.

Tuesday

Teacher:

- The teacher reads two emails from students, Kim and John.

- Since Kim asks a question about the essay assignment, the teacher responds and sends her a link where she can find an example of this type of essay. He asks her to post her question on the discussion board so he can share this information with the rest of the students.

- The teacher uploads instructions for John, who is having technical problems submitting his assignment, and refers him to the university's tech support call center.

Students:

- More students join in and start working on the unit.

- Most students continue to study the learning resources for the week.

- Some open the discussion forum and a few of them post their first comment to the week's thread. Others only read the postings.

- Kim posts her question about the essay on the discussion forum and includes the teacher's link to an example.

Wednesday

Teacher:

- The teacher logs on and reads the students' comments on the discussion forum. He posts follow-up questions that require students to support their comments with further analysis and examples.

- He notices that only two-thirds of the group has participated, so he adds a message inviting the other students—by name—to join in.

Students:

- Students continue joining in and studying the learning resources for the week.

- Some start doing the research for the essay that needs to be turned in by Sunday midnight.

- Most students open the discussion forum and read other participants' contributions. A few participate actively. Others post their first comments.

- John tries to upload his pending assignment with no success and calls the tech support number. A tech tutor walks him through the process until he finally succeeds.

Thursday

Teacher:

- The teacher receives an automated notification that John has handed in an assignment for grading. He sends John an email congratulating him for tackling the technical problem and lets him know that he will grade it by the weekend.

Students:

- Students continue to participate in the forum. Slowly, almost all of them post at least one message.

- Kim's comment has opened an exchange among students regarding the essay. More questions are raised, some of which are answered by peers.

Friday

Teacher:

- The teacher logs on to the course and opens the discussion forum. He is happy to see that students have responded to his questions with thoughtful remarks. He sees that there is still confusion surrounding an important point, so he clarifies it. He summarizes the key concepts studied that week and mentions open questions that will be considered in other units.

- He thanks Kim for raising her question and clarifies the requirements for the essay. He answers any questions that haven't been resolved by the group.

- He checks the report on students' activity to verify that Mary is still enrolled because he notices that she did not respond to his email and has not participated in the week's discussion. He calls her and finds out that her mother has a major health problem; they agree on a plan to make up missed work.

- He sends an announcement reminding students that the deadline for handing in the essay is Sunday by midnight and informs them that he will check back with them on Saturday at noon for questions.

Students:

- Students are working on their research and start writing the essay.

- Melanie recommends an article and an interesting database to explore the topic further. She adds both resources to the discussion thread created for that purpose. Other students share more resources.

- In the discussion forum, John asks his peers a couple of questions about citation standards. Terry recommends an online webpage that generates APA-style citations and John uses it successfully. None of the students can figure out how to quote a tweet, so they ask the teacher.

Saturday

Teacher:

- The teacher logs on at noon to check for questions in the discussion forum. He sees the question about the tweet and responds that he does not know the APA citation standard for tweets. He invites students to help him figure it out, and suggests using the conference format meanwhile.

Students:

- Students are doing research and writing their essays.

Sunday

Students:

- All students except Mary turn in their essays before midnight.

1.7 Time Expectation for Teachers

> Time is a teacher's most valuable commodity. How we spend our time and plan for our students to spend their time demonstrates our priorities.
>
> (Heidi Hayes Jacobs, personal communication)

In **asynchronous** courses, online teachers and students log on to the LMS and work through a series of activities whenever it is convenient for them. **The line between class time and homework can become blurred.** Time spent on your course can happen throughout the day, in between other activities, and throughout the days of the week. While this allows for a great deal of flexibility and independence, teachers and students also need to coordinate their work with others in the course to participate in group activities, meet deadlines, and give and receive feedback.

Weeks are used to organize student workload instead of classroom sessions. Most online courses operate on a schedule with a start and finish date, so learning and teaching have to be completed within a time frame. A common practice is to consider a "week" as a period of time to distribute learning activities and define deadlines. Organizing workload in weeks is helpful to coordinate the group's progress so that collaborative activities and group discussions are possible.

Teaching time is spent differently than it is in on-site courses. A weekly workload of online teaching may entail:

- Posting announcements (text, audio, or video clips) to keep the class on track. Some teachers record fresh announcements several times a week as a way to make the communication more current and interactive.

- Posting questions to a discussion forum and responding to students' postings.

- Reviewing students' work.

- Communicating with groups of students and individual students.

- Monitoring and analyzing student engagement.

- Assessing students' progress.

- Reviewing upcoming learning activities and adapting the plan as needed.

In addition to the time spent online, there are many teaching tasks that require offline time, such as grading papers and preparing instructional notes.

An online course gives you great freedom. **You can break the work down into tasks and do it at times that are convenient for you.** Many people find it helpful to allocate two or three longer blocks of time (an hour or more) each week for more complex instructional tasks. Shorter online sessions are used for impromptu feedback within the online forums and to respond to emails.

Most teachers want to know how much time it takes to teach a course online. The only real answer is—it depends. It depends on:

- your course design;

- how many students you have;

- your instruction and feedback methods; and

- the time parameters you put around the course.

The extensive planning that goes into an online course design saves you time during the semester. You can focus most of your time on tending to students' needs rather than preparing for class. Like most challenges, teaching online becomes more intuitive and less time-consuming with practice. We learn what works for us, what to expect from students, and to plan our time accordingly. It's a process of continual improvement.

Personal Reflection

Margaret Foley McCabe

The first time I taught an online course, I logged on many times a day to see if anyone had responded to my posts. I rerecorded my introductory remarks and polished my responses compulsively. I was unsure how each contribution would be received and was overly careful. With time and experience, the interactions become familiar and take less time. You understand the context in which your contributions are received. It becomes apparent that the instructional value does not lie in the technical craft, but in the insights you offer to students.

1.8 Summary and Standards

Online education stems from a long tradition of distance education. It offers an exciting context for teaching and learning while expanding access to education. Using digital networks, people from all over the world can learn together and share ideas in new ways.

Online students use a Learning Management System (LMS) to access content, interact with a teacher and other classmates, and perform learning activities that help them master the course goals. Teachers perform many of the same tasks online as they do in the classroom. They motivate students, provide instruction, clarify directions, track students' progress, and provide responsive feedback. Yet they need to consider the specific traits of the online environment (asynchronous communication, remote access, and networked learning) as they make decisions about the best ways to promote student learning.

Online instructional models vary widely from one program to another. Four instructional models are commonly used today: (1) seminar/workshop; (2) competency-based; (3) webcast/webinar; and (4) MOOCs. The strategies and standards presented in this book focus on course models that feature teacher-student interaction as an integral part of the online course design.

☐ Teachers and students are active participants in the learning process.

References and Further Reading

Allen, E., & Seaman, J. (2013). *Changing course: Ten years of tracking online education in the United States*. The Babson Survey Research Group and Quahog Research Group. Retrieved from http://online learningsurvey.com/reports/changingcourse.pdf

Allen, E., & Seaman, J. (2016). *Grade level: Tracking online education in the United States*. The Babson Survey Research Group. Retrieved from http://onlinelearningsurvey.com/reports/onlinereportcard.pdf

Barrett, D. (October 28, 2015). How a 40-year-old idea became higher education's next big thing. *The Chronicle of Higher Education*. Retrieved from http://chronicle.com/article/How-a-40-Year-Old-Idea-Became/233976.

Biggs, J., & Tang, C. (2007). *Teaching for quality learning at university*. Maidenhead, UK: Open University Press.

Chao, T., Essier, T., & Sai, T. (2010). Using collaborative course development to achieve online course quality standards. *International Review of Research in Open and Distributed Learning*, *11*(3).

Ho, A. D., Chuang, I., Reich, J., Coleman, C. A., Whitehill, J., & Petersen, R. (2015). *HarvardX and MITx: Two years of open online courses Fall 2012–Summer 2014*. Social Science Research Network. Retrieved from http://papers.ssrn.com/sol3/papers.cfm?abstract_id=2586847

Holmberg, B. (1989). *Theory and practice of distance education*. London, UK: Routledge.

Kearsley, G. (2000). *Online education: Learning and teaching in cyberspace*. Toronto, Canada: Wadsworth.

Kim, J. (2014). Why we need a new EdTech vocabulary, *Inside Higher Ed*. Retrieved from www.insidehighered.com/blogs/technology-and-learning/why-we-need-new-edtech-vocabulary#sthash.U7oqMPdu.dpbsm

Lowenthal, P. R., Wilson, B., & Parrish, P. (2009). Proceedings from AECT International Convention 2009: *Context matters: A description and typology of the online learning landscape*. Louisville, KY: AECT. Retrieved from http://patricklowenthal.com/publications/AECT 2009TypologyOnlineLearning.pdf

Moore, M. G., & Kearsley, G. (2005). *Distance education: A systems view*. Belmont, CA: Thompson/Wadsworth.

Stein, J., & Graham, C. (2014). *Essentials for blended learning: A standards-based guide*. New York, NY: Routledge.

Swan, K., Bogle, L., Day, S., & van Prooyen, T. (2015). A tool for characterizing the pedagogical approaches of MOOCs. In C. J. Bonk, T. H. Reynolds, & T. C. Reaves (Eds.). *MOOCs and open education around the world* (pp. 105–118). New York, NY: Routledge.

Vai, M., & Sosulski, K. (2016). *Essentials of online course design: A standards-based guide* (2nd ed.). New York, NY: Routledge.

Zabala, A., & Arnau, L. (2010). *Cómo aprender y enseñar competencias*. Mexico City, Mexico: Grao/Colofón.

Chapter 2 | Factors That Influence Online Teaching

> Effective teaching is not a set of generic practices, but instead is a set of context-driven decisions about teaching.
>
> (Glickman, 1991, p. 6)

How should I teach online? The best way to answer this question is to reflect on the reasons behind your current teaching practices and figure out how these driving principles apply to online instruction. There are several factors to consider, such as the:

- unique perspective of the teacher;

- target students;

- course content and specific learning objectives;

- online environment and technologies used; and

- host institution's priorities.

These factors can also be thought of as the **who/what/where/why** of teaching and learning.

You don't need to reinvent your entire approach to teaching to be effective online. We recommend that you stay true to your beliefs and draw from your experience as a classroom teacher. Then consider other factors that come into play when teaching online and use the standards presented in this book to guide your practice.

2.1 Online Teaching

In the 1990s, it was thought that the online learning environment favored some teaching methods over others (Harasim, 1990). It was proposed that the asynchronous environment promoted self-directed learning, thus teachers should adopt the role of "facilitator of knowledge acquisition" rather than director of classroom learning. The online teacher's role was described as a "guide-on-the-side" rather than a "sage-on-the-stage" (King, 1993).

Over the past decades, we have seen that the online environment can support a wide range of approaches to teaching and learning (Lowenthal, Wilson, & Parrish, 2009). There are virtual courses in which teachers serve as experts delivering information. Some teachers facilitate discussions, while others delegate inquiry-based research. Most teachers fulfill a variety of roles determined by their own beliefs than by the online environment (McCabe, 1998).

Educational research has long supported the notion that teachers' practices are strongly related to their beliefs (Munby, Russell, & Martin, 2001). Beliefs about teaching and learning are rooted in experience and are often unconscious. We tend to teach the way we learn and emulate our best teachers (Nespor, 1985). This presents a problem for teachers, especially those who have little or no experience as online learners and may not have mentors to emulate.

How can teachers who are new to online study make confident choices about online instruction? Through self-reflection, they can identify their values as educators and apply this criterion to their online strategies. The answers to basic questions can help instructors understand their preferences:

- What is your primary role as a teacher?

- What makes you a good teacher?

- What are the characteristics of a good learner?

- How do students learn best?

- How do you know when and what students are learning?

The diversity of teachers' beliefs leads to different kinds of teaching:

- Some teachers see their primary role as **experts in the subject matter**. They provide students with clear explanations and respond to their questions.

- Others see their role as **model learners**. These teachers tend to demonstrate the qualities they attribute to good students—searching for new connections, evaluating ideas, and asking follow-up questions that lead into new territory.

- There are also teachers who see themselves as **facilitators of learning**. They guide and prompt students' progress as a coach on the side.

Throughout the book, you will find examples of different online instructional styles. Table 2.1 introduces some teachers who collaborated in this book and presents how they perceive their roles in the online environment.

There are many other possible models to describe teaching. The point here is to encourage you, as an online teacher, to understand the role you play and the reasons behind your choices. Then you will be able to find the online means to support your personal approach to teaching.

Table 2.1 Meet Some of the Online Teachers Who Contributed to this Book

Carmen Coronado teaches two online courses: *Curriculum Design and Assessment* and *Projects I* for the Virtual University System at Universidad de Guadalajara (Mexico). "**I see myself as a companion and a guide.** I believe students need help understanding the content and the instructions for activities and assignments. Since I have a clear vision of the course structure and teaching strategy, I support them when they don't know what to do, or need clarification or further explanation of the content. Also, I give them feedback to help them assess their progress, identify their difficulties, and figure out how to overcome them."	
Tom Geary teaches *Advanced Writing* online for Tidewater Community College (United States). "**I see my role as a facilitator or coach.** I don't think of myself as the one with all the answers. Rather, I think of teaching as a strategic position. Students come to my online course with their own experiences and skill	

continued

Table 2.1 *continued*

sets. I want them to bring their understandings and questions to the table. I use my more advanced knowledge of the subject to push my students' thinking into new territory and help them collaborate to find their own answers."	
Damien Mansell co-teaches an MOOC about *Climate Change* for Exeter University (United Kingdom). "As online teachers, **we serve as resources for learning**. We frame the issues that relate to climate change, present information, and provide people with answers. Because our material stays online, students can learn at their own pace."	
Rosario Freixas teaches two online courses, *Research in Social Work I and II*, for the School of Social Work at Universidad Nacional Autónoma de México (Mexico). "**I see myself as a coach who helps students develop research skills.** I introduce research methodology and assist students as they apply it to their own projects. My role is to enable students to investigate social processes with rigor, precision, and integrity."	
Benjamín Mayer-Foulkes teaches a course on *Lacan's Discourses* online at 17, Instituto (Mexico). "**My role as a tutor** is to introduce the discussion topic, establish the guidelines for the week's work, and promote an active and constant exchange among the learners. Reading each other's communications and writing in a common forum, we note how concepts behave in particular linguistic contexts."	
Allen Stairs teaches *Philosophy* online at the University of Maryland (United States). "**I see my role as a model thinker.** I try to model for my students what it is to think like a philosopher. There are real advantages to doing this online because students can read what I say again and they can craft their expression of their own thoughts more carefully, practicing the logic and rhetoric of philosophy."	
Scott Thornbury lives in Barcelona, Spain, and teaches an online course called *English in the World* for The New School for Social Research (United States). "**My approach to teaching is activity-based.** Learners work in groups on tasks and I manage and scaffold the whole process. I'm rarely the "sage on the stage"—99% of the instruction and learning happens through discussion and feedback."	

2.2 Online Learners

Any discussion about teaching is intricately bound to the needs and characteristics of the learners. After all, it is their growth that determines the effectiveness of a course.

Ideally, online courses are designed for the particular student population they serve. General characteristics such as the age range of students, their educational level, and the number of students in a class may be known ahead of time to guide the course design process. However, the particular characteristics of the students enrolled will influence how it progresses. Students have very different needs and personalities. You may have a few students whose early enthusiasm and participation help to propel highly engaged interaction throughout the semester. Another semester, your students may be less active and more reluctant to take part in the interaction. The personalities, preferences, and needs of the particular students in your online class will influence your approach. It's important to take note of the characteristics of your students to make use of their knowledge, experience, and perspective while addressing their learning and motivational needs.

Pre-course surveys or introductory exercises help you and your students get to know one another and enable you to personalize instruction. Find out about students':

- motivation for taking the course;

- prior experience with the subject matter;

- where they live, study, and work;

- learning preferences and/or challenges; and

- access to and experience with the technologies used.

This information can help you tap into your students' realities and transform an online course from a computer-mediated connection into a personalized and shared experience. It can also help you identify students who may need extra support or tailored instruction.

 Refer to the book's website for an example of a pre-course online survey: www.essentialsofonlineteaching.com.

Personal Reflection

Carmen Coronado

I have learned after years of teaching online that it is very helpful to have some kind of "fact sheet" on each student. I like to take handwritten notes on a physical notepad. Here, I list my students and write if they are married or single, how old they are, where they work, in what city, country, or farm they live. I have had students living in Germany and the United States, as well as in small remote towns in Mexico. From what they tell me, I get an idea of what their lives have been like and how they are now, why they study, and what they expect to learn. This helps me understand them and approach them. I can empathize with each one.

A teacher may decide to adapt teaching strategies to meet the preferences and expectations of the learners. Or a teacher may ask the students to adapt their work habits to meet challenges that lay outside their comfort zones (both approaches could be seen as responsive to students' needs). In either case, it is important for teachers to understand where the students begin to know how to help them progress.

 Online teaching is tailored to meet the needs of the particular student population served.

2.3 Course Content and Learning Objectives

Content and learning outcomes influence instructional choices. Picture a math teacher introducing a fundamental concept, such as complementary angles. She explains the definition of the term, draws a diagram on the board to illustrate its meaning, and then uses the concept to solve a problem. She then gives students an assignment that requires them to demonstrate comprehension of complementary angles and to apply that understanding to solve problems.

Now picture a creative writing teacher introducing the elements of fiction. He assigns a text for the students to read as homework and then uses it as context to teach about plot, setting, characters, mood, and other literary devices. The lesson is discussion-based and the teacher's questions tend to be subjective in nature: "How would you describe the mood in this text?" There are several right answers. The focus is on the students' ability to back up their answers with examples from the text. The teacher assesses the learners' understanding by their ability to convey a sense of mood in their own writing.

These two vignettes illustrate teaching for different kinds of learning. The math teacher is concerned with explaining the concept clearly so that her students comprehend it. Her lesson is about acquisition of knowledge and application. The creative writing teacher is trying to get his students to think critically about the text, analyzing the writing and applying their reasoning.

As you select a teaching strategy, be aware of the specific level of thinking that you are targeting. Do you want to teach students to state a fact? Or to explain a concept? To synthesize information and generate new ideas? To propose a solution to a problem? From a teaching perspective, it is important to challenge students in all levels of cognition for them to thoroughly own and use new ideas. Ask yourself what actions you will take to support the named learning outcomes. You can reinforce the acquisition of knowledge, challenge students to analyze their reasoning, apply their knowledge to new situations, or develop an idea. Pay attention to the kinds

Bloom's Taxonomy of Learning

Benjamin Bloom (1956) created a well-known Taxonomy of Learning to distinguish six levels of thinking or cognition. He proposed that students learn on a continuum, beginning with knowledge acquisition and moving up through comprehension, application, analysis, evaluation, and synthesis. Many teachers find this taxonomy useful to identify the level of thinking they are targeting in a lesson.

of thinking your questions and comments promote. Your input online can challenge students to reach beyond their first answers and do more than complete the assigned tasks.

 Activities and instruction engage students in a range of thinking skills, including critical and creative thinking, analysis, and problem-solving.

Teaching Tip

Ask follow-up questions

Teaching critical and creative thinking skills often requires teachers to ask follow-up questions and to encourage students to dig deeper than their initial response. For instance, a teacher may ask a question that requires analysis: "Why do you think that is the right answer?" Or he or she may ask an evaluative question: "How does that relate to your research project?" Follow-up questions that respond to the particulars of a student's reasoning and personal contexts are important to drive the learning process further.

Follow-up questions are a natural part of a teacher's input in face-to-face classroom interaction. The skilled online teacher also presses the conversation forward, asking students to make new connections or reconsider their response with additional information or new perspectives. This enriches the discussion for all. **The teacher must be present and actively involved in the online interaction to do this.** See Chapter 8 for guidelines on facilitating online discussions.

2.4 The Online Environment and the Tools Used

Online courses can be offered through a Learning Management System (LMS) or a combination of software applications (i.e. websites, social networks, online editors, knowledge organization and sharing resources). The platform offers teachers a variety of tools that can be flexibly used to support different functions, such as:

- content presentation in various formats (text, video, audio, multimedia);

- teacher-student communication;

- group discussion;

- collaboration;

- assignments;

- peer review;

- learning assessments; and

- teacher feedback.

There are many choices of technologies that can help teachers accomplish the functions listed above. Institutions invest a great deal of time, money, and effort in choosing and implementing an LMS. Training and support services for faculty usually revolve around the use of tools within the institution's chosen LMS. A standardized template is produced so that all online courses within an institution look basically the same. This makes it easier for students, teachers, administrators, and support staff to have shared expectations about how an online course is delivered and facilitates course management.

An LMS includes a limited set of tools that perform the tasks needed for teaching and learning. While online teachers can opt to use tools other than those offered within this platform, the system's basic tools (the discussion board, the announcement features, the dropbox, assessment applications, etc.) tend to be used most frequently.

Coates and Baldwin (2005) examined the effects of Learning Management Systems on universities' teaching and learning. They conclude:

> LMS's are not pedagogically neutral technologies, but rather, through their very design, they influence and guide teaching. As the systems become more incorporated into everyday academic practices, they will work to shape and even define teachers' imaginations, expectations and behaviors.

(p. 27)

This suggests that the choices of technologies included in an LMS may bias instructional strategies. They point out the connection between popular LMS tools and online pedagogical trends. For example, many LMSs include tools that rely on forms of assessment that can be automatically "corrected." Automated tools cannot easily assess students' responses to open-ended problems. The authors express concern that such assessment tools may become dominant in higher education practices and limit the kinds of tasks used to evaluate students.

The specific media you use to deliver resources and interact online will affect students' experience. Text-based interaction may appeal more readily to those who are comfortable writing. Video resources may be more appropriate to represent certain kinds of information and may work better for visual learners. It is generally recommended that teachers select technologies that are aligned with the specific goals of the activity it services and use a variety of media to appeal to different modalities and learning preferences (Quality Matters, 2014).

Teaching Dilemma

What instructional tool should I use?

Choosing the simplest technology for the job is usually the best choice. It keeps the focus on the learning task rather than the mode of communication. When you are teaching, it is important to give students clear instructions about how to use the tools chosen and explain how they fit within the overall goals for the class. In other words, explain and justify your methods. Again, it is important that you begin with a clear understanding of the rationale behind your instructional choices so that it is **teaching**—not technology—that drives your decisions and actions. Refer to Chapter 3 for an in-depth discussion about learning resources and tools.

The LMS features and course design may influence online instructional choices. As we emphasize throughout this book, **it is imperative that learning, not technology, drive instructional decisions**.

☑ Learning activities and ease of use determine the best technologies to use.

2.5 The Mission and Priorities of the Host Institution

Institutions of education have different missions, values, and goals, and have different reasons for offering online programs. Many colleges and universities began providing online courses at a distance to serve students who could not physically attend campus-based classes (Bonk, 2002; Owston, 1997). Today, schools offer online courses for one or more of the following reasons: to reach more students, to serve a wider geographical area, to increase revenue, to provide greater flexibility, to improve instructional quality (Burke, 2005). The priorities placed on the various motivations affect strategic decisions about the development, implementation, resources, and evaluation of online courses. How will online courses be developed and by whom? How many students will online classes serve? What kinds of training, support, and resources will be given to the online teachers? What kinds of evidence will be gathered to evaluate the success of the course? Answers to these questions will have significant impact on how online courses are taught.

Best practices for online teaching need to be consistent with the norms and values of the institution as a whole. Some schools are known for their small student-teacher ratios and pride themselves on interactive, learner-centered instruction. They are likely to offer online courses with small class sizes (i.e., 10–25 students) and encourage high levels of student-teacher interactions. Institutions that traditionally offer large lecture courses may favor online teaching methods that serve larger numbers of students. To compensate for the size, effort and investment in these courses may be directed to the production of high-quality learning resources and methods that encourage student-to-student interaction. While these two examples oversimplify strategies to account for scale and student engagement, they illustrate an important assertion: by necessity, online teaching practices should be aligned with the priorities and practices of the host institution.

☑ Online teaching is aligned with the priorities and practices of the host institution.

2.6 Influences in Action: Sample Course

The following example shows you how all the influences come into play as the online teacher teaches a course:

Joyce Anderson teaches a *Technical Writing* course online for Millersville University in Lancaster, Pennsylvania, United States. It is an advanced composition course that focuses on professional writing in the fields of science, technology, and math.

Personal Factors

Joyce Anderson believes that:

- Students learn by doing.

- Learning is a social process.

- Her role as an online teacher is to be a model learner, expert resource, and facilitator of learning.

Each of Joyce's fundamental beliefs about learning influence her teaching in the following ways:

- **Students learn by doing.**

Joyce teaches her online classes as writers' workshops. Students learn to become better writers by analyzing techniques used in writing samples, applying their growing understanding to their own writing and critiquing each other's work.

- **Learning is a social process.**

Joyce organizes her class as a "community of learners" responsible for helping one another learn. Discussion forums serve as the central place for online instruction and interaction. She encourages students to share their writing, ask questions, respond to each other, and build knowledge together.

- **Her role as an online teacher.**

Joyce serves as a model learner for her students. Her course design and all of her online comments demonstrate clear, purposeful, and well-organized writing. She participates in the discussions, modeling the kind of inquiry and response she expects of her students. She also models self-reflective learning, sharing her thoughts about the course as it unfolds.

Joyce also serves as an expert resource and facilitator of learning. She uses the online *resource* area to share documents, writing samples, and criticism that she has created and collected over years of research. She weaves instruction throughout her postings in the discussion forum, responding to learners' contributions and seizing *teachable moments* in the written exchanges. Joyce spends time tracking every student's progress each week and sends emails to motivate participation when needed. She provides personalized feedback and asks follow-up questions that keep the discussion moving forward into new territory. She is careful to find a balance in her participation in the discussion forums so that she contributes to, but does not control, the flow of conversation.

Student Factors

Most of Joyce's undergraduate students are enrolled full-time at Millersville University, studying mathematics, engineering, and sciences. They take the course to become better professional writers in their fields of interest. There is a wide range of experience and competency in basic writing skills among the students.

Joyce sees the diversity of learners' fields of study, backgrounds, and abilities as an asset to the course. In her own words:

> These students are the kinds of people who will be reading each other's professional writing throughout their careers. They need to learn how to explain their subjects to people in other disciplines. So the online class gives them real-life experience in communicating with a diverse audience.

Joyce recognizes her online learners as unique individuals. She wants to get to know them and to understand their motivations and challenges. So she opens her online courses with an icebreaker exercise that helps the group get to know each other. The exercise is intended to be fun and to build rapport and trust among the group.

While many students are experienced users of new technologies, Joyce doesn't assume that they know how to use the selected tools of the LMS. She provides detailed instructions in case they are needed. She also includes a suggestion sheet, "How Do I Do Well in This Course?" that anticipates their concerns and addresses questions that have arisen in past semesters.

 Refer to the book's website to look at Joyce Anderson's icebreaker exercise and the document "How Do I Do Well in This Course?": www.essentialsofonlineteaching.com.

Course Content and Learning Outcomes

Joyce describes the content and learning objectives of *Technical Writing* within the course syllabus (see Figure 2.1).

Course Description

Technical Writing is an advanced composition course designed to develop the skills and expertise to compose effective technical communications: standard English, clarity and economy of style, visual literacy, graphics, and multimodal presentation.

Course Objectives

1. To participate in the learning process by using pre-writing, drafting, and revision strategies for writing purposes.

2. To apply stylistic and technical strategies to informal and formal writing.

3. To promote understanding of technical information and concepts using standard written English and clear, correct, and concise writing.

4. To demonstrate critical thinking in researching, collecting, and analyzing evidence to support technical writing.

5. To practice professional writing by composing four major writing projects: a Career Packet, an Instructional Memo, a Technical Report, and an Informative Project.

6. To contribute to the online discussion and *Technical Writing* community in a technical and professional manner.

7. To exhibit professionalism online and in the workplace.

8. To craft texts for multiple audiences in multiple forms/genres.

Figure 2.1 Excerpt from Joyce Anderson's *Technical Writing* Course Syllabus (reprinted with permission)

Joyce believes that the online environment is particularly well suited to teach writing because most online communication happens through text and sharing documents. Students have access to each other's work and do peer reviews through writing. The discussion board provides an additional opportunity for them to practice and improve their written communication skills. Joyce suggests that the importance of writing as a necessary skill is more evident to her online learners.

She is careful to model effective writing in all her online contributions and students follow her lead: "I notice that my students will mimic my salutations and general tone in their own posts. Their writing gets noticeably better through the daily communications."

Technological Factors

Millersville University currently uses Desire2Learn as its Learning Management System. The course home page has a banner that offers four pull-down menus: Resources, Communication, Assessment, and University Resources. Each menu lists tools that are available for teachers and students to use in their online courses (see Figure 2.2 for an example). Chapter 3 provides a description of common LMS tools.

Figure 2.2
Options Included Under the Resource Menu in Desire2Learn

The tools provided in Desire2Learn influence Joyce's teaching. She posts all course **documents** and **learning resources** in the content section of the LMS (i.e. syllabus, support materials, and grading rubrics). To communicate with students, Joyce posts **announcements**, and uses the **discussion forums** and **email**. Her students submit their work through the LMS dropbox feature. The **users' progress tool** helps her track student grades and participation (see Chapter 3 for a description of LMS tools and how to use them).

Joyce uses a few of the LMS features available to keep the course procedures as simple as possible. She begins the semester with the general course information and the first week's learning activities available to students. Each week, she initiates a new unit that focuses on a different writing challenge. She uses the same tools throughout the semester to provide instruction, give assignments, teach criteria to create and assess good writing, exchange ideas, and give students' feedback. The consistent procedures make it easy for them to understand what to do. She believes that this straightforward approach allows the learners to focus on effective writing and for her to focus on students' needs.

University Factors

Millersville is a public university located in central Pennsylvania, well known for its liberal arts programs. A matter of institutional pride is the student-centered learning model, with courses taught by professors who are highly engaged and responsive to the students. Most classes are small, ranging from 24 to 31 students. Larger lecture-based courses are supplemented with small group discussion sessions between lectures.

The university's online courses are accredited and have the same rigor and learning outcomes as campus-based courses. The online courses are developed and taught by faculty members and reviewed through the same course approval process as all of Millersville courses. Students must be admitted and enrolled to participate in their online courses.

The institution provides support for faculty as they design and teach their online courses for the first time. Faculty members participate in an extensive virtual workshop series that focuses on: (1) experiencing Web-based learning as a student; (2) learning the tools and options within the LMS; (3) designing an online course; (4) developing resources for virtual learning; (5) adopting online teaching strategies; and (6) assessing progress and strategies for improvement. The faculty development process also allows teachers to observe online courses in action.

Institutional priorities and practices influence Joyce's instruction. She usually has 22–24 students in her online *Technical Writing* course. This relatively small class allows her to get to know her students individually. She is able to provide every student with frequent and personalized attention. She can group students purposefully or work with them as a whole class. The small class size also makes the discussion board manageable; there are enough people contributing to keep the discussion lively, but not so many that it becomes hard to read. Since students are enrolled in the online course for credit, they all have shared incentive (a passing grade) to participate in the course as planned. This lends cohesiveness to the collaborative efforts.

Joyce taught her *Technical Writing* course in a classroom before redesigning it as an online course. The virtual faculty development workshop series helped her understand the potential of the online environment to support the same kind of personal engagement she shares with classroom students. She explained in a post-workshop survey:

> I was a bit hesitant at first . . . Now in this sixth week of the [faculty workshop], I am quite enthusiastic about offering my course online. It has been exciting, almost to the point of overwhelming. However, I now feel that I have a full understanding of what is required to teach an engaging and effective online course . . . It was exceedingly helpful to have an experienced online instructor guide us through this process and provide encouragement and support throughout. This modeling of good practice was an effective way to teach and learn.

Joyce uses many of the teaching strategies she experienced in both the faculty workshop and the online classes observed. The institutional support and collegial environment helped her to build a new repertoire of teaching practices.

2.7 Summary and Standards

Best practices of online teaching are influenced by the context in which the course is taught. In this chapter, we looked at the impact of the following factors:

- teacher characteristics;

- student characteristics;

- course content and learning objectives;

- online environment and technologies used; and

- host institution priorities.

We suggest that you take time to reflect on each of these five categories and identify how these factors influence your approach to teaching. The key to effective online teaching is finding methods that are aligned with your beliefs and the priorities of the institution while serving your students with the best resources available.

The following standards can serve as a checklist to evaluate your instructional choices:

☐ Online teaching is tailored to meet the needs of the particular student population served.

☐ Activities and instruction engage students in a range of thinking skills, including critical and creative thinking, analysis, and problem-solving.

☐ Learning activities and ease of use determine the best technologies to use.

☐ Online teaching is aligned with the priorities and practices of the host institution.

References and Further Reading

Ambrose, S. A., Bridges, M. W., Lovett, M. C., DiPietro, M., & Norman, M. K. (2010). *How learning works: Seven research-based principles for smart teaching*. San Francisco, CA: Jossey-Bass.

Anderson, L. W., & Krathwohl, D. R. (Eds.). (2001). *A taxonomy for learning, teaching, and assessing: A revision of Bloom's taxonomy of educational objectives*. Boston, MA: Allyn & Bacon.

Bain, K. (2004). *What the best college teachers do*. Cambridge, MA: Harvard University Press.

Bates, T. (2015). *Teaching in a digital age*. Vancouver, BC: BC Campus Open Textbooks. Retrieved from http://opentextbc.ca/teaching inadigitalage/

Biggs, J., & Tang, C. (2007). *Teaching for quality learning at university*. Maidenhead, UK: Open University Press.

Bloom, B. S. (Ed.). (1956). *Taxonomy of educational objectives handbook I: Cognitive domain*. New York, NY: Longman.

Bonk, C. J. (2002). *Online teaching in an online world.* CourseShare. com. Retrieved from http://publicationshare.com/docs/corp_ survey.pdf

Burke, L. A. (2005). Transitioning to online course offerings: Tactical and strategic considerations. *Journal of Interactive Online Learning, 4*(2), 94–107.

Chao, T., Saj, T., & Essier, T. (2010). Using collaborative course development to achieve online course quality standards. *International Review of Research in Open and Distributed Learning, 11*(3). Retrieved from www.irrodl.org/index.php/irrodl/article/ view/912/1644

Chickering, A. W., & Gamson, Z. F. (1987). Seven principles for good practice in undergraduate education. *AAHE Bulletin, 39*(7), 3–7.

Clark, R. (Ed.) (2012). *Learning from media. Arguments, analysis, and evidence. A volume in perspectives in instructional technology and distance learning* (2nd ed.). Charlotte, NC: Information Age.

Coates, J. H., & Baldwin, G. (2005). A critical examination of the effects of learning management systems on university teaching and learning. *Tertiary Education and Management, 11*(9), 9–36.

Dewey, J. (1897). My pedagogic creed. *School Journal, 54,* 77–80. Retrieved from http://dewey.pragmatism.org/creed.htm

Dewey, J. (1938). *Experience and education.* New York, NY: Free Press.

Fenstermacher, G. D., & Soltis, J. F. (1986). *Approaches to teaching.* New York, NY: Teachers College Press.

Glickman, C. (1991). Pretending not to know what we know. *Educational Leadership, 48*(8), 4–10.

Greene, M. (1978). Teaching: The question of personal reality. *Teachers College Record, 80*(1). Retrieved from www.tcrecord.org

Harasim, L. (1990). Online education: An environment for collaboration and intellectual amplification. In L. Harasim (Ed.). *Online education: Perspectives on a new environment.* New York, NY: Praeger.

Jones, C., & Binhi, S. (2011). *The next generation and digital natives: Implications for higher education.* A literature review commissioned by the Higher Education Academy. Open University. Retrieved from http://oro.open.ac.uk/30014/

King, A. (1993). From sage on the stage to guide on the side. *College Teaching, 41*(1), 30–35.

Knowles, M. (1975). *Self-directed learning: A guide for learners and teachers.* Chicago, IL: Association Press.

Lee, M. J. W., & McLoughlin, C. (2010). Beyond distance and time constraints: Applying social networking tools and Web 2.0 approaches to distance learning. In G. Veletsianos (Ed.). *Emerging technologies in distance education* (pp. 61–87). Edmonton, AB: Athabasca University Press.

Lowenthal, P. R., Wilson, B., & Parrish, P. (2009). Proceedings from AECT International Convention 2009: *Context matters: A description and typology of the online learning landscape.* Retrieved from http://patricklowenthal.com/publications/AECT2009TypologyOnline Learning.pdf

McCabe, M. (1998). Lessons from the field: Computer conferencing in higher education. *Journal of Information Technology for Teacher Education, 7*(1), 71–87. Retrieved from www.tandfonline.com/doi/abs/10.1080/14759399800200026#.VQDesUKhNfk

Moore, M., & Kearsley, G. (1996). *Distance education: A systems view*. Belmont, CA: Wadsworth.

Munby, H., Russell, T., & Martin, A. K. (2001). Teachers' knowledge and how it develops. In V. Richardson (Ed.). *Handbook of research on teaching* (pp. 877–904). Washington, DC: American Educational Researcher.

Nespor, J. (1985). The role of beliefs in the practice of teaching. *Journal of Curriculum Studies, 19*(4), 317–328. Retrieved from www.tandfonline.com/doi/pdf/10.1080/0022027870190403

Owston, R. (1997). The world wide web: A new technology to enhance teaching and learning? *Educational Researcher, 26*(2), 27–33.

Prensky, M. (2001). *Digital natives, digital immigrants*. Retrieved from www.marcprensky.com/writing/Prensky%20-%20Digital%20Natives,%20Digital%20Immigrants%20-%20Part1.pdf

Quality Matters. (2014). *Standards from the QM higher education rubric* (5th ed.). Retrieved from www.qaa.ac.uk/en/Newsroom/Documents/QualityMatters2014DelegatePack.pdf

Siemens, G., Gasevic, D., & Dawson, S. (2015). *Preparing for the digital university: A review of the history and current state of distance, blended, and online learning*. Athabasca, CA: University of Athabasca.

Xu, D. (2013). Adaptability to online learning: Differences across types of students and academic subject areas. *Journal of Higher Education, 85*(5). Retrieved from http://ccrc.tc.columbia.edu/publications/adaptability-to-online-learning.html

Chapter 3

Teaching with Digital Tools and Resources

"The right tool for the job" is a saying that can apply to online teaching. The best digital tool is determined by the instructional task that needs to be accomplished. If your course is already designed, many of these tasks will be defined for you. But there are different ways to accomplish the same task, so it's useful to know your options and understand the benefits of certain tools over others for your purposes. Similarly, the core learning resources may already be identified for your course. But you may want to add or modify resources as you work with your students.

This chapter covers some technical options for accomplishing different kinds of interactions and common instructional tasks. It also provides an overview of different kinds of resources to deliver content.

Before we begin, let's focus on a few reassuring facts:

- Technology can support the learning process without getting in the way.

- Successful online learning can happen with relatively simple tools.

- The right tools and resources can help you work more effectively.

We will walk you through the tools available online for basic teaching functions.

Think about ways that you can use them in your course.

Note: This is not a comprehensive list of tools and resources. Rather, we highlight some basic types of resources and tools that teachers can use and combine to create rich and interactive learning experiences.

3.1 Supporting Learning with Digital Resources and Tools

Digital resources and tools can support rich interaction between:

- teacher and student(s);

- student(s) and student(s); and

- students and content.

Usually, the resources and tools are integrated within a Learning Management System (LMS). This technological platform provides a closed and safe environment for teachers and students to interact. Working within an LMS has these advantages:

- Access is restricted through a username and a password.

- Tools and resources are in the same place.

- Courses can be created and managed easily.

- Data is stored centrally.

- Reports show student progress.

- Institutional support can be provided if all teachers are using the same LMS.

Note: Some institutions are now using a combination of independent tools to offer online courses. Refer to section 3.6 for more information.

The following overview of a unit from an online course in *Global Economics* illustrates how **learning resources and tools** (*in italics*) are woven together to create engaging and challenging activities.

Global Economics Course—Unit 3

Students' learning activities:

- Watch an *introductory video* explaining the globalization of economic systems.

- Read the *journal article* "Interest Rates and the Exchange Rate: A Non-Monotonic Tale" by Viktoria Hnatkovska, Amartya Lhiri, and Carlos A. Vegh, analyzing how interest rates in major economies can affect other nations' currencies.

- Use the *online discussion forum* to discuss the question: "How will fluctuations in major economies such as the United States, the European Union, Germany, or China affect the economic outlook in emerging economies?"

- Search for online *statistical data* from the World Bank and the International Monetary Fund to support the arguments presented in the discussion forum.

- Complete an automatically graded diagnostic *quiz* to assess comprehension of key concepts.

- Prepare a document listing five takeaways from this lesson and three questions to explore the subject further and submit using *dropbox*.

Figure 3.1 A Unit from an Online Course That Illustrates How Digital Resources and Tools Create Engaging Activities

In the example above, online activities provide information in a variety of formats to appeal to students with different learning preferences. They also use a variety of tools that enable students to work in different ways. In the discussion forum, students interact with classmates and the teacher to deepen their understanding of the subject. Individually, students take a quiz to assess their understanding of concepts or apply what they have learned in an assignment. In this rich digital environment, students can learn research skills, critical thinking, and teamwork, as well as economics.

Teachers help students to use digital tools and resources effectively to reach the learning outcomes for the course. Some teachers see this as a daunting responsibility because they are not confident in their technical know-how. However, you do not need to be an IT expert or know about all the tools available to perform a task online. You just need to choose an appropriate tool for your needs, practice using it, and show your students how it's done. Keep it simple and broaden your experimentation over time. **Your major contribution is your knowledge and expertise on the subject, not your technical skills.**

Personal Reflection

Patricia González-Flores

I have discovered that many teachers are not aware of how much they know about using digital tools. They already use applications in their daily lives to navigate the Internet, write documents, and send emails. They are familiar with clicking on icons to perform functions, selecting options from pull-down menus, and capturing and formatting information in boxes or cells. The LMS and other digital tools used for online teaching work with a similar logic. So my initial recommendation is: look first at the familiar aspects of each screen (icons, menus) and don't be afraid to try them!

Begin by learning how to use the basic tools for essential teaching tasks, such as:

- communicating with your students;

- sharing resources with students; and

- assessing student learning.

Once you feel comfortable with the basic tools, you will be able to guide your students through most learning activities.

☑ **Learning activities and ease of use determine the best technologies to use.**

3.2 Communicating with Students

If you are already familiar with the digital tools you will be using to teach online, you may want to skip this section.

Teachers and students can communicate online using several LMS tools:

- announcements;

- discussion forums; and

- emails.

They allow asynchronous interaction and are commonly used in online courses because of the flexibility they provide to learners. Familiarize yourself with the traits and functions of these tools. Then, as you teach, you will be able to select the best medium for each communication task.

Teaching Tip

Consider using synchronous communication

Synchronous communication tools (such as chat or live sessions) can be used for immediate interaction, allowing you to talk with students directly. You can also use them for guests or student presentations. However, keep in mind that scheduling might be difficult if there are students living in different time zones or learners with busy schedules.

Chat is an instant messaging tool that allows conversations through text exchanges in real time.

Announcements

Online teachers can communicate with their class using the announcement tool in the LMS. Figure 3.2 shows an example of an announcement from Sepi Yalda's *History of Meteorology* class at Millersville University.

News ▽

History of Meteorology Journal   x
Posted August 26, 2013 6:28 AM

As you are reading through your book and the course notes you may want to look at the titles in the History of Meteorology journal which can be accessed online at http://www.meteohistory.org/scholarship/journal.html.

I have also listed this under the area for the final research paper so you can look at it as a resource for your final paper. Also please check out the link on NOAA library photos that include a large number of pictures related to the history of meteorology. The link can be found under the link for the syllabus under the "Content" tab.

Show All News Items

Figure 3.2 An Announcement from Sepi Yalda's *History of Meteorology* Class at Millersville University

ONLINE TOOL

Announcements in LMS

What?

An announcement is a message posted by the teacher to all the students enrolled in the course. Usually, announcements are used for one-way interaction (the teacher writes to students and they do not reply).

Students read the announcement on the course home page when they log on to the course. It can include text, images, audio, and video in the body. Some LMSs (such as Moodle or Desire2Learn) use the term "News" for the announcement tool.

Why?

An announcement **provides timely information** to students regarding logistics, upcoming events, additional content, or other issues. Some common uses are:

- welcoming students to the course;

- sending reminders (i.e. upcoming assignments, due dates, participation requirements);

- introducing a unit or lesson;

- informing about newly added resources or special events (such as guest lectures, conferences);

- highlighting progress achieved or challenges to be met; and

- motivating students to stay on track.

How?

Teachers can post an announcement immediately or schedule its appearance for a later date and time. Here are some suggestions for writing announcements:

- send at least one announcement per week;

- keep them short and to the point;

- attach a file if lengthy explanations are needed; and

- create video or audio messages to vary the media.

Announcements are created by typing or uploading texts to an online editor as shown in Figure 3.3.

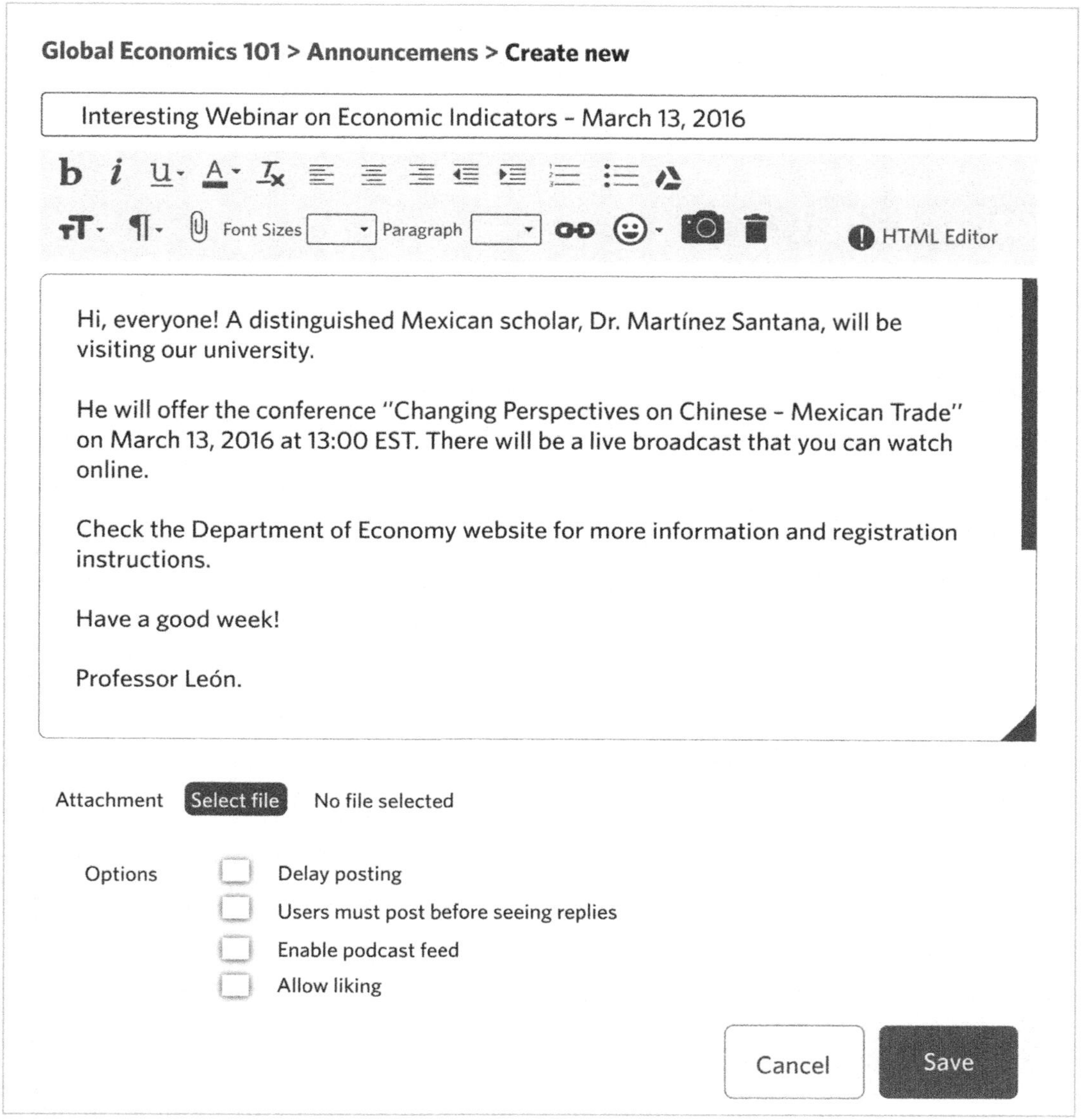

Global Economics 101 > Announcemens > Create new

Interesting Webinar on Economic Indicators – March 13, 2016

b *i* U· A· Ix ≡ ≡ ≡ ≡ ≡ ≡ ≡ ⚠

·T· ¶· 📎 Font Sizes ▾ Paragraph ▾ ∞ 😊· 📷 🗑   ❗ HTML Editor

Hi, everyone! A distinguished Mexican scholar, Dr. Martínez Santana, will be visiting our university.

He will offer the conference "Changing Perspectives on Chinese – Mexican Trade" on March 13, 2016 at 13:00 EST. There will be a live broadcast that you can watch online.

Check the Department of Economy website for more information and registration instructions.

Have a good week!

Professor León.

Attachment Select file   No file selected

Options   ☐ Delay posting
☐ Users must post before seeing replies
☐ Enable podcast feed
☐ Allow liking

Cancel   Save

Figure 3.3 An Example of the Dialogue Box for Creating Announcements (Simulating Canvas LMS)

☑ Weekly announcements call students' attention to important and timely course information.

Discussion Forums

Discussions are probably the most important tool for an online teacher because they provide the space for sustained conversations with and among students. Discussions can be used for many teaching purposes. Chapter 8 describes a range of ways discussions are used in online courses.

ONLINE TOOL

Discussion Forum in LMS

What?

Discussions are written conversations between two or more members of the class. They enable two-way communication and can be one-to-one or one-to-many. A discussion can include a teacher and the students or just the students.

Each discussion begins with an introductory message or prompt. Participants post replies that can be organized in two different ways:

1. in chronological order; or

2. threaded, with each reply presented under the comment to which it relates.

A "thread" is a series of messages that deal with the same topic. They are organized together so that users can identify them easily.

The introductory message and all replies have a subject and a body. The content is usually text, but video, audio, and hyperlinks can be embedded. Files can also be attached. Figure 3.4 shows an example of Professor León using a discussion forum to teach a unit of his *Global Economics* course.

Why?

Discussions allow people to exchange ideas. Students present their ideas (or questions) and receive feedback (or answers) from peers and the teacher. Since there are no time constraints, everyone can participate (read and write) and edit their postings carefully. Discussions are used as a space to:

- interact and explore course content as a group;

- post and respond to student questions;

- share information and links to resources;

- collaborate on group projects; and

- present a student project or presentation to the class.

For many courses, the discussion forums serve as the virtual classroom where participants meet regularly (see Chapter 8, pp. 210–212, for more information and examples).

How?

To set up a discussion, teachers create the introductory message in which the topic, the purpose, and the guidelines for the conversation are established (see Figure 3.5).

Participants post their comments at different times, and can reply to each other. The teacher monitors the conversation and may provide information and feedback to keep it on target.

Teachers can open and close a discussion manually or establish the day and time when it will be open and closed. They can also open discussions to an individual or a small group.

Note: Most discussion forums in an LMS can be configured so that students are able to open discussions on their own. It is an interesting option if you want to share some course responsibilities with them.

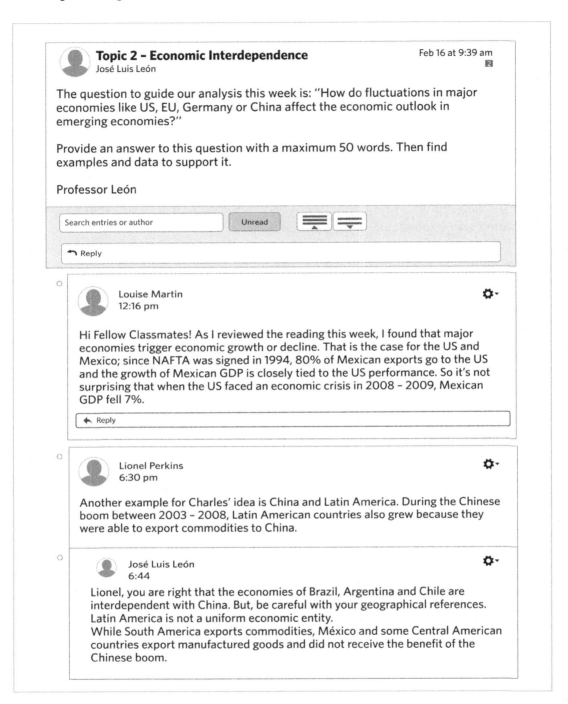

Figure 3.4 An Example of a Discussion Forum in a *Global Economy* Course. The discussion is threaded, so responses are filed under the related comment.

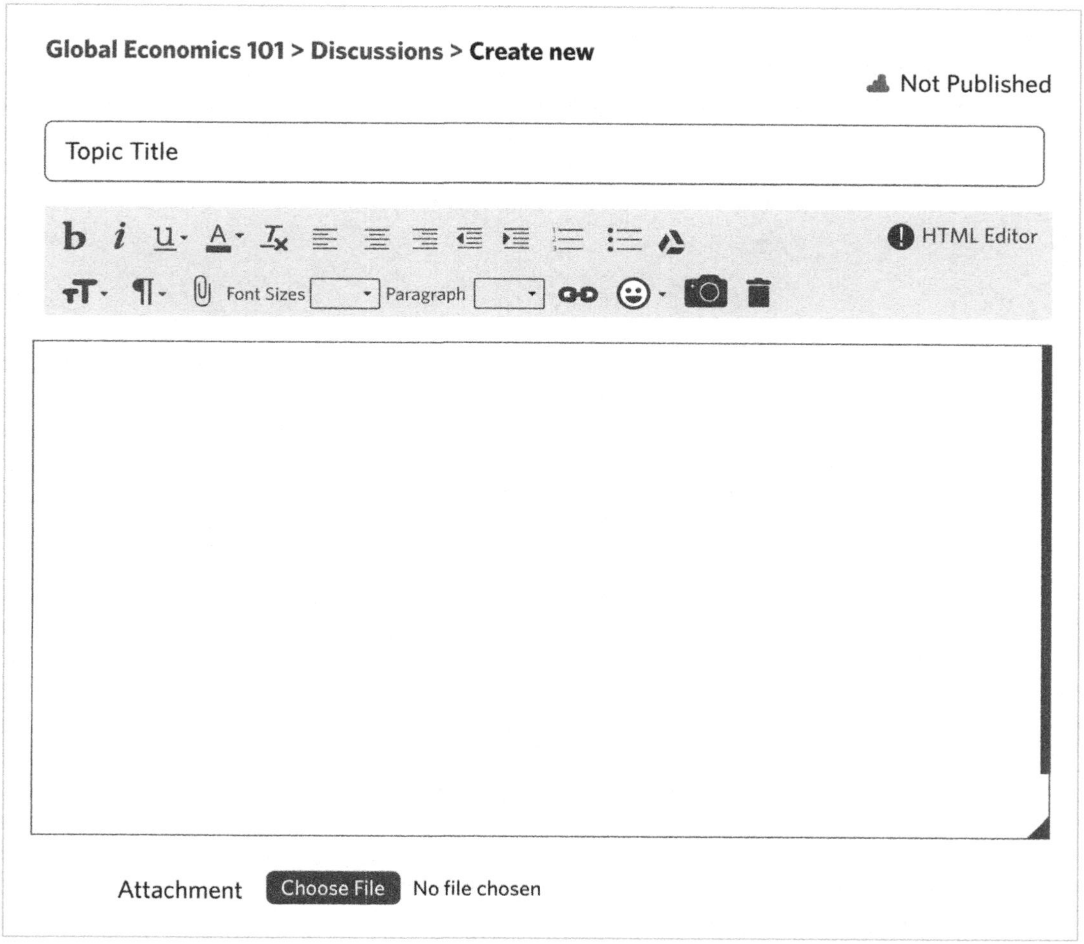

Global Economics 101 > Discussions > **Create new**

🔊 Not Published

Topic Title

b *i* <u>u</u>· <u>A</u>· *I*ₓ ≡ ≡ ≡ ≡ ≡ ≡ ≡ ⬧   ❶ HTML Editor

▪T· ¶· 🔗 Font Sizes [　▾] Paragraph [　▾] ∞ ☺· 📷 🗑

Attachment [Choose File] No file chosen

Figure 3.5 The Screen for Creating a Discussion in Canvas LMS

Most LMS include configuration options that allow you to establish a specific communication dynamics in online discussions. You can combine grouping, timing and structure in different ways (see Figure 3.6).

<u>Note</u>: A "group set" is one way of dividing students into teams (i.e. for discussions: two teams of six students; for final projects: four teams of three students). The teacher can create as many group sets as necessary within a course.

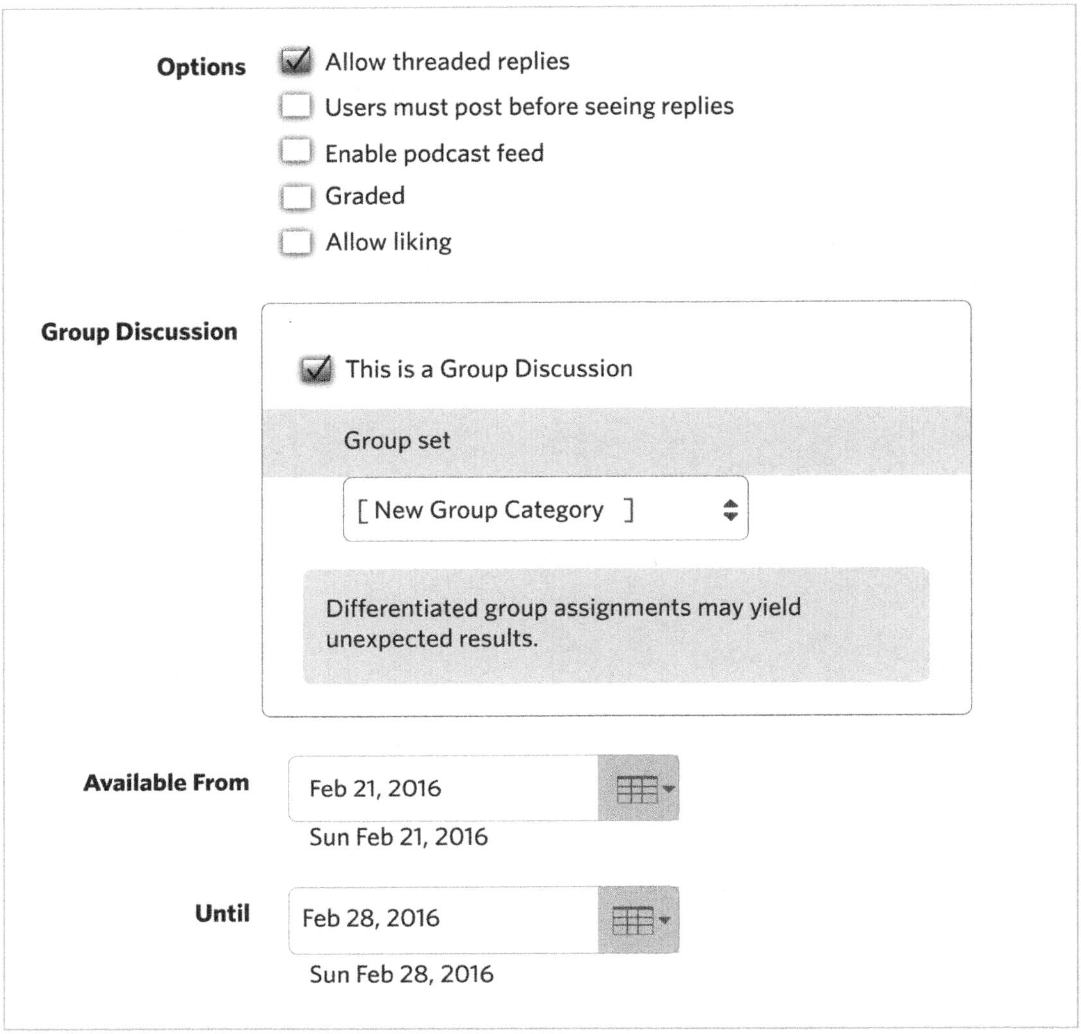

Figure 3.6 Discussion Configuration Options in Canvas. The group discussion option is checked so that each small group will have its own private discussion. Notice that a starting and ending date can be configured.

☑ Discussion forums are used to support online course interaction.

Email

Most LMSs include an email tool for interaction between registered users. Communicating with students individually helps to establish connections and increases students' personal investment in the course. However, one-to-one communication is time-consuming and can lead to redundant work on your part. Once a personal exchange has been made through email, most teachers redirect the conversations back to the online group discussion. Whole-group interaction is efficient and allows all the students to benefit from exchanges between participants. A general rule of thumb is to use email to address personal concerns or matters that pertain to students individually.

Teachers use email to:

- check on a student that has not participated and invite him or her to log on;

- discuss inappropriate behavior in the online environment; or

- address an issue that relates to an individual student.

Teaching Tip

Use email addresses that your students check frequently

Some teachers prefer to use students' personal email addresses rather than the accounts provided within the LMS because students are more likely to check their personal email regularly.

☑ Email facilitates private conversations between teachers and students, or among students.

The three communication tools described (announcements, discussions, and emails) will allow you to interact with students in different ways. It is a good practice to use multiple modes of communication. You can then select the best media for each need and, if necessary, send redundant messages that reinforce the communication.

☑ **Teachers use a variety of means to communicate with students throughout the course.**

3.3 Sharing Resources with Students

An online course is situated within the greatest network of resources ever imagined—the Internet. This presents opportunities and challenges for teachers—you have access to a huge array of content to enhance your students' learning, but you don't want to overwhelm them or shift the focus too far from the course objectives.

During the course design phase, the core learning resources are usually identified and/or created for the course. So your course may already have readings and video lectures uploaded to the LMS, as well as slideshows, worksheets, and websites identified for students to use during the lessons.

While you are teaching your course, you may need to add resources to address different learning needs that arise (Figure 3.7 summarizes common reasons to add resources to your course).

There are many kinds of online resources to consider adding to your course. They include:

- **digital resources**, that is text or multimedia files that are distributed and viewed;

- **people** (guest experts) with whom students interact; and

- **archived and real-time databases**.

Let's look at how these different kinds of resources can serve your students.

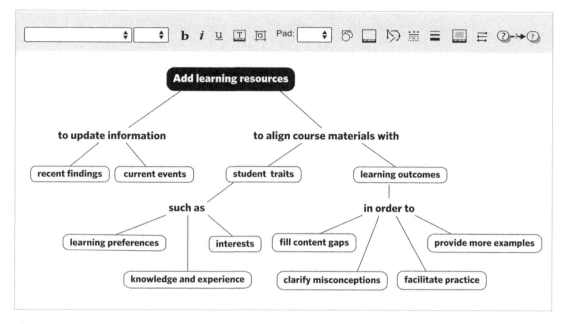

Figure 3.7 A Concept Map Summarizing Reasons for Adding Resources to a Course. This is an example of a concept map created with Cmap Cloud, a free online digital tool.

Digital Learning Resources

Digital resources are the primary way most content is delivered to students in asynchronous courses. Course designers and teachers often produce video lectures to give an overview of the week's topic or provide instruction. They post documents for students to read and links to multimedia presentations to view. Databases, online journals, podcasts, images, simulations, and multimedia presentations offer a rich variety of ways for students to engage with course information.

The choice and variety of resources matter. Media differ in the extent and ways that they represent content. Words and symbols might be the best way to communicate some ideas, while a picture or animation might be better suited for others. Imagine you are teaching an architecture course. Text could describe a building in words. A blueprint could illustrate the plan and dimensions. A video could take you on a tour around the space and allow you to hear the sounds of the environment. All these ways of experiencing the building could make the exploration more engaging and broaden students' understanding of the subject. Reading, viewing, and listening also challenge different learning skills and require us to synthesize information in distinct ways. Incorporating a variety of resources into your course can deepen students' understanding and appeal to different learning preferences.

Learning resources can be shared through the LMS. The media file can be:

- uploaded to the LMS resource repository; and/or

- attached to or embedded in an announcement or within discussions.

If the resource is available on the Internet, the corresponding link can be included in the text of the teacher's messages or within a lesson. The editing toolbar in most LMSs has icons to click to attach files or embed links, images, video, and audio (see Figure 3.8).

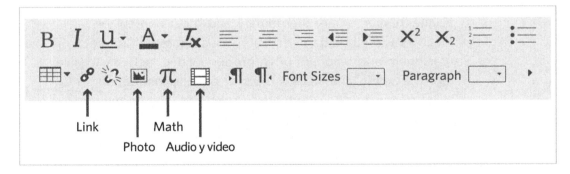

Figure 3.8 The Editing Toolbar in Canvas LMS with Options to Attach Files and Embed Links, Images, Audio and Video

Teaching Tip

Include real data as learning resources

Many academic, professional, or international organizations around the world gather real data and make them available to others on the Internet. Statistics and descriptive information can be gathered about all kinds of phenomena, such as weather, trade, scientific research, and political and social trends. Access is usually free, but might require registration.

Introducing real data in a course gives students the opportunity to analyze authentic problems and become familiar with primary sources of information. Teachers can include links to real data sites within announcements, assignments, or discussions. They can also provide instructions about how to access and process real data.

Figure 3.9 provides an example of the use of real data in a meteorology course at Millersville University. The assignment requires students to use real-time databases that record weather variables to understand physical interactions in the climate system.

Note: Databases provide access to organized and searchable information. For example, international organizations such as the International Monetary Fund offer historic data on economic indicators such as gross national product in countries. A live feed is a system that tracks changes in a variable in real time. For example, weather platforms track meteorological phenomena, such as hurricanes, in real time.

Assignment 2

Sepi Yalda

Feb 24 at 6:59 pm

For this assignment, you will gather and analyze data from different real-time databases to recognize patterns, departures, detectable cycles and signals in weather phenomena. Please look at temperatures as well as land and surface data –especially when using global datasets. Consider:

* Local variability
* National variability
* Global variability

In order to do an in-depth analysis, you will need to review and generate plots and graphs using information on:

* Global mean monthly surface temperatures estimates
* Automate Surface Observing System (ASOS) temperature departure and degree day maps.
* Upper atmospheric temperatures
* Global anomalies

You can access the above information, including other data types at:
www.ncdc.noaa.gov/monitoring-references/faq/anomalies.phs
You can access the local data at:
www.atomos.millersville.edu/p-wic/html/climatology.htm

Figure 3.9 An Example of an Activity Using Real Data from Sepi Yalda's *Climate Dynamics* Course at Millersville University

Teachers often indicate the type of media and the length of videos or podcast so students can plan their study time appropriately (Figure 3.10 provides an example list of resources from a statistics course).

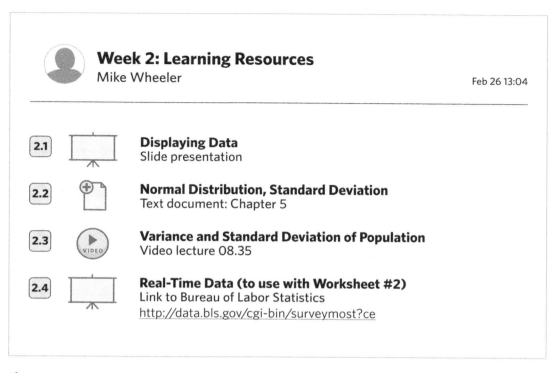

Week 2: Learning Resources
Mike Wheeler

Feb 26 13:04

2.1 **Displaying Data**
Slide presentation

2.2 **Normal Distribution, Standard Deviation**
Text document: Chapter 5

2.3 **Variance and Standard Deviation of Population**
Video lecture 08.35

2.4 **Real-Time Data (to use with Worksheet #2)**
Link to Bureau of Labor Statistics
http://data.bls.gov/cgi-bin/surveymost?ce

Figure 3.10 List of Digital Learning Resources in a *Statistics* Course

Media Selection

Incorporating diverse media into your course can add interest and support different learning styles and preferences. Text, images, video, and audio all have their advantages for certain content and purposes. As you select media, be aware of the applications needed to share and view files. Learning resources must be accessible to all students.

Text

Most online communication happens through text because it is easy to type and send messages or documents. Text documents can be supported with graphics and data. The reader can view text online or print it out. Text can be edited, added to, and annotated.

Images

Images can convey ideas succinctly and powerfully. They can provide graphic representation of concepts and present relationships among elements. Images can be real (photos) or created (graphics, charts, illustrations).

Audio

Spoken words can offer a more personal perspective about the topic, with the subtleties of meaning and personality communicated through one's voice. For example, recording a conversation in a foreign language can have a very different effect than sending it as a text document. Music can also be shared as audio files. Audio files can be downloaded from sites such as Amazon and iTunes.

Video

Videos combine the elements of text, audio, and images. For online students, "seeing" their teacher personalizes the instruction. Simple videos are easy to create with video recorders or computer cameras. They can also be downloaded from sites such as Vimeo and YouTube.

Multimedia Presentations

Slideshows and other kinds of computer presentations combine audio, visual, and graphic elements to explain and illustrate information. Simulations and quizzes can be included to provide practice opportunities. There are many applications to create multimedia presentations, such as PowerPoint, Prezi, HaikuDeck, and Powtoons.

As you gather or create learning resources to add to your course, consider these points:

- Effective online courses use a variety of learning resources to present information in engaging ways and appeal to students' learning preferences.

- The medium affects the message. Think about the information you want to share and imagine the best way to explain it. Would you say it in words? Draw a graphical representation? Demonstrate it with a moving visual? All of these forms of communication are common online today.

- Consider time factors. Remember that the purpose is to give clear and informative instruction. So don't spend more time than they are worth.

- Share resources in formats that are accessible to all students.

Personal Reflection

Tisha Bender

In the syllabus for my *International Children's Literature* course, I list all the reading materials the students are meant to have. Some of the materials are books they have to purchase—so they have time for that. Some of the reading material I post online in the resource area. I also provide links to web pages and articles.

Each week of the semester, I post a written mini-lecture. It is a short piece—just a page or so—that I post to the resource area. I use these to highlight different aspects of the literature we are studying.

I suppose I could do the mini-lectures as a video of me talking, but I choose to share these as text-based documents because it seems appropriate to the course, *International Children's Literature*. And also because I get immersed in—and really believe in—the power of words to convey meaning and emotion. I'm a storyteller and I teach through narrative. These pieces are my way of sharing my insights and hopefully inspiring the students to do the same.

When I notice in the discussions that the students could use some additional information or might have missed something in the text, I create a mini-lecture to address it. I then post it in the resource area and let the students know that it is there for them to read. It works out quite well.

See the book's website (www.essentialsofonlineteaching. com) for more suggestions about using digital media for online teaching.

☑ Courses include a variety of relevant multimedia to support learning and appeal to individual preferences.

☑ Learning resources are shared in formats that are accessible to all students.

☑ Learning resources include authentic materials and relate to real-life applications.

Guest Speakers

One of the advantages of the online environment is that anyone with access to the Internet can interact with your students. Experts or practitioners can participate in a course and add authentic and up-to-date information. They can add fresh and informed perspectives to the discussion and motivate student engagement.

Teachers invite guest speakers to participate in the course and make arrangements for them to gain access to the LMS. Guest speakers interact with the students using the communication tools available, either asynchronously or synchronously. Some ways of setting up interaction with guests are:

- posting learning resources that introduce students to the guest speaker's work or ideas (i.e. texts, videos, podcasts);

- sending the expert a list of questions prepared by students after analyzing his or her work;

- having the guest participate in a discussion thread for a week or a couple of days; and

- organizing a chat or live online videoconference at a fixed date and time.

Teaching Tip

Record live sessions

If you use synchronous media for guest speakers, you can record the session and upload it to the LMS. Then the recording can serve as a resource for students who were unable to participate in live sessions. The recording can also serve as a resource in future courses.

 Learners are encouraged to interact with others (classmates, guest speakers, etc.) and benefit from their experience and expertise.

Promoting the Use of Resources

Digital media, guests, and real data can provide students with varied, relevant, and updated content. Many teachers assume that because an article or video is included in the course, students will study it. Yet, this is not always the case. It is not uncommon that students decide to skim or skip through some of the resources, maybe even ones that are critical to the core content.

Teachers play a very important role in providing students guidance in how to use the course content effectively. At the beginning of each unit, it's helpful that teachers promote the use of resources:

- Explain how each resource contributes to learning goals and why it is important.

- Provide prompts to help students focus on key content elements of learning resources, such as outlines, guiding questions, and graphic or textual prompts.

- Describe how each resource relates to graded activities.

- Remind students of technical requirements for viewing resources.

- Distinguish between required and optional resources in the course.

Figure 3.11 provides an example of an announcement posted at the onset of a modern poetry unit.

Announcement | ▽

Introduction to Unit 2 - Modern Poetry
Oct 10 18:20

Peter Thomas
This week we explore the work of two great American modern poets, James Dickey and Randall Jarrell. The resources include poems, a podcast, videos, and literary criticism. Each resource brings a different aspect to our exploration. The poems serve as our primary source material. Read these carefully – to yourself and aloud – before listening to the podcast. Notice how different media affect your interpretation.

Pay attention to the narrative storytelling quality and the disjointed sense of time in these poems. What is a happening and what is a memory? I explore these questions in my lecture this week. It will give you some ideas to consider in your weekly assignment comparing these two poets.

The literary criticism by Jarrell is a pdf file; make sure you have the Adobe Acrobat reader installed.

I've included supplemental essays by Randall Jarrell and some more of my favorite Dickey poems. These are not required reading, but feel free to bring any thoughts they inspire to our discussion. Enjoy!

Remember that informed weekly participation in discussions and carefully crafted assignments will contribute to your course grade. Check the rubrics and if you have any questions about the expected work.

Let's get started...

Show All Announcements

Figure 3.11 An Announcement Explaining the Use of Learning Resources

☑ Teachers provide students with guidelines for using resources.

3.4 Assessing and Grading Student Learning

Teachers assess students' progress toward learning outcomes to gauge the effectiveness of the instruction and to assign grades. Frequent and diverse opportunities to gather evidence about students' performance is essential. There are several tools in the online environment that contribute to this purpose:

- dropbox or assignment tool;
- rubric editor;
- quiz or exam editor; and
- gradebook.

This section describes the tools and their functionality. Chapter 9 provides more information on strategies to assess your students and provide them feedback.

 The course includes ongoing and frequent assessment.

Assignments

Teachers use LMS assignments to manage students' coursework.

ONLINE TOOL

Assignments

What?
The LMS assignment feature includes tools to post instructions and handle submissions. In some LMSs, the submission tool is called "dropbox;" in others, it is simply a button in the assignment screen (see below).

Why?
This online tool makes it easy for teachers to create assignments and manage students' products:

- Assignments are uploaded, stored, organized, and tracked within the LMS.

- Rubrics and other files can be attached to an assignment.

- Due dates and grading conditions can be established.

- Grades are automatically inserted in the gradebook.

- Alerts or notices are sent to teachers when assignments are turned in.

- Some LMSs include plagiarism checkers.

How?

Teachers upload instructions for each task using the assignment tool. They include due dates and assessment information. The students read the instructions, do the assignment, and submit the work through the dropbox or upload it directly within the assignment tool.

Week 5 Assignment

Submit Assignment

Due:	Monday by 11:59 pm **Points** 10
Submitting:	a text entry box, a website url, a media recording, or a file upload
File types:	doc, docs, and pdf
Available:	March 7 at 12:00 am – March 13 at 11:59

Please review all resources and submit a short paper answering the question: What are the required digital competencies for employees in the Society of Knowledge?

Figure 3.12 An Online Assignment in Canvas LMS

Rubrics

Rubrics serve as a guide for grading and self-assessment. Students can use them to monitor their own learning. They also spell out the criteria that teachers will use in grading assignments, discussion participation, and presentations. Table 3.1 presents an example.

Table 3.1 An Example of a Grading Rubric for Slide Presentations

	Excellent 4	Good 3	Average 2	Poor 1	Points
Content	Content is accurate and includes all information needed to communicate the topic.	Content is accurate and includes most information needed to communicate the topic.	Content has some minor inaccuracies and is missing key concepts needed to communicate the topic.	Content has multiple inaccuracies and is missing key elements needed to communicate the topic.	
Slide organization, transition, and development	Information is organized in a clear and logical way. Slide transitions are smooth and the sequence develops the message.	Most information is organized in a clear, logical way. One slide or item of information seems out of place.	Some information is logically sequenced. Some slides seem out of place and transitions are inconsistent.	There is no clear plan for the organization of information presented.	
Pictures, art, graphics, and background	Images are appropriate, imaginative, and support the topic. The layout is easy to read and pleasing to the eye.	Images are appropriate and creative. Layout is cluttered and/or disjointed.	Most images are appropriate, but lack in creativity. Layout is cluttered and/or disjointed.	Images are missing or inappropriate.	
Spelling, grammar, and mechanics	No spelling or grammatical errors. Correct number of slides.	Few spelling and/or grammatical errors. Correct number of slides.	Some spelling and grammatical errors. Correct number of slides.	Many spelling and grammatical errors. Too few slides.	
Sources	All sources are accurately documented in the correct format.	All sources are accurately documented but one or two citations are not in the correct format.	Some sources are not accurately documented and are not in the correct format.	Sources are missing and several are not accurately documented.	

Rubrics can be complemented with model examples of assignments that comply with the criteria established at different levels. Students will then have a very clear picture of their target.

Most LMSs include a tool to create and share rubrics for activities (see Figure 3.13). They can also be prepared as word processor or spreadsheet files, and uploaded as LMS resources or attached to announcements or discussions.

Title:	Slide Presentation Rubric					
Criteria	**Ratings**				**Pts**	
Content view larger description	Content is accurate and includes all information needed to communicate topic. 4 pts	Content is accurate and includes most information need to communicate topic. 3 pts	Content has some minor inaccuracies and is missing key concepts needed to communicate the topic. 2 pts	Content has multiple inaccuracies and is missing key elements to communicate the topic. 1 pts	4 pts	⊕
Slide organization, transition and development view larger description	Information is organized in a clear and logical way. Slide transitions are smooth and the sequence develops the message. 4 pts	Most information is organized in a clear, logical way. One slide or item of information seems out of place. 3 pts	Some information is logically sequenced. Some slides seem out of place and transitions are inconsistent. 2 pts	There is no clear plan for the organization of information presented. 1 pts	4 pts	⊕
⊕ Add Criterion 🔍 Find Outcome					**Total Points: 8**	

Cancel   Create Rubric

Figure 3.13 The Rubric Editor in Canvas LMS

☑ Criteria/rubrics clearly inform learners about how they will be assessed on specific assignments and online participation.

Quizzes and Exams

LMSs make it easy for teachers to quiz students about their understanding of the content. Figure 3.14 shows an example.

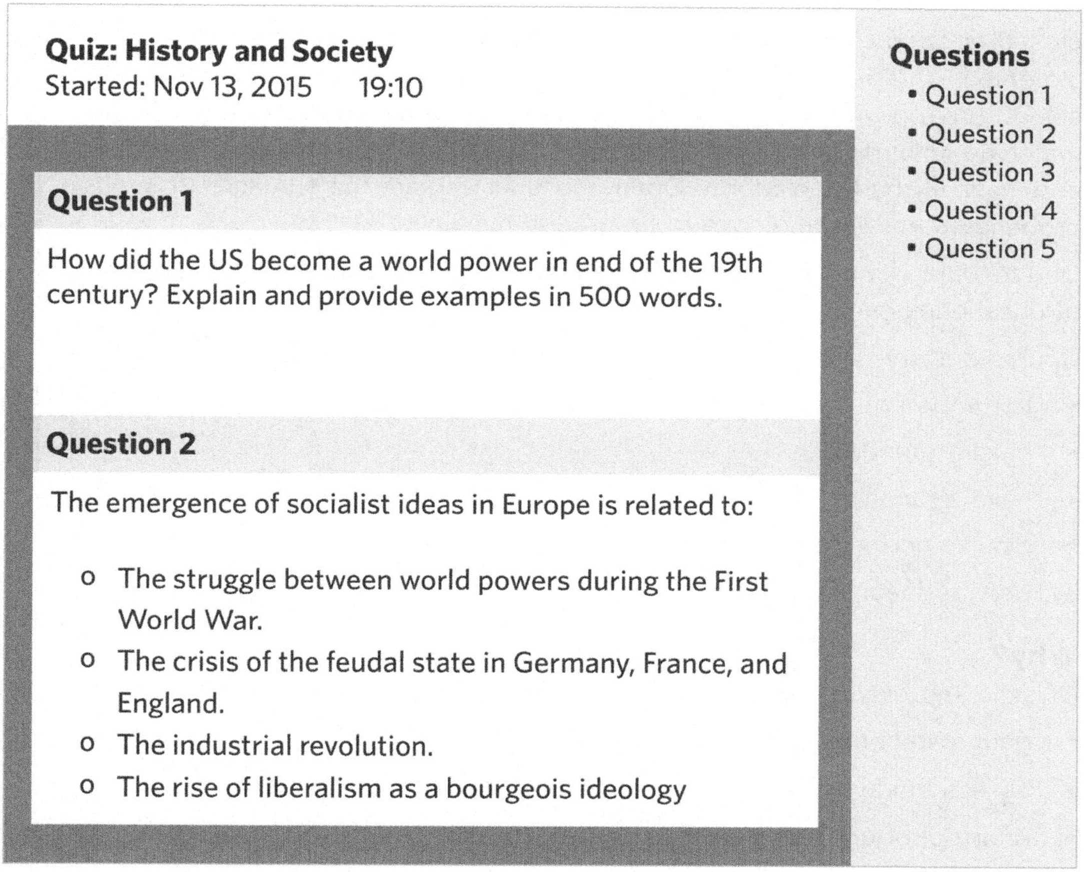

Quiz: History and Society
Started: Nov 13, 2015   19:10

Questions
- Question 1
- Question 2
- Question 3
- Question 4
- Question 5

Question 1

How did the US become a world power in end of the 19th century? Explain and provide examples in 500 words.

Question 2

The emergence of socialist ideas in Europe is related to:

o The struggle between world powers during the First World War.
o The crisis of the feudal state in Germany, France, and England.
o The industrial revolution.
o The rise of liberalism as a bourgeois ideology

Figure 3.14 An Example of a Quiz

Surveys can also be created with the quiz editor tool to gather information about different issues. For example, teachers use the quiz editor to create an end-of-course survey. In this case, the students' responses would be collected but not graded.

ONLINE TOOL

LMS Quiz and Exam Editor

What?

Teachers can create and send their students assessment instruments with closed or open-ended questions. Closed questions include a problem statement or direct question, and present options that students have to select, drag, or match. They can have different formats (i.e. multiple-choice, matching columns, true/false, drag-and-drop). Closed questions are graded automatically by the platform. Open questions require the students to produce an answer and have to be graded manually.

Quizzes and exams include an introductory section for instructions and a set of questions (see Figure 3.14).

Course designers and teachers can configure quizzes to:

- be graded or not;
- have a due date;
- have a time limit;
- display correct answers; and
- provide feedback.

Why?

Quizzes and exams can be inserted at strategic points in a lesson to:

- gauge students' previous knowledge on the topic;
- assess students' understanding of course material;
- offer opportunity for students to self-assess;
- promote the application of concepts;
- provide practice exercises; and
- encourage further analysis.

How?

Creating a quiz or exam is a two-stage process:

1. The questions are prepared. They can be typed in or uploaded from a file.
2. The instructions are posted and the questions to include are selected and sequenced. The due date can be set at this time or defined later.

Gradebook

The online gradebook manages students' grades. Teachers can concentrate on reviewing students' performance and providing feedback. No more time-consuming calculations!

ONLINE TOOL

Grades and Gradebook

What?

The gradebook is a tool for monitoring student progress. It calculates and records grades for all graded activities: participation in discussions, assignments, quizzes, and tests. Most grading tools provide a space where teachers can add comments.

Why?

Assessing progress and providing feedback is a critical teaching task. The online gradebook makes teachers' work easier by automating grade calculations, tracking students' progress and providing detailed reports. It can also offer students immediate feedback.

How?

Teachers set up the gradebook by selecting the learning activities that will be graded and defining their weights toward the final grade. During the course, teachers review students' work, assign grades, and provide feedback.

Grades can be assigned automatically (usually for quizzes with closed questions). Teachers also record grades in the gradebook after assessing work or collecting peer-review information. Teachers have access to all students' grades and each student can see his or her grades at any time. Figure 3.15 shows an example.

		Individual View	Showing All Section

All Grading Periods ▾ | Filter by student name or secondary ID | ⬇ Import ▾ | ➔ Export ▾ | ⚙ ▾

Student Name	Secondary ID	Pre test Out of 5	Information Survey Out of 5	Peer review round 1 Out of 10	Final assignment Out of 30
Josefa Ayza History 101-01	joayza@gmail.com	4	5	✕	A 28
Adrienne Margain History 101-01	margain.adri@hotmail.com	3	5	EX	C 18
Max Johnson History 101-01	max.johnson@yahoo.com	5	5	—	B 25
Julian Cameo History 101-01	j.cameo@gmail.com	2	5	EX	B 23
Louse Martin History 101-01	martin556@gmail.com	3	5	✕	A 30

Figure 3.15 The Gradebook Screen—Teacher's View—in Canvas

Constant assessment opportunities help the students know if their learning strategy is working or whether they need to adjust it. Teachers and students can benefit from the online assessment tools that simplify grade management and provide immediate access to assessment information.

☑ Teachers and students can easily track learners' progress.

3.5 Creating Collaborative Resources

Most LMSs have tools that allow students to create digital resources together. Using these tools, students can develop media production skills that are relevant today.

Collaborative Editors

Collaborative editors allow people to work together on a document or some other kind of media at the same time or asynchronously.

ONLINE TOOL

Collaborative Editors

What?

Collaborative applications (i.e. Google Docs, wikis) enable two or more users to create and edit together web pages, documents, spreadsheets, or presentations. The file is generated and saved on a server connected to the Internet. Any user's edits are recorded in the shared version. Users can work on the file at the same time or make edits at different moments. They have a toolbar to perform editing, formatting, and viewing functions. They can include comments for each other to discuss issues. A history of revisions made by each user can be displayed.

Wikis were one of the first collaborative tools available; they are used to create one or more web pages, with no specific format. Formatting options might be limited and their functionality can be awkward. Today, there are word processors, spreadsheets, and presentation tools for collaborative editing that are easy to use and very similar to the desktop version of these applications.

Why?

Instead of having one person create the product, all members of a group look at the same content and make edits directly. This shared space is useful for:

- working on small group projects;

- revising and editing a document; and

- creating a shared knowledge base (i.e. an annotated bibliography, a resource list, or a glossary).

Use collaborative editors when you want the students to construct new meanings from each other's ideas, and your goal is to achieve a collective product.

How?

A student or teacher creates the new document and gives permission to others to view or edit it (see Figure 3.16). All changes are saved in the document's "history of revisions," so that each user can look at what individuals have contributed. Users can also decide to go back to a previous version.

The file is saved in the Internet server, but can be downloaded and printed. Thus, the document can be turned in through the dropbox.

A note of caution: It can be difficult to grade individuals' contributions when collaborative editing tools are used. Although the teacher can view the history of revisions, each person's edits are hard to track (and thus to grade). Such tools are better used for creating collaborative products than demonstrating the group process.

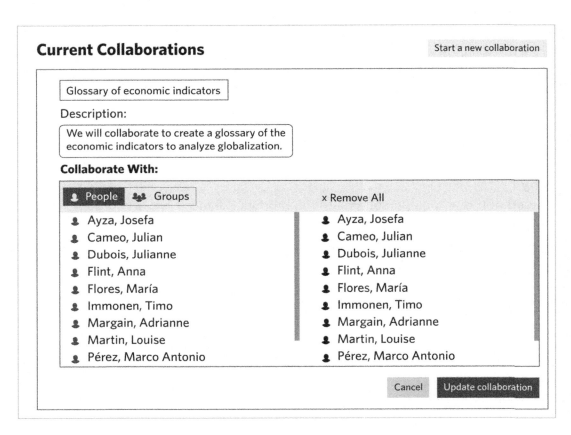

Figure 3.16 Managing Online Collaboration in Canvas. Teachers can create a group assignment using collaborative editors such as Google Docs.

Blogs

Individuals can publish web pages that can be commented on by others using blogs.

ONLINE TOOL

Blogs

What?

A blog is an easy-to-use tool for publishing web pages without being a programmer. Usually, one individual—the teacher or a student—is responsible for creating blog entries. The content can include text, images, video, audio, and links. Other members of the group can post comments about each entry, so a conversation is established.

Entries are usually classified chronologically, but other categories can also be used.

Why?

Writing about the course topics, projects, or one's own process can promote research skills, in-depth analysis, and self-reflection. They also provide teachers with important information about the students' thought process. Peer and teacher comments can make the experience even richer.

Some common uses of blogs are:

* student learning journals;

* readings logs; and

* research projects.

How?

The teacher provides instructions for the assignment. A student creates his or her own blog and writes entries. The teacher and other students read and write comments to which the author responds.

Some LMSs include blogging tools that are linked to the gradebook (so blogging activities can be graded). There are also free options that can be used (e.g. Blogger, LiveJournal, Typepad, Movable Type, and WordPress).

☑ Teachers are competent in the use of the digital tools and resources necessary to teach the online course.

3.6 Beyond the LMS

LMSs are created to facilitate online teaching and learning. They provide a structured, closed, and secure environment for teaching and learning. Yet, there are many other online tools available that can perform the necessary communication, content delivery, and assessment functions.

Some institutions are using a combination of independent tools to offer online courses instead of the LMS. For example, Figure 3.17 shows a an excerpt from the course *Ventures in Learning Technologies* (ETEC-522) at the University of British Columbia, offered in the fall of 2015 using:

- **A blog** (in this case, WordPress) to create the course website and enable discussions. Blogs are easy-to-use tools for personal website creation that don't require specialized knowledge. They include entries that can be categorized by different criteria. Readers can post comments to each entry.

- **YouTube videos** and **podcasts** to deliver multimedia content (Bates, 2015).

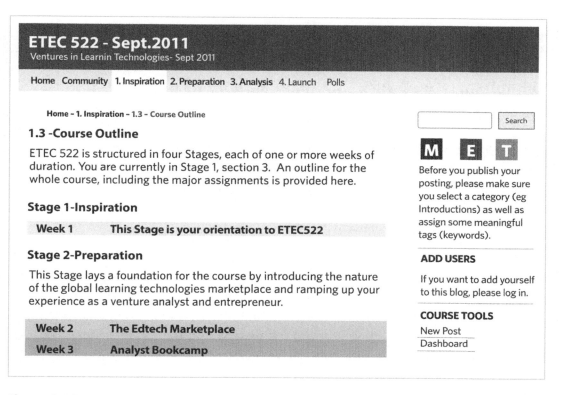

Figure 3.17 The WordPress Screen from the ETEC-522 Course at the University of British Columbia

Teachers who work in LMSs are also integrating tools from the Internet. For example, Tom Geary teaches an online writing course at Tidewater Community College using Blackboard as the LMS. He incorporates a tool called WordCloud to help learners summarize concepts at the end of a discussion. Scott Thornbury teaches language courses in The New School's LMS, Canvas. He schedules one-to-one live sessions with his students using an external videoconferencing application (Skype).

Whatever platforms are used to offer online courses, there are a few important things to remember:

- External tools can be used in courses offered in an LMS to enrich students' experience.

- It is possible to combine digital tools and resources to teach an online course without an LMS.

- Good teaching principles apply within and outside of an LMS.

Teaching Dilemma

Should social networks be used as part of online course interaction?

Many online learners and teachers are active on social networks such as Facebook, Google+, and Twitter. These networks can provide a familiar platform to extend online course interaction. But should a teacher incorporate social networks into the instructional realm? This is a hotly debated topic among educators.

On the one hand, online learning can be a somewhat isolating experience, as students do not physically interact with each other. Social networks can provide an arena for students to get to know each other "outside of class." This kind of bonding can have a positive effect on the learning community within the LMS because students build friendships and trust in their peers (Lee & McLoughlin, 2010). Students can also use social media as a platform to do collaborative projects and share study materials. In many ways, these online networks provide an informal space that function as a social campus surrounding the online classroom. Some reasons for using social networks to connect with students include:

- Many students are already using them enthusiastically.

- Students can create profiles to share information about themselves.

- The networks are accessible through mobile devices.

- Users tend to check and respond to messages sent via social networks frequently.

On the other hand, formally integrating social networks into course procedures has some implications to consider:

- Interaction outside of the security wall of an LMS is not protected under privacy acts governing academic institutions.

- There are different norms and criteria for interacting on social networks than within a course.

- It blurs the line between personal and academic realms.

Some teachers view social networks as part of the digital world students live in and use them as an extension to their online courses. Tom Geary is active on social networks and doesn't see a problem with allowing students to use them as a communication option: "I'm OK with them messaging me through Twitter or working on a project together on Facebook." Tom explains his reasoning:

> Today's students are digital natives. They learn a lot from social media interactions, from visiting websites and from just being online on a daily basis. I feel that online learning is just an extension of that. I take students to multimodal websites and have them create multimodal projects. They work in all sorts of digital spaces and on Twitter and look at social networking and offer that kind of analysis in their projects. It's where they are and what they do. So why not use it?

Tom does occasionally have problems when his students use a social network for group projects instead of the space he has designated for collaboration within the LMS:

> When students work outside the boundaries of the LMS, I can't see their process. I can't tell if they are on track. When this happens, I ask students to send me progress reports. But sometimes they don't and they don't get their work done on time or their work is off target. This is a problem that wouldn't happen if they were working in the LMS.

Other teachers, such as Scott Thornbury, choose not to use social networks in their online teaching. Scott explains:

> For teaching, I keep well away from social networks, actually. I keep the two things very separate. I don't friend students on Facebook and I don't refer to my Twitter feed. If people find it, that's fine. It's not just to keep a separation of public and private life. I feel I have two public lives in the sense: I have a professional life within the university representing the Masters Program and the work I do outside of that professionally—the videos I post on my website, my papers, talks I've given at conferences. I let people find that stuff, but I don't refer them to it because I think there is a danger that you might skew the agenda. I think there are two different agendas: (1) there is the narrow focus [the course] that has certain criteria; and (2) a broader professional arena. Students mustn't think that they are being assessed on criteria that are broader, more elusive, and not well spelled out. If the students know that I have a particular approach, they may try to tow some particular line or orientate their thinking toward that. I don't want that to be an issue within the course.

There are two kinds of boundaries to consider between an online course and the rest of the Internet. First, there is a security parameter that surrounds most LMSs. Within a password-protected environment of an LMS, users can feel relatively safe that their privacy and rights are protected. As teachers, this is an important condition to keep in mind, and one to make your students aware of too.

But there is also a perceptual boundary created in the minds of the participants that separates an online course as a distinct space. Inside a virtual classroom, interactions adhere to certain norms and values that are determined by the academic setting, the teacher, and the students. Extending course interaction to include social networks invites a broader range of influences into the dynamics.

We recommend that you consider the benefits of using social networks as you would any resource. Think about whether its use will:

- support students' attainment of the learning outcomes for the course;

- facilitate ease of communication among all participants (including you);

- support the kind of learning community you want in the course; and

- respect and protect the rights of students to participate in course interactions freely and comfortably.

 Check the book's website for a list of tools and resources that can be used for online teaching: www.essentialsofonlineteaching.com.

3.7   Summary and Standards

Teaching an online course is made possible through digital tools and resources that are usually integrated in an LMS. In some cases, online courses are offered outside of an LMS, using a combination of tools and resources available on the Internet. Whatever the platform, teachers select the communication tools needed to teach the course and for the students to engage in the learning activities.

Content is distributed to learners through digital media (text, image, video, audio, or multimedia) by uploading the file to the platform or including the corresponding link in their messages. Guests and real data are often used to enrich the course content, and familiarize the students with authentic tasks. Assessing students' progress is facilitated with rubrics, quizzes, and a gradebook tool that automates calculations and provides immediate information to participants.

It is important that teachers learn to use the basic tools and resources before their course starts. Feeling comfortable with the technology will let them concentrate on tending to students' learning needs.

- [ ] Learning activities and ease of use determine the best technologies to use.
- [ ] Weekly announcements call students' attention to important and timely course information.
- [ ] Discussion forums are used to support online course interaction.
- [ ] Email facilitates private conversations between teachers and students, or among students.
- [ ] Teachers use a variety of means to communicate with students throughout the course.
- [ ] Courses include a variety of relevant multimedia to support learning and appeal to individual preferences.
- [ ] Learning resources are shared in formats that are accessible to all students.
- [ ] Learners are encouraged to interact with others (classmates, guest speakers, etc.) and benefit from their experience and expertise.
- [ ] Learning resources include authentic materials and relate to real-life applications.
- [ ] Teachers provide students with guidelines for using resources.
- [ ] The course includes ongoing and frequent assessment.

☐ Criteria/rubrics clearly inform learners about how they will be assessed on specific assignments and online participation.

☐ Teachers and students can easily track learners' progress.

☐ Teachers are competent in the use of the digital tools and resources necessary to teach the online course.

References and Further Reading

Bates, T. (2015). *Teaching in a digital age*. Vancouver, BC: BC Campus Open Textbooks. Retrieved from http://opentextbc.ca/teachingina digitalage/

Clark, R. (Ed.) (2012). *Learning from media. Arguments, analysis, and evidence* (2nd ed.). Charlotte, NC: Information Age.

Lee, M. J., & McLoughlin, C. (2010). Beyond distance and time constraints: Applying social networking tools and Web 2.0 approaches to distance learning. In G. Veletsianos (Ed.). *Emerging technologies in distance education* (pp. 61–87). Edmonton, AB: Athabasca University Press.

Chapter 4 | Preparing to Teach Online

Teaching an Online Course

| Preparing to Teach Online | The Beginning Weeks | The Middle Weeks | The Final Weeks |

Preparing to teach online means getting yourself and your course ready to engage students. It requires a deep understanding of the course design and a personal action plan for how you will support students' progress. **It's helpful to put yourself in the shoes of the learners to anticipate their needs.** Imagine the following scenario:

Kim logs on to her online course for the first time, feeling excited and a bit nervous. There it is: CS001 *Digital Marketing*. She clicks on Module 1. Dr. Martin Milton's announcement welcomes her. Wow! He says that there will be students from six countries in the class! Her professor's enthusiasm is contagious. OK, so she has to start by reading the syllabus and introducing herself.

The course sounds ambitious and demanding: a weekly discussion with readings, videos, and case studies to analyze. There are three projects throughout the semester: two individual campaigns and a group presentation. Discussions will account for 30% of the grade and projects for the other 70%.

She will need to organize herself. Saturday mornings will be a good time to review the resources before participating in discussions. The syllabus says that one of the projects will be done as a group. How does that work online?

A little overwhelmed, she opens a video Professor Milton has posted introducing himself. He looks friendly and his credentials are impressive. He has worked on interesting campaigns in Silicon Valley and certainly seems to know his subject. **Kim is relieved to learn that he will be active throughout the course, participating in discussions, giving feedback, and even offering individual support if she needs it.** She joins the first discussion called "Building Our Community" and posts her introduction to the class.

The student in this scenario logged into a course that was ready for her. Each step of the student's initial experience was anticipated and carefully planned by the teacher. He welcomed the student with excitement and provided information to help her move logically from one step to the next. He made a video introduction to let students know that there is a real-live teacher participating in the course with them. The teacher took time to think through the students' needs, plan his role in the course, and set the stage for success.

This chapter shows you how to prepare to teach an online course. Before the semester begins, it's important to:

- plan your teaching;

- define the course time frame;

- ready the discussion forums for interaction;

- check all course resources; and

- fill in information needed.

Careful preparation pays off. With a thorough understanding of the course design, you can set up routines that will help you and your students to work effectively throughout the course.

4.1 Planning Your Teaching

First impressions are very important in online learning. At the onset, students are often unsure about how an online course will function and what is expected of them. They might have questions about their own technical skills or ability to learn online. They may feel anxious about not meeting their teacher and classmates in person. A well-prepared online course eases students' transition into online learning. It's the teacher's job to make sure that all the components of the course are ready for students. A well-organized first week lays the groundwork for a successful semester.

Review the Syllabus and Introductory Materials

A good understanding of the course design is necessary for teachers to plan their instruction. The syllabus and other introductory materials (such as suggestions for online study, rubrics, guidelines for participation, technical guides, etc.) present this information. Review these documents before your course starts. Identify how the activities, resources, outcomes, and assessment fit together. Comb through the plan considering:

- what students learn in each unit;

- how the learning activities lead to the outcomes;

- how students work online; and

- how they are assessed.

Your students will also need to have a clear picture of the course's goals and the strategy to achieve the learning outcomes. So make sure all essential issues are addressed in the syllabus and that the content reflects the current semester. **If you find that the syllabus does not provide enough information, you may need to revise it or provide additional documents to fill in the gaps.**

Figure 4.1 provides an outline of the components of a thorough online course syllabus.

Syllabus Components

Basic Course Information

1. Session (e.g. Fall 2016).

2. Course title and number/section.

3. Instructor name and email.

4. Academic credits.

5. Prerequisites.

Course Timeframe and Format

1. Format (i.e. asynchronous or blended, with an explanation).

2. Number of weeks online.

3. First and last day of the online course. Note any holidays.

4. Weekly start and end day for each lesson (e.g. the online week begins on Tuesday and ends on Monday).

5. Due date/time zone: due dates are expressed in day, hour, and time zone (e.g. GMT, EST). Students are responsible for adjusting the due date to their time zone. The time zone expressed will most likely be that of the teacher.

Course Description
A summary overview of the course.

Learning Outcomes
These express what the learner will know or be able to do at the end of the course.

Communication Strategy
Provides a space and place for the teacher to clearly outline his or her availability and response time within the online course.

Figure 4.1 Syllabus Components

Source: Vai and Sosulski (2016) (reprinted with permission)

Technical Requirements

The contact information for online technical support and resources.

Course Requirements

1. **Assignments**. The overview of assignments, such as number of papers, projects, participation in discussion forums, texts, quizzes, group projects, readings, etc.

2. **Assessment and Feedback Plan.**

3. **Activity Grade Percentage.** List how grades will be determined and the weight of each type of activity in determining the final grade.

4. **Criteria for Class Participation.** Students should be required to contribute substantially to the discussion forum, a minimum of three times per week. A rubric that outlines the criteria for evaluating class participation leaves little room for confusion (see Chapters 8 and 9).

5. **Policy on Due Dates and Lateness.** Establishes clear rules and penalties for late assignments.

6. **Submission of Graded Assignments.** The manner of submission for graded assignments is clearly stated.

Link to Institutional Academic Policy

Statement on plagiarism and cheating, and honor code.

Course Schedule

The online course schedule is a calendar, to-do list, and presents a sequence of events, assignments, readings activities, and course deliverables. (See Table 4.1 for an example.)

Figure 4.1 *continued*

Table 4.1 A Partial Example of a Course Outline from an *Introduction to Educational Psychology* Course

Dates	Lesson & Topic	Resources	Learning Activities
Unit 1—Learning theories and their educational application			
Week 1	**1. Behaviorism**	Woolfolk, Chapter 7	**Activity 1:** Group discussion
		Skinner, *Teaching Machines*	**Activity 2:** Written assignment (Behavioral Case Study Analysis)
Week 2	**2. Cognitivism**	Woolfolk, Chapters 8 and 9	**Activity 3:** Group discussion
		Mayer, Chapter 3	**Activity 4:** Written assignment (Cognitive Case Study Analysis)

Institutions around the world have different guidelines for syllabi. Templates and elements vary.

Teaching Tip

Check institutional policies

Most institutions have policies about making changes to online courses. Check with your academic department to find out if you have permission to edit the course syllabus.

 A syllabus including contact information, a course outline, requirements, and expectations for student participation is accessible from the start of the course and throughout.

Choose Your Teaching Strategy

Before the semester begins, you need to figure out what actions you will take to support your students' learning as they move through the various activities. Start with the first week;

imagine each step of a learner's process. What will they need to know and be able to do to succeed in the assigned activities? What will you do to help them? Think about how you might:

- provide instructions;

- clarify concepts or procedures;

- give feedback; and

- motivate them to participate and learn.

Let's look at an example that shows how a teacher prepares to teach the first week of her *Creative Writing* course. Figure 4.2 walks you through the teacher's analysis and decision-making process. Notice that the teacher begins by imagining what students will do as they log on to the class and participate in the first activities. She considers how these activities are designed to lead to the learning outcomes identified. Then the teacher figures out what she can do to help the students reach those outcomes.

Some teachers analyze all the course units and plan their interventions for the whole semester. Others only prepare for the first few weeks. While an in-depth knowledge of the whole course is necessary to inform your teaching, you may not know at the beginning what students will need down the road. We recommend that you prepare as much as possible, but allow for adaptation of the plan as the course evolves.

Teaching Tip

Review and revise a preexisting course plan

If you have taught this course before, review your notes and records from the past semester. Were there any activities that didn't work out as planned? How can you make the experience more rewarding for students? Take time before the new semester begins to make revisions to improve the course and your teaching strategies.

My Teaching Plan for Week 1

Creative Writing

Activity #1: Orientation to the LMS and the Course

What students will do:

- Log onto the course and review all the material under the START HERE menu.

- Ask questions about course procedures and expectations in the Q&A discussion forum (see Chapter 8, p. 211, for an example).

Learning outcomes:

- Students will demonstrate an understanding of the course procedures and requirements by successfully completing the week's learning activities.

- Students will understand how to access learning resources within the LMS, interact in the discussion forum and use the dropbox to submit an assignment.

What I will do before the course begins:

- Post an announcement welcoming students and directing them to the START HERE menu.

- Check that the syllabus and other introductory documents are complete and up to date.

- Open a Q&A discussion forum for students to ask questions about course procedures and include instructions for how to use this forum.

- Post an icebreaker activity.

What I will do during the first week:

- Welcome students online.

- Respond to students' questions.

Figure 4.2 An Example of a Teacher's Preparation for Initial Course Activities

Activity #2: Introduction to Course Content

What students will do:

- Read Chapter 1: Principles of Plot Development.

- View Grammar Review and take self-assessment quiz.

- Submit a writing sample to the dropbox.

Learning outcomes:

- Students build a knowledge base of plot development for the following week's discussions and assignments.

- Students gain an understanding of their grammatical strengths and weaknesses.

What I will do before the course begins:

- Check that the Grammar Review resource and automated quiz are available and working correctly (upload if necessary).

- Prepare an announcement to post midweek to:

    o   direct students to the reading activity;

    o   assign a due date for the writing sample;

    o   provide a link for students to purchase the textbook; and

    o   give instructions for the writing sample.

What I will do during the first week:

- Answer questions about the assignment in the Q&A forum.

- Check students' writing sample and provide feedback.

Figure 4.2 *continued*

4.2 Defining the Course's Time Frame

Asynchronous courses offer a great deal of flexibility in terms of when teachers and students participate. However, weekly routines and due dates are necessary if students are expected to work together and move through the activities as a group. Teachers also need to define their weekly teaching schedules to be able to provide learners with timely support and maintain an active presence throughout the course.

Establish a Weekly Routine for Students

As discussed in Chapter 1, online time is usually organized in weeks. Keeping the basic learning activities similar from one week to the next makes it easier for students to plan their schedules.

Personal Reflection

Sepi Yalda

In my online course, *History of Meteorology*, students know that they are required to do the following learning activities each week:

- Read and watch a set of learning resources.

- Gather data from online sources.

- Participate in an online discussion forum.

- Submit a progress report on their research project.

In addition to these weekly requirements, they take quizzes, give online presentations, take tests, and submit final projects at scheduled times throughout the semester. Knowing the task that they are expected to perform each week helps students to plan their time accordingly.

Set the Course Calendar

Most online course designs establish a recommended number of weeks for the completion of each unit. **We recommend that you identify a start and end date for each unit. Also specify the due dates for all assignments.** Remember to factor in holidays and official breaks in the semester schedule. This will help everyone move through the units within the same time period.

Personal Reflection

Benjamín Mayer-Foulkes

My online course at 17 Instituto (Mexico) uses critical theory as a tool to analyze phenomena. It focuses on an in-depth analysis of the different texts. We focus on the body of work each week, with a required reading and some recommended ones. I provide questions to guide the analysis. Students are expected to read each text very carefully, contribute to the discussion in a well-documented fashion, and then produce rigorous and singular monthly essays.

After several experiences, I found that it was best to open a new unit on Friday because students were then able to use the weekend to read the texts. Then, during the week, they could participate in the discussions with solid arguments. The quality of the discussions increased.

Table 4.2 shows the activities that a teacher and his students do in the first week of a course offered by 17, Instituto in Mexico. The weekly routines for your course will depend upon the course design and the teaching activities that you have planned.

Table 4.2 The Weekly Routine for Online Courses at 17, Instituto

Weekday	Teacher Activity	Students' Activity
Friday	9:00 a.m. CST Open weekly discussion and post comment: • Introduce the author and text. • Clarify the week's work.	Read week's intro and guidelines for study of the author.
Saturday Sunday	Teache off.	
Monday thru Thursday	**10:00 a.m. CST** • Set the appropriate atmosphere for fruitful exchanges. • Enrich the discussion. • Respond to students' questions. • Identify students that have not participated and address them individually. • Post a closing comment. • Close the weekly discussion.	• Read and post comments responding to course questions. • Enrich the discussion. • Observe the relation between conceptual content and written form.

 A consistent routine of weekly course activities is established to help online learners organize their schedules.

Here are some tips that will help your students form productive work routines and meet deadlines:

- Establish consistent deadlines. Many teachers launch discussions and activities at a set time each week. Similarly, consistent time and day of the week serves as the weekly deadline for submission of assignments (i.e. Sundays at midnight).

- Consider the time students need to review content before participating in a discussion or doing another activity. Asynchronous interaction happens over days, so allow at least four or five days for productive discussion to take place.

- Specify when you want students to move on to a new discussion.

- Schedule any live session that you plan during the semester so that students can plan ahead. It is a good idea to make them optional and upload recorded versions available for those learners that cannot attend.

- Remember that online students have multiple responsibilities besides studying. Allow sufficient time for them to complete all the learning activities.

- Specify the time zone along with the deadline. Online courses may serve participants that live in different regions.

Learning activities (discussions, assignments, tests and quizzes) may be configured in the LMS to be accessible for a specific time period (see Figure 4.3). For example, you can set a discussion forum to open on a specific Monday and close the following Monday. Configuring start and end dates within the LMS will help you implement the schedule according to the timeline described on the syllabus.

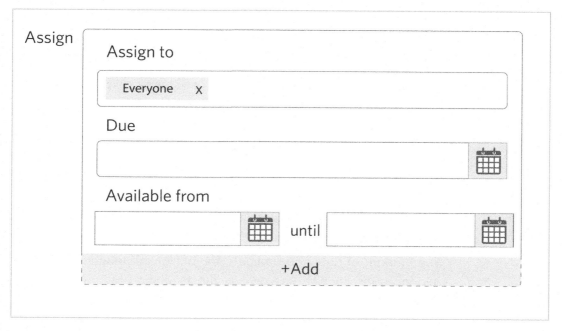

Figure 4.3 Screen in Which Teachers Designate Dates When an Assingment is Due and Available to Students in Canvas. Discussion forums may be configured in a similar way.

Teaching Dilemma

Do I make all lessons and resources visible from the beginning?

The LMS allows the teacher to program the dates when a lesson will be made visible to students. Therefore, it is possible to provide students with all the course content from the beginning or reveal a lesson each week. The former option gives learners the possibility to move forward at their own pace; the latter helps to ensure that everyone is moving through the material together.

When most of the coursework relies on individual work, learners may benefit from the flexibility of moving forward at their own pace. If the course features group discussions and collaborative learning, it's a good idea to open the activities one at a time. The right decision for you will depend upon your course design.

☑ Due dates for submission of assignments are clear.

☑ Sufficient time is allotted for students to complete the learning activities.

Plan Your Teaching Schedule

Teaching an online course requires good time management skills. It's up to you to set up an effective work schedule that allows you to fulfill your responsibilities to support your students within a reasonable time frame.

The amount of time you dedicate to your online teaching will depend upon your course design and teaching practices. To estimate the number of hours you will require each week, analyze the weekly routine you have established for students and the teaching interventions that you have planned for the first weeks. Approximate the time you will spend:

* reviewing course content and activities of each lesson;
* gathering and adapting additional materials;

- providing instructions and orientation;

- opening and monitoring online discussions;

- tracking students' progress;

- supporting individual students; and

- grading assignments and providing feedback.

Descriptions and examples of each of these instructional tasks are provided in Chapters 5–10.

Most online teachers find it best to designate blocks of time (two or more hours) several times a week for substantive review of the students' online activity, to compose instructional contributions, and to evaluate students' work. They usually check in with the online course every day in shorter intervals to keep up with the online discussion and add comments. Setting up a consistent teaching schedule will help you manage the workload while providing a consistent online presence in your course.

Personal Reflection

Margaret Foley McCabe

Many teachers are concerned that online teaching will be too time-consuming. Based on our own online teaching and our experience working with hundreds of online teachers, we estimate the average time a teacher dedicates to an online course ranges between 8 and 15 hours per week. Of course, individual practices vary widely online, as they do in classroom-based instructions.

There are several factors that contribute to the belief that online teaching is more time-consuming:

- Online courses require substantial time and effort in planning and preparation before the semester begins.

- Teaching online for the first time involves a learning curve that may require additional time.

- Increased student enrollment in some online courses requires more time for evaluation and feedback of students' work.

- There is a perceptual hangover from the early days of online education that were fraught with technical difficulties in an unfamiliar online environment. Thankfully, today's technologies are faster and easier to use, and more people are familiar with online communication.

4.3 Setting the Stage for Interaction

Online courses can function as learning communities with teachers and students interacting and learning together. But this does not happen automatically; teachers need to set the stage for interaction and create a climate of mutual trust and respect. They anticipate students' needs and concerns before the course begins and post instructions and welcoming remarks to get the students personally invested and engaged from the start. They also open discussion forums for the different kinds of conversations that will take place in the course.

Post a Welcome Announcement

As students log on, they need to know where to start. The syllabus and other introductory materials are usually found in a prominent place within the course home on the LMS. However, it's helpful for teachers to point to these documents and make sure that students read and understand them as they begin the course.

Figure 4.4 provides an example of an announcement that directs the students to the "Course Introduction" file with links to the syllabus and all support materials needed for students to understand how the course works. The teacher had to think this all through before her students began the course.

Announcement ▽

Posted Jan 12, 2015

Hello and welcome to Introduction Computer Programming. I'm Prof. Harbin and I look forward to working with all of you throughout this semester.

Please begin by exploring the materials found within the Course Introduction file.

Here you will find:

- **A short video I made to introduce myself and the course to you.**
- **The course syllabus.**
- **A calendar that includes due dates for all projects and test dates.**
- **The grading policy and rubrics for projects.**
- **The first weeks' activities**

As you watch and read this material, the whole plan should become clear. We'll meet in the discussion forum called "Introductions". As you may have guessed, this is where we will meet each other and begin the adventure into computer programming. If you have questions about any of this, please bring them to the introductory discussion.

Enjoy the course!
Prof. H.

Show All Announcements

Figure 4.4 A Welcome Message Explaining to Students Where to Start

 Instructions direct students to initial course activities.

Open Discussion Forums

Before your course starts, it is important that you set up the discussion forums. As we explained in Chapter 3 and elaborate upon in Chapter 8, discussion forums are spaces in which students can interact by posting comments (see pp. 64 and 210). Teachers often create the discussion forums before the course begins and then make them visible to students at appointed times throughout the semester. For instance, a teacher may create 15 discussion forums—one for each week of a 15-week semester—and then open them to students one at a time.

As you prepare your course for students, consider opening the following discussion forums.

- **An Icebreaker Activity**

Structured introductory activities are very useful to open the dialogue. Icebreaker activities are exercises that give each student a question or challenge that requires them to participate online. They give people opportunities to get to know one another and build rapport among the online class.

Icebreaker activities are effective when they:

- are clearly described;
- encourage participation;
- set the tone for interactions;
- provide opportunity for participants to get to know one another;
- allow people to share their experience and/or expertise;
- promote cooperative learning; and
- familiarize students with online interaction.

Check if an icebreaker activity is included in your course design. If so, does it promote the kind of interaction you want? You may need to adapt the activity to suit your teaching style and the kind of relationship you wish to establish with and among your learners. If an icebreaker activity has not been planned, it's a good idea for you to plan this kind of introductory exercise.

There are many versions of online icebreaker activities with different emphasis and purpose. Some are like games that invite a personal response. Other icebreaker prompts are more academically focused; students may be asked to share their previous experience with the subject matter and interests in the course. The point of an icebreaker activity is to get students participating and to connect to the course and each other. Figure 4.5 below shows an example of an icebreaker activity from Scott Thornbury's linguistics studies course, *English in the World*.

> Oct 20, 2014 at 4:36 pm
>
> ## Unit 1: DB1. Me myself and I
>
> As a 'warm-up' exercise, introduce yourself and list some of the names (formal and informal) people call you (as in Example 3 on page 3 of the extract from Holmes 2008).
> Show the connection between your relationship with them and this name (mother, son, colleague, old friend etc.) and in light of the **social dimensions** listed on p. 10. Any pattern? Any anomalies? How (and why) has this changed over time?
>
> (This discussions is NOT graded)

Figure 4.5 The Icebreaker from Scott Thornbury's Course. The Holmes article he quotes refers to formal and informal speech. He is incorporating the content of the course into this initial exercise.

 Check the book's website for more examples of icebreaker activities: www.essentialsofonlineteaching.com.

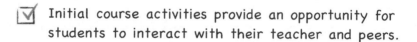 Initial course activities provide an opportunity for students to interact with their teacher and peers.

- **Forums to Discuss Course Content**

Many online courses include discussion forums that correspond in topic to weekly units indicated on the course schedule. This is usually where most of the course interaction takes place. Students' participation grades are based on the comments they post to the weekly online discussion forums.

To start these off, a teacher posts instructions and questions to which students respond. Good discussion prompts include questions that encourage critical thinking and a range of responses from students (see Chapter 8 for uses of discussion forums and suggestions for effective discussion prompts).

- **Question & Answer (Q&A) Forum**

Teachers often create a discussion forum for students to post questions about procedural or technical issues they encounter.

Having a Q&A forum open throughout the semester has several advantages. It:

- organizes all logistical questions and answers in one place;

- keeps the course discussions focused on content without getting bogged down by logistical questions;

- lessens the burden on teachers to respond individually to similar questions by many students because everyone can read the answer posted in the Q&A forum; and

- enables students to help one another by posting responses and suggestions to their classmates' problems.

Figure 4.6 shows a prompt that a teacher posted to designate a discussion forum for Q&A.

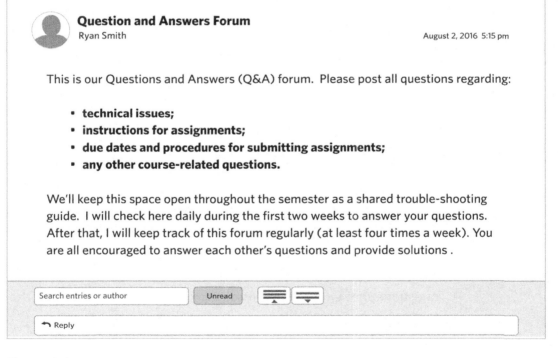

Question and Answers Forum
Ryan Smith   August 2, 2016 5:15 pm

This is our Questions and Answers (Q&A) forum. Please post all questions regarding:

- **technical issues;**
- **instructions for assignments;**
- **due dates and procedures for submitting assignments;**
- **any other course-related questions.**

We'll keep this space open throughout the semester as a shared trouble-shooting guide. I will check here daily during the first two weeks to answer your questions. After that, I will keep track of this forum regularly (at least four times a week). You are all encouraged to answer each other's questions and provide solutions .

Search entries or author   Unread

Reply

Figure 4.6 A Prompt Used to Open a Q&A Forum

Prepare Your Personal Introduction

In online courses, students need to know their teacher and establish a personal relationship with him or her. Teachers often introduce themselves within the icebreaker activity. The tone and style of a teacher's introduction create a first impression and give students a sense of how the teacher will relate to the class. Figure 4.7 provides an example. This is Scott Thornbury's introductory response to the icebreaker in his socio-linguistics course (cited above in Figure 4.5). Here, Scott describes various names he has been called throughout his life.

 Scott Thornbury's introduction to icebreaker excercise
Jan 27, 2015

I'm called Scott mostly - it's the kind of no-nonsense name that doesn't lend itself to shortenings or cute forms. Very rarely I tolerate Scotty: a (now deceased) Scottish friend used to use it almost instinctively and, whenever he could, manage to work 'Beam me up, Scotty' into the conversation – which, in his case, I didn't mind in the least. Another New Zealand friend calls me Scotto - but she is the only one.

At high school I was Thornbury —which says something about the hideous colonialist pretensions of that particular institution. I don't think I've ever been called Thornbury since.

When I was a teacher, I insisted on Scott, but when I taught in Egypt, the respect which teachers are held meant that students —even much older than me— insisted on Mr. Scott. Or Mr. Skoot, in actual fact.

Now that I teach in a US university context, I've had to accept Professor as an address term —often on it's own— or, even more respectfully —Professor Thornbury. In UK terms, I am not actually a Professor (defined there as 'a university teacher of the highest status' whereas in the US a Professor is 'any full-time teacher at a university'). I have tried to insist on Scott, but —for some students at least— I sense that this violates their sense of propriety. So I live with it, although I feel a little like an impostor!

Figure 4.7 Scott Thornbury's Introduction in the Icebreaker Exercise

Many teachers choose to make a short video to introduce themselves. Seeing your face and gestures and hearing your voice gives students a better understanding of the person behind the digital instruction. The personal and visual reference offered by a video is more important than the production quality. You can use the camera in your phone, tablet, or computer to record a simple introductory video.

See the book's website (www.essentialsofonlineteaching. com) for basic guidelines for preparing a video and examples of teachers' video introductions.

In whatever ways you decide to introduce yourself to your students online, consider sharing:

- **Your background and areas of expertise.** Your subject knowledge and work within your discipline makes you a valuable asset to online discourse. You are able to see connections between students' efforts and new territory that lies ahead for their exploration. Your credentials help to establish students' trust in your instruction.

- **Your enthusiasm.** As a teacher, your passion for learning is one of the most powerful tools you have to engage students. Your excitement can be contagious, igniting students' interest and personal investment.

- **Personal anecdotes and point of view.** The more authentic you can make your introduction, the better. Sharing personal stories gives students a living context to better understand your online contributions.

- **Your teaching style.** Let students know what you enjoy about teaching and how you like to interact with students.

- **The support you will be offering.** Reassure learners that you will be helping them during the course and describe what kind of support you will provide. Invite them to contact you whenever they need help.

- **Your contact information.** Tell students how to get in touch with you. It is recommended that you provide several means of communication, both inside and outside the LMS—email, discussion forum, chat office hours (see Chapter 5, p. 130).

☑ A teacher's introduction within a course personalizes his or her online interaction with students.

Teaching Tip

Introduce teaching assistants and online facilitators

Large-scale online courses are sometimes divided into sections with smaller class sizes. Teaching assistants or online facilitators often lead these online sections, facilitating the discussion board, answering students' questions, reviewing students' work, and participating in other interactive parts of the online course. In such cases, the teaching assistants or facilitators should share an introduction online (in addition to that of the lead teacher). Here again, the students need to learn about their knowledge and experience in the field to trust their instruction. Their enthusiasm will motivate them.

4.4 Preparing Course Materials

Core learning resources for a course are created or identified during the design phase and may be uploaded to the LMS at that time. Before a course begins, teachers need to upload any additional materials they have prepared to clarify the syllabus, reinforce concepts, add examples, or update information. In Chapter 3, we described different options that the LMS offers to handle additional resources:

- uploading materials to the LMS;

- sending them as an attachment in announcements or discussions; or

- including links in discussions, announcements, or emails.

It is recommended that teachers check that all course materials are available and functioning correctly before the course starts. **Non-working links or resources frustrate students and make them feel that their course is not well prepared.** So verify that links are functional and point to active web pages or resources. Try out the quizzes and tests to make sure they are working properly. Also check discussion forums, wikis, and blogs that students will use. Identify and correct any problem before your students log on to the course.

☑ Correct, working links are provided to course materials and resources.

4.5 Establishing Procedures for Technical Failures

While technology has come a long way, students may encounter technical problems that prevent them from fulfilling online course requirements. It is important that teachers prepare and communicate a contingency plan to handle such situations. Figure 4.8 provides an example.

What to Do in Case of Technical Difficulties

If technical problems prohibit you from completing course requirements, you must:

- Contact the tech support (1-800-TEC-SUPP or techsuppor@que.edu).

- Inform your teacher of the problem by email BEFORE an activity or assignment is due. (Note that the email will indicate the date and time sent.) The teacher will determine the best way to proceed.

Failure to comply with these guidelines may affect your grade.

Figure 4.8 An Example of a Teacher's Contingency Plan Included in the Course Syllabus

There are also some work habits that can help you and your students handle problems associated with LMSs, personal computers, or connectivity failures.

Here are some suggestions that can be used to avoid frustration:

- Write online contributions in a word processor, save them as files, and then paste the text to the LMS. If there is a problem while posting to the LMS, you will have your writing saved on your computer.

- Save a back-up copy of your course files regularly (i.e. course projects, presentations, essays) to prevent information loss in case your computer fails. You can use online storage systems (such as Google Drive or Dropbox) to be able to access your information from any device.

- Establish an external email address to be used as an alternate means for communicating in the event of LMS problems. As we have suggested, it is important to have multiple means for interacting with students. Redundancy is a safeguard.

☑ **Students are informed about procedures to follow in the event of technical difficulties.**

4.6 Summary and Standards

A thorough review of the course design will help you plan your teaching interventions to support the students as they work through learning activities.

You are ready to teach your course if you have:

- planned how to support students' learning throughout the semester;

- defined a course calendar, weekly routine, and due dates;

- configured the dates for learning activities and resources in the LMS (if required);

- uploaded your personal introduction to the LMS, as well as any other necessary resources;

- reviewed or created an icebreaker exercise;

- checked that all resources and links work correctly;

- prepared the discussions for the first week; and

- established a contingency plan for technical failures.

The time and investment you put into preparing the course and yourself for teaching your online course will pay off. It allows you to make informed decisions while the course is in progress and frees you to focus on your students' engagement with the material instead of planning the next task.

☐ A syllabus including contact information, a course outline, requirements, and expectations for student participation is accessible from the start of the course and throughout.

☐ A consistent routine of weekly course activities is established to help online learners organize their schedules.

☐ Due dates for submission of assignments are clear.

☐ Sufficient time is allotted for students to complete the learning activities.

☐ Instructions direct students to initial course activities.

☐ Initial course activities provide an opportunity for students to interact with their teacher and peers.

☐ A teacher's introduction within a course personalizes his or her online interaction with students.

☐ Correct, working links are provided to course materials and resources.

☐ Students are informed about procedures to follow in the event of technical difficulties.

References and Further Reading

Carnegie Mellon Eberly Center. (n.d.). *Design and teach a course: Instructional strategies*. Retrieved from www.cmu.edu/teaching/designteach/design/instructionalstrategies/discussions.html

Conrad, R., & Donaldson, J. (2004). *Engaging the online learner*. San Francisco, CA: Jossey-Bass.

Jacobs, H. H. (Ed.) (2004). *Getting results with curriculum mapping*. Alexadria, VA: ASCD.

Ko, S., & Rossen, S. (2004). *Teaching online: A practical guide*. New York, NY: Routledge.

Mayes, R., Luebeck, J., Ku, H. Y., Akarasriworn, C., & Korkmaz, O. (2011). Themes and strategies for transformative online instruction: A review of literature and practice. *The Quarterly Review of Distance Education, 12*(3), 151–166.

Stein, J., & Graham, C. R. (2014). *Essentials of blended learning: A standards-based guide*. M. Vai (Ed.). New York, NY: Routledge.

Vai, M., & Sosulski, K. (2016). *Essentials of online course design: A standards-based guide* (2nd ed.). New York, NY: Routledge.

Van de Vord, R., & Pogue, K. (2012). Teaching time investment: Does online really take more time than face-to-face? *The International Review of Research in Open and Distributed Learning, 13*(3). Retrieved from www.irrodl.org/index.php/irrodl/article/view/1190/2212

Chapter 5 | The Beginning Weeks: Launching an Online Course

Teaching an Online Course

The Beginning Weeks	The Middle Weeks	The Ending Weeks

Imagine that it's the first day of the online semester and your course is ready for students. You've uploaded all the resource materials and prepared the weekly assignments and discussions. You've posted a welcome announcement on the LMS for students to see as they log on.

Now it's time to meet your students and begin teaching. It's an exciting time that unfolds over a few days as students log on and find their way to the course. One by one, students enter and introduce themselves to you and each other. What was once just a course design and a collection of digital tools and resources is now a shared experience. The online course has begun!

Teachers fulfill many important roles during the beginning weeks of a course. The first one is to help students understand how the course works. The syllabus and introductory information provide detailed information explaining this to students. However, they often need a tour through the course to understand how it all fits together. The teacher serves as the tour guide.

Teachers also act as hosts, welcoming students and getting them excited about the adventure ahead. You share your enthusiasm about the course and your interest in what the students bring to the experience. Students see right away that the course is interactive and requires personal investment and active participation.

The teacher is also a living resource for the students. You are the one participant in the class who knows the intricacies and rationale for the course design and has expertise in the subject matter. You are there to clarify, amplify, and extend students' learning as opportunities arise.

For many students, this may be their first online course. So **the first weeks must provide students with an orientation to online learning, as well as the start of the actual course**. Instruction:

- helps students to work effectively in the online course environment;

- motivates them to engage in the course activities and reach the learning objectives; and

- encourages them to develop work habits that will serve them well throughout the semester.

This chapter emphasizes teaching strategies to get students on board and moving in the right direction.

5.1 Helping Students to Work in the Environment

As the course tour guide, you walk students through the first week's activities. You demonstrate how to communicate in the LMS and make sure they know how to perform all the different kinds of tasks required. You model the use of digital tools. You also point students toward the various types of resources and workspaces they will use and answer their questions along the way.

Familiarize Students with the Learning Environment

There are just a few basic things students need to understand to be able to work in the LMS, and it is important they do so as early as possible. They need to know how to:

- log on to the course and review lessons;

- access and use online resources (texts, video, audio, presentations);

- communicate online (discussions, announcements, email);

- create products with digital tools (wiki, blog, word processor, etc.);

- take quizzes or exams;

- upload assignments; and

- check their grades and review the teacher's feedback.

Many teachers use the opening learning activities to teach and test the students' mastery of competencies required to perform the course activities. For example, Tom Geary of Tidewater Community College begins his online course with a scavenger hunt. To earn full credit for the scavenger hunt exercise, students need to:

- locate learning resources within the LMS;

- find a resource on the Internet;

- post a comment to the discussion board;

- take a (non-graded) quiz; and

- submit a writing sample using the dropbox.

If students have trouble with any of these activities, Tom is able to help them or direct them to the institution's tech support for help.

During the first week of a course, learning the technology can demand a lot of the students' time and attention. Give students ungraded or low-stake opportunities to gain mastery in these competencies. Gauge the students' technical performance and help them feel comfortable and confident navigating the online environment before grades become an issue. A key task for you as a teacher is to make sure that students focus on learning the content and don't get bogged down with the technology.

Teaching Tip

Call or email your students

Remember that if students have problems understanding how to work in the LMS, you can reach them through more familiar forms of communication—telephone or personal email.

 Introductory activities help students master technical competencies required to participate in the course.

Review the Course Syllabus

Make sure students review the course syllabus and other introductory material carefully. The course design and your welcome announcement should point them to these materials. Some teachers give a low-stakes or ungraded assignment that asks students to answer questions about information found in the syllabus to check students' comprehension of the plan, such as:

- Name the three learning resources you are to read/view next week.

- How many times a week are you supposed to post comments on the discussion board?

- What is the title of the first assignment? And when is it due?

- How does the first assignment relate to the "Learning Outcome" identified for Week 1 on the syllabus?

- How many points is the 1st assignment worth toward your final grade?

- Name three ways you can get help in this course.

Keep a close eye on students' progress through the first week's activities to see if they understand the procedures.

☑ Information on the syllabus and introductory course material is reviewed with students at the beginning of the course.

Establish Ways to Communicate with Students

In Chapter 3, we described how the different communication tools of the LMS function. During the first weeks, it's a good idea to use all, or most, of the communication tools you will use throughout the semester so students get a full picture of how course interaction works. Here are some ways teachers use communication tools in the first weeks:

- **Announcements** are used to post messages for students to see as they log on to the course. Your first announcement is a welcome message (see p. 62). A couple of days into the first week, you may want to post a second message, pointing students to some important course information. This will let students know that announcements change and they should always read them on their way into the course. Figure 5.1 shows an example.

 Mid-week issues   Sep 2 at 9: 32 am
Nanette Bristol

Hello Psychology 101 Students. I have a few issues that need your attention:

1. I will use this Announcement feature to communicate important course information throughout the weeks. Please check here each time you log on.
2. I just opened our first content discussion, "Biology of the Mind." The discussion prompt included there explains what to do.
3. Let's finish up our introductions by t tomorrow (Thursday) to move on to Unit 1.

Figure 5.1 An Example of a Second Announcement a Teacher Posts During the First Week of a Course

- **Discussion forums** are used to interact with the whole class. Your first discussion is likely to be an icebreaker or some other kind of introductory activity. We provide some suggestions for facilitating the opening discussion in the next sections below. Chapter 8 offers more about facilitating different kinds of discussions for different purposes.

- **Email** is used to have private interactions with students. LMS mail services have an option to do an email "blast," meaning you can write one email and send it to each student. This is an easy way to introduce email as an option for students to communicate with you. Figure 5.2 shows an example.

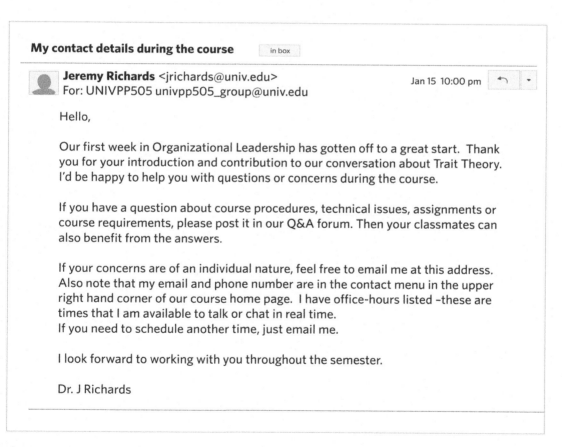

My contact details during the course | in box |

Jeremy Richards <jrichards@univ.edu>   Jan 15 10:00 pm
For: UNIVPP505 univpp505_group@univ.edu

Hello,

Our first week in Organizational Leadership has gotten off to a great start. Thank you for your introduction and contribution to our conversation about Trait Theory. I'd be happy to help you with questions or concerns during the course.

If you have a question about course procedures, technical issues, assignments or course requirements, please post it in our Q&A forum. Then your classmates can also benefit from the answers.

If your concerns are of an individual nature, feel free to email me at this address. Also note that my email and phone number are in the contact menu in the upper right hand corner of our course home page. I have office-hours listed –these are times that I am available to talk or chat in real time.
If you need to schedule another time, just email me.

I look forward to working with you throughout the semester.

Dr. J Richards

Figure 5.2 A Teacher's Initial Email to Students

- **The feedback tool in gradebook** provides another option for you to communicate with each student individually. When students turn in work online, the LMS feedback tool allows you to post comments in the margins (look for suggestions on offering feedback in Chapter 9, pp. 254–258). Some teachers use this tool extensively to provide individual feedback and open a dialogue with students about their progress over time. Offering feedback on students' first assignment will establish this tool as another avenue for communication between you and your students.

Using all these tools during the first weeks establishes different pathways for group and individual communications. It lets students know what to expect from you and how to reach you and each other.

 Teachers use a variety of means to communicate with students throughout the course.

Offer Support

As mentioned in Chapter 4 (p. 117), many teachers create a Question & Answer (Q&A) discussion to provide a space for students to ask procedural questions and seek advice from the teacher and fellow students about assignments. This online space can be left open throughout the semester.

Some students may be too shy or feel that their questions are too obvious to post in the Q&A forum. We suggest that you post a notice during the first few weeks of the semester reminding students that they can contact you with any questions or concerns about the class. You may choose to send this invitation out to students as an announcement on the course home page or as an email (see Figure 4.4 on p. 115 for an example).

If advising and tech support services are available at your institution, remind students that the contact information is in the syllabus. Also mention all other resources that may support their learning (digital library, digital tools such as plagiarism and grammar checkers, learning communities, etc.).

 Students are provided with several options to receive support for procedural, technical, and content-related issues.

Track Students' Participation

At the end of the first week online, check to see if all the students who have enrolled in your course have logged on successfully. **If students have not logged on, email them to inquire about their absence.** They may not be aware of the procedure to join the course, or may be experiencing technical difficulties. It is best to address nonparticipation issues during the beginning weeks of a course, before students fall too far behind to catch up.

Some LMSs can be configured to send teachers notifications when a student has not logged on to the course for a period of time.

There may be students who have logged on but have not posted comments. Email these students to let them know that in an online course, no one can see or benefit from their presence unless they contribute. In many courses, students are required to contribute three or more times a week. Share with them grading criteria for participation (in Chapter 6, pp. 166–170, we describe how to track students' progress; Figure 6.6 shows a detailed report of student logins).

Most LMSs have tracking software that allows you to see who has logged on to the course. Figure 5.3 shows an example.

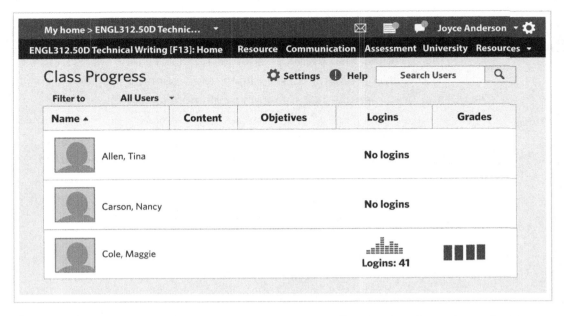

Figure 5.3 The Class Progress Report in Desire2Learn. The fourth column shows that two students have not logged in.

☑ Enrolled students who have not participated in the course during the first weeks are contacted.

5.2 Encouraging Communication

At the onset of the course, some students may be apprehensive about joining the discussion. Or, they may add a comment with minimal information because they are uncertain about expectations. It's natural for them to want to dip their toe in the water before jumping in. So it's important that you are there when they do, affirming their efforts and encouraging them to take the plunge.

Once the students have joined in the introductory discussion, welcome them and ask them follow-up questions. Help them become more comfortable by letting them know about your teaching and your expectations for their participation in the course. And promote students' interaction with one another.

Respond to Students' Initial Postings

When students introduce themselves online, give them feedback as soon as you can. This will show them that you are present during the course—guiding and supporting their learning—and that personal interaction is an important element of the online environment.

The following excerpt from a course on *Global Issues* illustrates how a teacher's response can be reassuring, initiate connection, and invite further input. The teacher encourages other students to respond to the first student's introduction.

Student: Hello everyone. My name is Sarah and this is my second online course. I'm a sophomore and my major is International Relations. I've studied music most of my life and have always found it interesting how artistic movements are shared and influenced by one another throughout the world and throughout history. The question I'd like to pose to the class is: Do you think globalization promotes diversity or homogeneity across cultures?

Teacher: Welcome Sarah! Congratulations on being the first to jump in. What kind of music do you study? I studied art history as an undergraduate and have found it immensely helpful as way to learn about world history. Economic interdependencies, struggles for power and resistance, and evolving perceptions of value are expressed through artistic movements. They map out an interconnected global history. We will trace several current artistic trends backwards over the next few weeks. I look forward to your input.

Great question about diversity vs. homogeneity—I'll let your classmates answer that.

Notice in the example above how the teacher:

- Uses the student's name, and refers to specifics within her response. These kinds of connections let students know that online interaction is personal and responsive.

- Asks a question to invite a follow-up comment from other students. The challenge is to open the discussion with the whole group.

A teacher may respond to the first one or two students promptly and then allow time for others to interject before posting again. This gives an opportunity for students to interact with each other and promotes a group dialogue rather than a back-and-forth conversation between the teacher and an individual student. Here's an example from a writing course that shows how a teacher greets students while encouraging group interaction.

Student 1: Hi! I'm Amy and I signed up for this course to fulfill my writing requirement. I'm a computer science major, so I haven't done much writing except papers and stuff like that. I hope to get better at it. How many people will be in this class?

Teacher: Welcome Amy. Glad to have you on board. There are 24 students enrolled in this course (and I'm looking forward to getting to know you all).

Writing skills are increasingly important in all fields because email, text, and shared documents have become the norm for communicating ideas. We'll consider the best uses and practices for different writing tasks.

Student 2: Hello Prof. Heinz, Amy, and other students who follow. My name is Brook and I'm in the Honors College, with double majors in Biology and Chemistry. I enjoy reading and find writing to be a good way to organize my thoughts.

This is my first online class, so I look forward to the experience.

Student 3: My name's Carter and I'm in the same boat as Amy. I don't really enjoy writing, but I understand how important it is (and required to graduate). One thing I've noticed is that people often use text to plan things when a simple telephone call would be so much more efficient. Does this bother anyone else?

Student 4: Hello everybody. This is Alex. Yes, Carter—it drives me crazy! Text should be used for quick messages—not long back-and-forths. Sometimes I think people just want to control the discussion and leave it whenever they want. Text is good for that—but it leaves a lot of room for misinterpretation.

Brook—I also find writing to be the best way for me to understand my own ideas. Sometimes I don't know what I think about something until I sit at a keyboard and begin to type. It's like the ideas come through my fingers. Did I mention that I am a media student?

Teacher: Welcome, Brook, Carter, and Alex. I love the conversations that have started. Writing involves a certain kind of thinking that combines logical, creative, and organizational skills. I agree with Brook and Alex, that writing can produce different ideas than other forms of communication.

And Carter and Alex have hit on an important theme of this course: finding the right form of communication for a particular purpose and audience.

Note: You'll find that we develop our own style of writing in this discussion forum. Let's keep it conversational without worrying too much about grammatical rules. Just be your (respectful) self and "talk" directly to others.

Notice how the teacher mentions individual students by name while addressing the whole class. This technique personalizes the dialogue without making the exchange between the teacher and a particular student exclusive. Everyone is invited to join in and comment on all that has been said (see Chapter 8 for more tips on facilitating online discussions).

Personal Reflection

Margaret Foley McCabe

The icebreaker exercise sets the tone for group communication. As a teacher, I tend to the interactions that take place in this initial exercise very carefully to make sure that each student is recognized by me or another student. I usually check in on my course two or three times a day during the first week to welcome students into the fold. Students may feel a little vulnerable after posting their introductory comment—unsure about what others will think of them. Students have told me that they feel reassured once someone has addressed them. It's like being invited into a circle of conversation. After I get the first few students interacting, I can sit back and let the students take over. They tend to mimic what I have started—greeting each other and asking follow-up questions. I usually jump in once a day with brief comments and general remarks to show that I am present. I often conclude the icebreaker activity with a roundup of information we have learned about each other. I try to do this in a fun, light-hearted way that highlights personal connections.

☑ Initial course activities provide an opportunity for students to interact with their teacher and peers.

☑ Teacher feedback is provided in a timely fashion.

Share Your Approach to Teaching

Online students want to know what kind of teacher you are. They are curious about your background and what you offer them. They want to know what you value and what you expect in the online interactions. They look to you for clues about the underlying criteria that will shape the course experience.

In Chapter 4, we suggested that you prepare and upload a personal statement or video introducing yourself to your students. This helps students connect to you as a person. But don't leave it there. Weave information about you and your teaching through your interactions with students during the first weeks of the semester. It helps them understand how you teach and what you expect from them. The following sections offer examples and suggestions for helping students understand how you teach and what you expect from them.

Lend Your Expertise

Ken Brain's research for his book *What the Best College Teachers Do* (2004) suggests that subject matter expertise is an important factor in engaging students:

> **Without exception, outstanding teachers know their subjects extremely well** . . . They know how to simplify and clarify complex subjects, to cut to the heart of the matter with provocative insights, and they can think about their own thinking in the discipline, analyzing its nature and evaluating its quality. That capacity to think metacognitively drives much of what we observed in the best teaching.
>
> (pp. 15–16)

Your subject knowledge and work within your discipline makes you a valuable asset to online discourse. You see connections between students' efforts and new territory that lies ahead for their exploration. Posting follow-up questions to students' responses and adding insightful comments within online discussions or in response to students' blogs challenges learners to go further and to press their inquiry into new territory. Your informed intervention can elevate a closed exchange (question/answer) into an open dialogue that inspires new layers of thought.

Personal Reflection

Allen Stairs

Every discipline has its own body of research and professional practices. A teacher's online contributions can demonstrate discipline-based thinking for students. For example, on the discussion board, I try to respond to each person at least once a week, adding on to his or her comments in a way that frames it in philosophical terms. I'm trying to model for them what it is to think like a philosopher. There are some real advantages for doing this online because the exchange is there [online] for study. You can slow down, read the students' responses again, and analyze what is behind a comment or a question. You can find the teachable moments—it's like threading a needle.

Whether you have designed your online course or you are teaching from a predesigned course, it is important for you to own your expertise in its subject matter. Your willingness to share that knowledge will help to keep them engaged in the process.

Share Your Teaching Values

In addition to the course requirements (described in the syllabus), students are curious about the teacher's expectations and preferences. How formal and strict are you as a teacher? What is the relationship that you invite between you and your students? What are your teaching priorities and preferences? As students log on to the course, they are looking for answers to these kinds of underlying questions. Let them know:

- **What should students call you?** When you post online, your first and last name appears on the message. Students may not know what to call you. Do they use your title? First or last name? Your choice in this matter—along with the tone and language you use—helps to establish the kind of relationship you want to have with your students.

Example 1

Tom Geary's students at Tidewater Community College call him Tom. He explains why:

> I want to encourage the whole group to become a community of learners rather than me as the teacher at the front of the class. I like to keep it informal and want students to feel comfortable just conversing with me online rather than composing answers to the teacher's questions.

Example 2

Joyce Anderson of the University of Maryland asks her students to refer to her as Prof. Anderson. She explains her choice:

> Because this course is designed to help students become better professional writers, I model openness with a sense of professionalism. Calling me Prof. Anderson reinforces my relationship to the student as a mentor, editor, and professional writer.

- **What are the firm and negotiable course rules?**
  Asynchronous online learning has a certain amount of flexibility built into the design to allow for different schedules and styles of participation. But students need to know the limits of that flexibility. Let students know where there is "wiggle room" and what guidelines need to be followed precisely. Every teacher puts emphasis on different aspects of the plan. Let your students know where you stand. In the following examples, two teachers post comments that help students to understand their expectations about online participation.

Example 1

Teacher: I want to emphasize that **it is a course requirement to log on and participate in the discussions three or more times throughout a week.**

This allows your classmates and me to respond back to you and build a conversation together. Logging on once a week and posting three comments is not the same. Your grade will reflect timing as well as content. See the participation rubric included in the syllabus and contact me if you have any questions.

Example 2

Teacher: A few students have asked me about my expectations for your weekly reflection blogs. Don't worry too much about length and format for this assignment. The point is for you to reflect on and respond to the questions I post in a way that captures your experience and thoughts. I will award 2 points each week for addressing the questions in any way you see fit.

- **What do you value in students' participation?** Students tend to want to please teachers. This goes beyond grades—they want you to think of them as capable people. It can be hard for students to gauge teachers' expectations online. Take the guessing game out of it by naming the attributes you value in online participation. This will lessen students' anxiety and encourage them to contribute effectively. Here is an example from a teacher's post in a weekly (content) discussion.

Teacher: I'm pleased to see students discussing controversial issues with such respect and honesty. This shows a desire to learn—not just to prove a point. I appreciate when students:

- Summarize issues raised and ask for confirmation that they have characterized their peers' points of view correctly. This is a powerful way to help us all focus on the salient issues and gives the original author a chance to clarify if needed.

- Back up their positions with support from the learning resources and personal experience.

- Take risks in expressing personal perspectives.

- Build on what others have added to the conversation and tie ideas together.

- Ask authentic questions.

Keep up the good work!

Model Participation

Teachers' online comments carry considerable weight with students. They look to you as a model of how to participate online. If you want students to participate three or more times a week, log on and contribute at least that many times.

Personal Reflection

Scott Thornbury

I can't overemphasize the importance of teachers being present online. In course evaluations, this is the one area that students consistently value most. They want their teacher there and they want to hear from him or her.

You can't just sit back and watch; you have to actively participate by posting comments, otherwise students don't know you are there. This may seem obvious, but you can't make assumptions about such things. For instance, we had one teacher in our program that was new to online teaching. She's a very conscientious and attentive teacher. She logged on every day and read the students' posts on the discussion board, but didn't add any comments. Her students complained that their teacher was never online and this upset them. We [the administration] had to tell this teacher that she needed to post comments every time she logged on to the discussion for students to know that she was there with them. It wasn't her fault—no one explained this to her. But this is something that is critical to online teaching.

If you want them to be inquisitive about other students' remarks, model asking follow-up questions.

Participating frequently in online discussion forums, through email, and through other feedback loops lets students know that you are there learning with them. Your constant involvement in the course sends students a very clear message of your commitment to their learning.

Write to Connect

Academics often use formal language when writing that can seem stiff in online conversation. Try to work against this tendency and write to connect with students when interacting with them online.

- **Use a conversational tone and informal language in online interactions.** Don't be afraid to relax the academic standards of writing a bit when interacting with your students online. While you model intellectual inquiry through your participation, you also want to make the online dialogue inviting and easy for students to enter. The goal is to achieve the kind of relaxed, conversational tone that comes naturally when face-to-face with students and colleagues.

> **Teacher:** OK, Josh . . . I'm glad you brought up the Higgs boson controversy. As a philosopher, it's been fun for me to see how the media's coverage of this scientific breakthrough has sparked a public debate about determinism and free will. So what do you think? Does the discovery of the "God particle" change the balance of the arguments?

- **Show your personality and share your reactions to students' comments.**

> **Teacher:** That's fantastic! Where did you learn that poem? I haven't heard that reference since I was a kid.

These kinds of interjections are directed toward the student as a person. They invite personal and genuine dialogue.

- **Convey the emotional content of your comments.**
  Without physical cues, the sentiment of our communication can get lost.

> **Teacher:** Theresa, it's great to have you back in the conversation. Thanks for letting us know about the accident. Very scary! I'm so relieved to know that everything's OK now.

- **Make posts visually easy to read by using the following conventions:**
  - Break up long blocks of text. Write succinctly and use short paragraphs with space in between.
  - Divide comments that cover multiple issues into different posts. That way students can attach a response that relates to a specific point.
  - Use bullets or numbers when listing items.

As you teach, you fulfill many roles and will probably use a different tone in different contexts. You may use a supportive, second-person conversational tone in discussions and more academic writing in delivering content. Announcements and emails will have their own style, depending on the message. It's a good idea to discuss writing conventions with your students. Let them know how your expectations for written assignments may differ from conventions used for online interactions.

☑ A supportive conversational tone is used throughout the course.

Encourage Student-to-Student Interaction

Student-to-student interaction is one of the great advantages of online learning. The lack of time constraints in asynchronous courses allows all students to contribute to all conversations and activities, and take their time to compose their comments. It's not practical or beneficial for the teacher to respond to all of it. It's better to encourage students to learn with and from each other—right from the start.

Students can support and motivate each other, as shown in the students' exchange in Figure 5.4.

Student 1: My name is Maggie. This is my first class in over 10 years since I dropped out of college with only a few credits to go. I'm finally back to finish, but feel like I don't know what I'm doing. It's been a long time since I've written a paper—let alone studied for a test. I chose this course because I need the credit and the *Sociology of Work* seems like something that may tap into my more recent experience.

Student 2: Hi. I'm Louis and I'm a sophomore psychology major. Maggie, welcome back to school. I've thought about taking a gap year but worry that I would never come back. You may not have written a paper in a while, but I bet you have more interesting work experiences than many of us (myself included) to write about. What's the funniest job you've ever had?

Student 1: **(Maggie)** Thanks, Louis. I can't tell you how nice it was to read your comment. I have had some pretty funny jobs over the years. I was a professional princess for kids' parties for a while. Not sure if this counts. ☺

Figure 5.4 An Example of a Student-to-Student Supportive Exchange Online

These are the kind of simple responses that build camaraderie and encourage students to come back for more.

Teaching Dilemma

When do I respond in discussions?

As a teacher, finding the right points to interject in students' conversations and knowing when to hold back is a delicate balance. You want students to know that you are present online, reading their contributions, answering questions, and providing insight as the situations warrant. But you don't want to be overbearing, robbing the students of the opportunity to figure things out together. Every teacher will have a different idea about what the optimum level of his or her participation is. It will depend upon your particular course and your teaching style.

Our advice is to provide feedback and support frequently at the beginning of the course and then taper off as students begin to respond to one another (see Chapter 8 for more on this topic).

Here are some strategies that can encourage student-to-student interaction:

- Don't take every other turn in the online discussions. Give time and space for students to respond to each other's comments and questions.

- Include instructions for students to post follow-up responses as part of the discussion prompt.

> **Teacher:** This week we will discuss [topic and questions inserted here]. Please respond to these questions as an original post and then comment on at least two of your classmates' posts. Think the problem through and ask each other substantive questions and build on each other's comments.

Some teachers include "follow-up" responses as a graded category within online participation assessment (see Chapter 8, p. 215, for an example participation rubric).

- Open students' questions and comments up for the whole group to consider.

> **Teacher:** Good questions, Peter. I'd like to hear what others have to say about this issue.

- Give positive feedback about students' interaction.

> **Teacher:** Karen, great response to Ronan's question. I encourage everyone to jump in, answer each other's questions, and offer your insights to us all. This is what our discussions are all about.

 Learners are encouraged to interact with others (classmates, guest speakers, etc.) and benefit from their experience and expertise.

5.3 Building Self-Directed Learning Skills

Online learning requires many of the skills attributed to self-directed learning. The flexible time frame of asynchronous courses and the independent nature of online participation requires students to:

- establish a personal work schedule;

- stick to it;

- take initiative to solve problems and seek support as needed;

- collaborate with others;

- plan and manage long term projects; and

- assess their progress and make adjustments as needed.

This can be challenging for many people—especially for less mature students.

In the first weeks, teachers set up guidelines and structures to help students establish effective work routines. Students need to know what kind of time they should devote to:

- participating online;

- reading and viewing the learning resources;

- completing assignments;

- studying; and

- working on long-term projects.

Provide Structure for Learning

With support and practice, students will need less direction over time and will be able to handle more leadership responsibilities and open-ended tasks in the middle and ending weeks of the semester. **More structure at the beginning will allow for more freedom and creative options later.**

Teaching Tip

Support the development of self-directed learning skills

"Scaffolding" refers to the support that a teacher provides to students in order to help them learn. The term is borrowed from the temporary frame used around a building during construction.

> Cognitive scaffolding allows learners to reach places that they would otherwise be unable to reach . . . And when the building is finished or the renovation complete, the scaffolding is removed, it is not seen in the final product.
>
> (Holton & Clarke, 2006, p. 129)

Consistent weekly course routines, defined due dates, and clear instructions about how and when to complete tasks provides the scaffolding for students to create their own work habits. It's important to establish these routines from the first week of the semester so students don't fall behind and lose motivation. Over time, students will rely less on the external structures and more on their own work habits.

Help Students Plan a Weekly Routine

Most online courses are designed to have fairly consistent work routines from week to week. It's helpful to point this out to students. Students need to know what order to move through the course activities and how much time they have to dedicate to each. Figure 5.5 offers an example of a "worksheet" a teacher gives to her students to help them establish a personal work routine.

Suggestions for Planning Your Learning Routine

Online learning offers a great deal of flexibility within our schedules. But each of us must find time to complete all the learning activities each week. The schedule below represents the tasks you will need to do to fulfill the course requirements and succeed.

I've included a rough estimate of the time I expect each of these tasks will take. However, recognize that learning is a highly individualized sport. Some people may need more time reviewing resources and others more time for participation or assignments. Plan your schedule so it reflects the time you need.

Weekly Tasks

- Read the assigned chapters and articles and view the lecture. (2–3 hours)

You will need to review the learning resources BEFORE participating in the discussions or completing the assignments.

Suggestion: Do this on Monday or Tuesday.

- **Participate in the weekly discussion forum.** (2–3 hours spread out throughout the week)

Participating in a discussion means reading what everyone has said, as well as contributing thoughtfully throughout the week. Plan to spend about 30 minutes to one hour composing your first response to the prompt (taking into consideration the week's resources and other students' comments). As the week progresses, there will be more comments to read. Plan on checking in and adding comments at least two more times. See the participation rubric in the syllabus for guidance.

Suggestion: Begin posting in the discussion on Tuesday or Wednesday.

Figure 5.5 A Worksheet Distributed to Students to Help them Plan their Online Course Routines

- **Complete weekly assignment.** (½–3 hours due by Sunday at midnight)

The assignments vary in length and complexity. The first three are independent writing tasks that can be done when you are ready to do it. Later assignments are collaborative and will require coordination of timing with your peers.

Suggestion: Read the instructions for the assignment at the beginning of the week. Then do the assignment after you have read the material and participated in the discussion for a few days.

- **Miscellaneous tasks.** (1 hour)

Allow time for other course-related tasks such as: keeping track of your course progress and upcoming assignment; interacting with classmates outside of the discussions; exploring optional course resources and researching related interest on the Internet; and getting help as needed.

Suggestion: Allow about an hour each week for miscellaneous course activity.

Note: This course is worth three credit hours. It is equal in content, quality, and rigor with an on-site course. That means **you are expected to spend approximately nine hours a week** completing the course requirements (this is equivalent to three in-class hours plus six hours of homework expected of students for a three-credit on-site course).

Here's a sample of how your time may be distributed. Plan and track your actual time to determine a schedule that will work for you.

Sample Schedule							
	Mon	**Tue**	**Wed**	**Thu**	**Fri**	**Sat**	**Sun**
Review Resources	1.5 hrs	30 min	30 min				
Discussion		45 min	30 min		15 min	15 min	30 min
Assignment		15 min			2 hrs		45 min
Miscellaneous Task	30 min		15 min		15 min	15 min	

Figure 5.5 continued

☑ Learning activities and course requirements are clearly defined and explained to students.

☑ A consistent routine of weekly course activities is established to help online learners organize their schedules.

5.4 Reflective Teaching: Learning as You Go

At the end of each week, review your online teaching experience and reflect on the achievements and difficulties. We recommend formalizing this practice by keeping an online teaching journal. You may choose to create a personal blog within the LMS or in another form that works for you. It's important to keep notes as you go through each week to capture your impressions, questions, and concerns as they arise. Writing a brief review of the week online will help you to identify situations that may require attention or a change in your instruction.

Journaling does not need to be extensive to be effective. Consider the following questions:

1. What has occurred online throughout a week?

   - Describe the students' pattern and quality of participation in each of the online activities and the coursework completed.

   - Which students are excelling? Which students are struggling? Characterize their online participation and work habits.

   - Describe your participation. How are you supporting the students online?

2. What aspects of the online course are going well? Are there areas that concern you?

   - Why do you think those aspects are going well? What do you think is contributing to the problem areas?

3. How you can build upon success? What can be done to improve areas of concern?

Tracking your journal notes from week to week will help you recognize patterns that are emerging. By the end of the first third of the semester, you will have enough information to take targeted action to improve your online teaching.

WEB Refer to the book's website to view sample teacher journal entries: www.essentialsofonlineteaching.com.

☑ Reflection on teaching provides information for course improvement.

☑ Course evaluation and improvement is an ongoing process.

5.5 Summary and Standards

During the first weeks of an online semester, the teacher serves as a host, a tour guide, and a resource, for students' learning. They help students learn how to work with the tools and dynamics of the LMS. They review the course design with the students and make sure they understand how it works and how it all fits together.

Teachers actively help students engage in the course by sharing their knowledge, enthusiasm, and expertise as facilitators of learning. They help students establish effective and efficient work routines that are important for learning throughout the online semester.

Teaching is a process of continual evaluation and improvement of students' progress and one's own practice. It is recommended that teachers keep track of their impressions about the course in progress in a journal. Such self-reflective practice provides a means to understand and improve online instruction and student learning.

The following standards were identified in connection with instructional issues that are commonly the focus of the first weeks of an online course:

- [ ] Introductory activities help students master technical competencies required to participate in the course.

- [ ] Information on the syllabus and introductory course material is reviewed with students at the beginning of the course.

- [ ] Teachers use a variety of means to communicate with students throughout the course.

- [ ] Students are provided with several options to receive support for procedural, technical, and content-related issues.

- [ ] Enrolled students who have not participated in the course during the first weeks are contacted.

- [ ] Initial course activities provide an opportunity for students to interact with their teacher and peers.

- [ ] Teacher feedback is provided in a timely fashion.

- [ ] A supportive conversational tone is used throughout the course.

- [ ] Learners are encouraged to interact with others (classmates, guest speakers, etc.) and benefit from their experience and expertise.

- [ ] Learning activities and course requirements are clearly defined and explained to students.

- [ ] A consistent routine of weekly course activities is established to help online learners organize their schedules.

- [ ] Reflection on teaching provides information for course improvement.

- [ ] Course evaluation and improvement is an ongoing process.

References and Further Reading

Bain, K. (2004). *What the best college teachers do*. Cambridge, MA: Harvard University Press.

Conrad, R., & Donaldson, J. (2004). *Engaging the online learner*. San Francisco, CA: Jossey-Bass.

Dabbagh, N. (2007). The online learner: Characteristics and pedagogical implications. *Contemporary Issues in Technology and Teacher Education, 7*(3), 217–226.

Garrison, R. D., Anderson, T., & Archer, W. (2004). *Critical thinking, cognitive presence, and computer conferencing in distance education*. Retrieved from http://cde.athabascau.ca/coi_site/documents/Garrison_Anderson_Archer_CogPres_Final.pdf

Garrison, D. R., & Cleveland-Innes, M. (2005). Facilitating cognitive presence in online learning: Interaction is not enough. *The American Journal of Distance Education, 19*(3), 133–148.

Gascoigne, C. (2014). Distance education readiness assessments: An overview and application. *Online Journal of Distance Learning Administration, 17*(4). Retrieved from www.westga.edu/~distance/ojdla/winter174/gascoigne_parnell174.html

Holton, D., & Clarke D. (2006). Scaffolding and metacognition. *International Journal of Mathematical Education in Science & Technology, 37*(2), 127–143.

Lehman, R. M., & Conceicao, C. O. (2010). *Creating a sense of presence in online teaching*. San Francisco, CA: Jossey-Bass.

McInnerney, J. M., & Roberts, T. S. (2004). Online learning: Social interaction and the creation of a sense of community. *Educational Technology & Society, 7*(3), 73–81.

Mandernach, B. J., Gonzales, R. M., & Garrett, A. L. (2006). Examination of online instructor presence via threaded discussion participation. *Journal of Online Learning and Teaching, 2*(4). Retrieved from http://jolt.merlot.org/vol2no4/mandernach.htm

Mayes, R., Luebeck, J., Ku, H. Y., Akarasriworn, C., & Korkmaz, O. (2011). Themes and strategies for transformative online instruction: A review of literature and practice. *The Quarterly Review of Distance Education, 12*(3), 151–166.

Smith, R. M. (2008). *Conquering the content*. San Francisco, CA: Jossey-Bass.

Sosulski, K., & Bongiovanni, T. (2013). *The savvy student's guide to online learning*. New York, NY: Routledge.

Yan, Z., Hao, H., Hobbs, L. J., & Wen, N. (2003). The psychology of e-learning: A field of study. *Journal of Educational Computing Research, 29*(3), 285–296.

Chapter 6 The Middle Weeks: Facilitating Online Learning

Teaching an Online Course		
The Beginning Weeks	The Middle Weeks	The Ending Weeks

During the middle weeks of the semester, the course is in full motion. Students are engaged in the online activities and busy completing assignments. It's an active time for the teacher too. You guide students through the lessons and help them keep pace with the course schedule. It's also important to continue to reinforce the social aspects of online learning to keep students personally invested in the course. Let your students know that you see them as individuals and humanize the digital environment. It can be a great relief for students to realize that online communication is simply a means to connect real people.

The middle weeks are also a time to step back and evaluate the course in progress. Are there aspects of the course that are not working as well as you would like? Are there students who are underperforming or not keeping up? There are many easy ways to gather information about students' progress online. You can use this information to understand how to support students better and adapt the course as needed.

As a teacher, you are a decision-maker, constantly evaluating situations and deciding what to do next. You anticipate and respond to students' needs while keeping the course goals and process squarely in view. This chapter highlights issues that are likely to occur during the middle weeks of your course and require your intervention. It focuses on how to guide your students through the curriculum, make personal connections with them, and improve your course and instruction as you go.

6.1 Guiding Students Through the Plan

Picture an air traffic controller, monitoring many flights coming and going from different directions, signaling planes to take off and others to land. Watching the flow of traffic on a monitor, the controller guides each plane safely to its destination. Online teaching during the middle weeks can feel a bit like this. Students participate at different times as they complete various tasks throughout the week.

As the teacher, you have a unique vantage point in the class. You have a thorough understanding of the material ahead and know the important benchmarks students need to meet to achieve the learning outcomes for the course. In the middle weeks, you also have a growing understanding of each student and can fine-tune your instruction to speak to his or her particular interests and needs. As you guide your students through the course, introduce each study unit thoroughly, connect with students on a personal level, and provide the support needed for them to achieve the learning outcomes.

Introduce Each Study Unit

By the middle phase of a course, students know the basic online work routines. However, each learning activity will require something new of the learner. Before you present a new unit to your students, **review all of the planned activities**. Think about each student's performance on assignments during the previous weeks. Did students reveal gaps in understanding that may make this week's activities difficult? Do any of the coming exercises require new instructions or clarification? It's essential to troubleshoot the week's plan ahead of time and give students advice and help upfront (see Figure 6.1 for an example). Emails and announcements are easy ways to communicate suggestions to your students. Invite students to respond or contact you if they have further questions or need help.

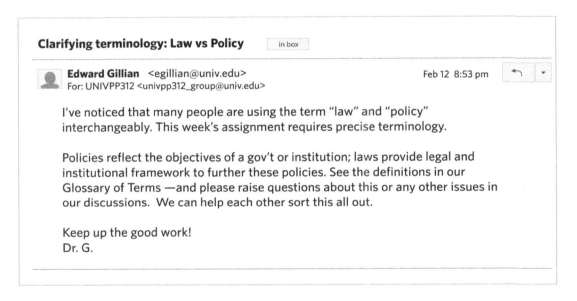

Figure 6.1 Teacher's Email Clarifying Terminology Used in the Course

Many teachers post an announcement at the onset of each new study unit, letting students know how the coming unit fits within the overall course design. These regularly scheduled announcements help to establish a predictable rhythm for the course progress and keep students on track. They can also be used to promote the use of resources (see Chapter 3, p. 62, for recommendations). Figure 6.2 shows a teacher's announcement that presents a unit in an *Introduction to Public Policy* course.

☑ Learning activities and course requirements are clearly defined and explained to students.

Announcement ▽

Introduction to Public Policy Course
Posted Dec 6, 2015 8:06 AM

Hi Everyone,

I've nearly finished grading your essays and will have them ready for you by tomorrow, December 7th, at 9 am EST. Check the dropbox for my feedback and please reply if you have questions or would like to discuss any points raised.

As we begin week 6, we shift our focus from the historical and structural context of policy to policy analysis. We will practice identifying the perceived problem(s) addressed by policies. I can't overemphasize how important this skill is. So often, elaborate policies are developed and implemented at great cost, but have little to do with the actual problems they were intended to fix. It's illuminating to be able to pinpoint matches and mismatches between a policy and its stated purpose.

Before you watch the video, "Agenda Setting, Power and Interest," read the study questions that frame this week's discussion (step 1 in the assignments). At the end of this week, you are required to cite a policy that affects or interests you and name the problem the policy addresses.   So think about that as you watch and read the resources.

I'm speaking at a conference in Toronto tomorrow, so I will not check in with the discussion until Tuesday. Please keep the ball rolling and keep each other in check.

Reminder: Your topic for the Policy Analysis paper is due on Saturday, December 12th at midnight EST. Email me before then if you have questions.

JW

Show All Announcements

Figure 6.2 Teacher's Announcement to Introduce a Unit

Help Students Keep Pace with the Course

Effective time management becomes increasingly important as the course progresses. You can help all the students to stay on track by posting reminders of upcoming due dates as announcements.

You can also suggest (or require) interim progress updates to discourage procrastination and help students plan their work schedules effectively. Figure 6.3 shows an example from Joyce Anderson's course.

Announcement | ▽

Technical Report
Posted Apr 9, 2016

Here are the steps and due dates to complete your Technical Report:
First, be sure that your topic is approved

10.9	Receive approval on topic/memo
11.05	Working bibliography due
11.07	Outline of topics due
11.12	Front Matter due
11.14	First Draft due
11.25	Final Technical Report due in dropbox

Show All Announcements

Figure 6.3 Example of Interim Check Points for Term Project in Joyce Anderson's *Technical Writing* Course

Joyce grades and offers feedback at each stage of the writing process. Other teachers simply break down large projects into interim steps with a suggested timeline and post reminders, such as the example in Figure 6.4.

Announcement | ▽

Research in Education
Posted March 9, 2015 10:11 AM

Remember that your research designs are due on April 23. That gives you two weeks to define:

1. **a statement of the problem and research question**
2. **the methods for gathering information**
3. **analysis procedure**

If you would like feedback or help with defining these steps, post your questions or attach your drafts to our open discussion forum: HELP and FEEDBACK. You can also email me to discuss your project.

Show All Announcements

Figure 6.4 Example Announcement Suggesting Interim Steps to Meet a Deadline

Some teachers post short video clips that provide students with a visual aid to explain activities and encourage students to stay on track.

Personal Reflection

William Archibald

William Archibald has taught *Advanced Composition* online for many years at Millersville University in Pennsylvania. Over time, his course and his teaching strategies have evolved. He advises faculty who are new to online teaching, "Be patient. It takes time to mature an online class." One of the practices he has added to clarify the activities and help students stay actively engaged is what he calls a "Daily Jing." He uses a screencast software called "Jing" to make short videos using the camera on his computer. In the videos, William talks directly to his students about an activity. He may simply explain the exercise, point to relevant learning resources, or give advice. He makes the videos available through the LMS and posts a simple question that requires viewing the "Daily Jing" to answer. Students answer the question for a point toward their participation grade.

William says that asking students to answer questions after watching the short videos makes it more likely that they will understand the lesson and to do the required activities on time. Students tell him that they find the videos helpful and appreciate his active presence throughout the learning process.

Refer to the book's website for an example of William Archibald's "Daily Jing" and links to screencast software: www.essentialsofonlineteaching.com.

6.2 Humanizing the Online Environment

Online dialogue—particularly text-based interaction—can have an unnatural formality to it that seems to highlight the distance rather than the connection between people. Michael Moore, one of the foundational writers on distance learning, refers to the sense of space between the teacher and learner as "transactional distance" and warns that it can be a barrier to learning. Somehow, teachers have to cross this barrier and meet their students as real people and let them know that they are invested in their learning. This is an implicit bond between teachers and students that is often missing in the digital environment.

> Transactional distance is "a psychological and communication space to be crossed, a space of potential misunderstanding between the inputs of instructor and those of the learner" (Moore, 1991).

Personal Reflection

Margaret Foley McCabe

I often write extensive evaluative feedback on students' papers and assignments. I also use feedback as an opportunity to open a one-to-one discussion with students by including questions and an invitation for them to respond back to me. The assignments give the students and me a shared context for a real conversation. It's a great way to get to know my students and for them to feel comfortable reaching out to me.

I find that I get to know more of my online students than I do in the classroom. By the end of a semester, I will have worked with each of them individually and have a real sense of who they are as learners.

Open Dialogues with Individual Students

Asynchronous online courses offer more opportunities to work individually with students than is often possible in onsite classroom situations. Students can communicate with you privately any time through email and don't have to wait until after class or to schedule a meeting during your office hours. The same is true for you. If you want to follow up on a topic that does not involve the whole class (a student's question about his or her topic for a project), you can carry on the dialogue easily through email exchanges.

Many teachers find it helpful to have student conferences midway through the semester. They reach out to students to find out how they are managing the workload and to help them become more successful in their efforts.

Personal Reflection

Scott Thornbury

Somewhere around the midpoint of the semester, I schedule Skype sessions with each of my students. These are normally 20 minutes or less. It gives me a way to touch base and see how students are getting on. If a student is having problems, this gives us a chance to work it through together.

If it is impractical to meet with all of your students, you may decide to narrow the focus to students whose participation or quality of work suggests that they are struggling. Email these students and invite them to schedule a conference with you. Or you can open the invitation to all students and let them decide if they could benefit from a student-teacher conference (see Figure 6.5).

☑ Opportunities for frequent teacher-student interaction are provided.

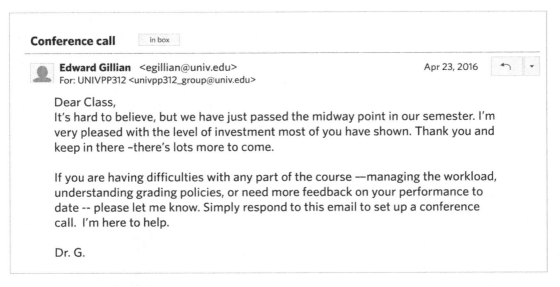

Conference call   in box

Edward Gillian <egillian@univ.edu>   Apr 23, 2016
For: UNIVPP312 <univpp312_group@univ.edu>

Dear Class,
It's hard to believe, but we have just passed the midway point in our semester. I'm very pleased with the level of investment most of you have shown. Thank you and keep in there –there's lots more to come.

If you are having difficulties with any part of the course —managing the workload, understanding grading policies, or need more feedback on your performance to date -- please let me know. Simply respond to this email to set up a conference call. I'm here to help.

Dr. G.

Figure 6.5 Sample Message Inviting Students to Schedule a Student-Teacher Conference

Tend to Group Dynamics

Facilitating student interaction requires the skills of a gracious host. You want to include everyone while moving the conversation forward. Sometimes certain students dominate discussions and others barely contribute. A teacher can help balance the dialogue by calling attention to a "quiet" student's comment or directing a question toward a less active participant. In the following example, Jeremy is a dominant student. He makes a point that contradicts a comment posted earlier by a less active student (Tobias). The teacher sees this as an opportunity to get Tobias more involved. The teacher frames the issue and asks Tobias to share his thoughts:

Student (Jeremy): I don't think that I agree with the author of the article we read this week. What if the focus of NASA's research fluctuated with the whims of supply and demand?

Teacher: Jeremy raises an interesting point. Tobias, considering your experience in research and development, how do you think funding for long-range, less consumer-driven research would be funded by the private sector?

Teachers also encourage students to respond directly to one another's questions and comments. They may turn questions that are directed toward them over to the class to answer:

> **Teacher:** Jeremy raises an interesting point. I'd like to hear other people's thoughts on this issue.

There is also a time to sit back and "listen." In the middle weeks, teachers often pull back and let students take the lead in discussions. They give students a chance to interact with each other, develop ideas together, and answer one another's questions. You may find that your role during this phase shifts to a supportive position. You read along and enter the discussion as needed to give instruction or ask a question that encourages students to dig deeper. If discussion strays too far away from the intended focus, you may need to redirect the conversation to keep the learning moving toward the outcomes. Here again, you serve as the bridge between the course as planned and as your students experience it (see Chapter 8, p. 211, for more suggestions about facilitating online discussions).

 Learners are encouraged to interact with others (classmates, guest speakers, etc.) and benefit from their experience and expertise.

6.3 Gathering Information About Your Students' Progress

In an online course, everything that is posted to the LMS is stored for the duration of the course. This provides a wealth of information that can help you understand students' learning process. You can review all that has been posted in your course, check students' performance on assignments, quizzes, and tests, and even see how much time students have spent in the various online activities. This makes it relatively easy to get a bird's-eye view of the online course in progress.

Statistics generated by tracking tools cannot tell you about the quality of students' engagement with the material, but the numbers can provide a map of their progress through the online activities. Your knowledge of the course design and your experience with the students will help you understand how to interpret the information gathered.

Tracking Students' Online Activity

It's essential to understand what students are doing online. A record of students' login times tells you when and how often they check in with the course to view information, read comments, complete assignments, submit work, or post contributions. Tracking students' online activity allows the teacher to see if they are connecting to the course at any level. If you notice that a student is logging on regularly but not contributing, that is a different problem than if the student has not logged on at all or very infrequently. When you understand students' work habits, you can take appropriate actions to guide those who may be falling behind.

Tracking students' online activity can help you understand the rhythm of interaction that emerges in your course over time. You may find that students tend to be more active on certain days of the week. Some teachers arrange their teaching time to coordinate with peaks in students' activity online. Teachers also find it helpful to recognize when students are likely to begin submitting assignments so they can dedicate appropriate time to assessing the work and giving feedback. Tracking helps teachers set realistic expectations and plan their schedules accordingly.

Patterns of students' online activity are easy to recognize in LMS reports. Figure 6.6 shows the login history of three students from Joyce Anderson's course over 30 days (the full report shows all the history of all 24 students in the class). It also gives a bar graph of each student's grades on assignments during the same time period.

Figure 6.6 Sample of Progress Report of Student Logins and Grades Generated by Desire2Learn

The full progress report of all 24 students' activity shows that most students logged on to the course several times a day with an average of 46 times over the month. All the students had done well on their assignments, with grades ranging between 75% and 100%.

Most LMSs can also generate reports about the number of posts students contribute to discussion forums. While this statistic does not tell you about the quality of their comments, it provides an easy way for teachers to see which students are participating each week. For example, Figure 6.7 on the next page shows how many "threads" and "replies" each student has made to the discussion in Joyce's course after five weeks. The "threads" are the primary comments students post in response to the discussion board prompt. The "replies" are the comments they post to other students' contributions.

Joyce noticed that one student, Heidi, had not contributed enough to meet the participation requirements for the week. This prompted Joyce to investigate. She saw that Heidi had logged on regularly (as shown in the Student Login History Report generated by the LMS) but had rarely posted comments. Joyce emailed this student, reminded her of the grading criteria for participation, and encouraged her to be more active in the discussions. Heidi had not realized that she needed to post a comment to participate in the course.

[First_name]	[Threads]	[Replies]
Alisonv	5	6
Bob	5	7
Cassie	5	5
Dan	5	5
Edward	5	8
Frank	5	5
Gabriella	5	6
Heidi	2	7
Izzy	5	4
Jose	5	5
Kyle	4	5
Laura	4	7
Mary	5	5
Nuri	5	6
Olphelia	5	8
Paul	5	5
Quincy	5	5
Rett	5	6
Suji	5	3
Thomas	5	3
Una	5	4
Vikram	3	8
Wyatt	5	4
Xavier	8	5

Figure 6.7 A Report of Student Participation in Discussion Forums within the *Technical Writing* Course. Students' names have been changed to protect privacy.

☑ Clarifying the requirement to participate in discussions can prompt students to be more actively involved.

Monitoring Students' Learning Progress

Learning outcomes are what students know and are able to do as the result of the course activity. The various kinds of work required by students—papers, projects, quizzes, tests, contributions to online forums, peer reviews, and student blogs—provide evidence about their progress. As explained in the box below, well-planned online courses have clearly articulated learning outcomes for each unit of study throughout the semester. The learning outcomes are often included in the online course syllabus so that students have a thorough understanding of the work expected of them.

Course Design Issue: Writing Learning Outcomes

Well-written learning outcomes:

- are specific;

- are clearly and concisely written;

- clarify for learners why they are doing what they are doing;

- support and help to provide a framework for the online development process by:

  - defining the knowledge and/or skills to be acquired;

  - helping to determine the content and activities for the course by pointing to the kinds of thinking skills needed; and

  - providing goals for assessment;

- help to ensure the quality of the course; and

- set up an agreement between teacher and learner as to their relative responsibilities.

Source: From Vai and Sosulski (2016, p. 184)

Most LMSs have an online gradebook tool to record students' grades (see Chapter 3, p. 87). This makes it easy to gather information on each student's progress in reaching learning outcomes as the weeks go by. Looking at trends in grades across the whole class can help you to see what is working at a course level. In Figure 6.8 you can see that most students did well on the "Career Packet" assignment. The grades ranged from 82% to 96%, with an average score of 88.79%. This would suggest that the learning activities and resources that surrounded this exercise prepared the students sufficiently for the assignment.

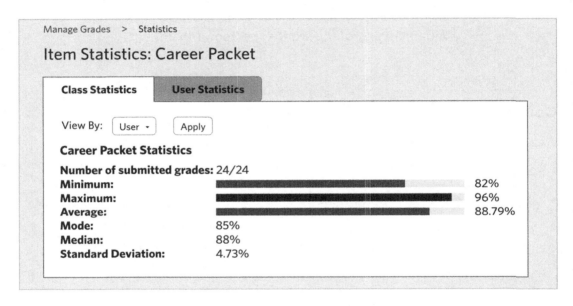

Figure 6.8 LMS Gradebook Report of Students' Performance on an Assignment (reprinted with permission)

Using Self-Reflection to Understand Students' Progress

An online course is experienced—not transmitted. A teacher's interpretation about what is happening in a course is key to understanding students' progress. In Chapter 4, we suggested that you keep an online teaching journal to track your thoughts about the course in progress. This can be a valuable tool in helping you gauge and improve your online teaching during the middle weeks of the course.

However you take note of your reflections about the course in progress, it is helpful to consider evaluative questions that help you target problems and recognize success. Ask yourself:

- Are you satisfied with the way students are engaging with the material, you, and each other?

- Are the students able to keep up with the requirements? Are the requirements rigorous enough to challenge them?

- Are the online resources adequately supporting the students' progress?

- Are students able to successfully complete the activities?

- Does the students' progress in reaching learning outcomes demonstrate the level of effort and growth you expect?

It is very useful to reflect upon these issues every time you finish a unit, or whenever you identify a teaching problem. Your answers to such questions will help you target what information you need to gather to understand the situation better. For instance, if students are not keeping up with the requirements, you can analyze their login history to see if they are investing enough time. Gathering and interpreting information about students' progress is a two-way street; one informs the other.

Transparency in Data Collection

Tracking students' online activity can improve instruction by enabling the teacher to make data-supported decisions. It's important to tell students how and why their online activity is tracked and the limits of its use to assure privacy and encourage trust.

- **Explain to students what kinds of information you will track and how you will use it to improve your instruction and the course design.** Tracking information provides quantitative information (i.e. how many times students log on, view resources, and post comments in a discussion) that helps teachers identify students' work habits and the way learners are using course materials. Explain to students that this data is used for teaching decisions and course improvement, not for grading, because the quantity of time spent online is not a measure of engaged learning.

- **Assure students that all policies intended to protect students' rights within the host institution are respected in the online course setting.** In the United States, student data can be used for instructional purposes "because the provider is only using [the protected] information for the purposes for which it was shared" (U.S. Department of Education, 2015). Specific laws governing online privacy policies vary in different countries, but most institutions apply similar standards online as they do on campus.

In most instances, activity within the learning environment is password-protected, so only enrolled participants can see or engage in the course activity. Only teachers and approved administrators are granted permission to use tracking tools to view activity within the course. Students cannot see their classmates' information, track their online activity, or view other students' grades.

☑ Course evaluation and improvement is an ongoing process.

☑ A variety of information (student performance data, feedback, etc.) is used to evaluate the effectiveness of course design and instruction.

☑ The rights and privacy of students are protected in accordance with the laws and policies that govern all the institution's courses.

6.4 Improving Your Course

As you track your students' progress through the various learning activities, you are likely to notice things that could be improved. You may discover trends that are problematic, such as dwindling student participation. Or perhaps a specific activity is not working successfully. What can you do to improve the situation? The trick is to be able to define a problem clearly, tease out the factors that may contribute to students' difficulties, make needed revisions, and monitor students' progress as a result of the change (see Figure 6.9).

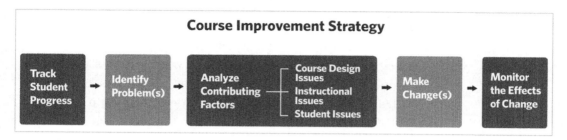

Figure 6.9 The Course Improvement Strategy

Identify a Problem

Define a problem as clearly as possible. Focus in on the specific concern you have regarding the situation and describe it in detail. For example, consider these two problem statements:

Vague problem statement:
Peer reviews aren't working.

Clear problem statement:
The criteria that students are using to evaluate each other's work in the peer review exercises are inconsistent.

A clearly stated problem zeroes in on the specific issue that needs to be addressed.

Consider Factors That May Contribute to a Problem

Focus on the "problem" that you want to address and identify factors that may cause or contribute to the situation:

1. **Course design:** Are there aspects of the design that are causing this problem? Check to make sure that the learning resources and instructions provide enough information for students to successfully complete the assignments. Make sure that the activities give students the kinds of experience they need to achieve the learning outcomes.

2. **Your teaching:** Are there ways to improve your teaching to increase students' success in the problem area? What could you do differently to reach students more effectively or provide greater support?

3. **Students:** Some problems are related to one or more students—but not the whole class. Consider the characteristics and performances of your students and try to understand what special conditions or circumstances are involved. Why might some students be struggling more than others? Do they understand the requirements and course expectations? Do they lack prerequisite knowledge or experience needed to succeed? Do they require more direction in their learning habits? What can be done to help?

Analyzing the problem systematically can help you target strategies for improvement.

As you seek solutions to a problem you have identified, think about the standards of best practice explained throughout this book. The list in Appendix A organizes all the standards topically. You can use these as checklists to improve your course in progress.

<u>Note</u>: If you suspect there is a course design issue, refer also to the standards in *Essentials of Online Course Design* (Vai & Sosulski, 2016).

Implement Changes

An online course functions as a system with all the parts working together to produce desired outcomes. Changing one part of the system can have a ripple effect that alters the whole learning situation. When you make a positive change, it can improve students' motivation, participation, and the quality of their work. **But change must be handled carefully so as not to unintentionally disrupt the parts of the system that are working well.** We recommend the following:

- Think through a proposed change from the students' point of view. How will it affect their work routines? The time they dedicate to the course? Their participation online? Their efforts toward learning outcomes, particularly term projects?

- Make small changes rather than radical revisions.

- Present the change in a positive light to your students. Make sure to communicate the reason for the change and what it will require of the students.

- Review the effects of the change.

Here's an example of a problem a teacher may come across with two proposed solutions:

Teaching problem: Too few students viewed the video lectures before participating in discussions and doing assignments.

Inappropriate solution: Limit the access of the lectures from Sunday to Tuesday in order to prompt students to watch these videos before participating in activities.

 This is not a good solution within an asynchronous course because it introduces a new time requirement in the midst of the semester. Students may have enrolled in the course because their schedules require flexibility. You cannot change the fundamental time requirements while a course is in progress.

Appropriate solution: Remind the class that their discussion participation grades are dependent on supporting their comments with materials from the learning resources—including the lectures. Inform students that a portion of the test questions will be drawn from the information presented in the video lectures.

This provides incentive for students to view the lectures and connects videos to the learning outcomes.

 Changes made to a course in progress are clearly communicated to students and respect the established workload and time requirements.

Monitor the Effects of Course Revisions

Teaching is a process of continual improvement. As you make changes in your course, monitor the effects of the revisions. Seek feedback from students and track their progress after the change is implemented. Do you see a difference in students' learning? If the change has had a positive effect, you may be able to apply what you have learned to other situations that need improvement. If it has not had the desired effect, reconsider your definition of the problem and the factors involved. Are there other revisions you can make to the course or your instruction? Seek advice from colleagues who have experience teaching online. They may have insight or advice that can shed light on the situation and help you improve your approach.

With practice, interpreting events and figuring out the best next move will become a part of your everyday teaching strategy.

6.5 Example of the Course Improvement Strategy in Action

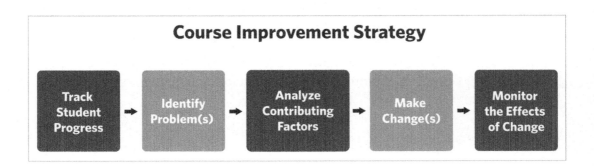

The following scenario walks you through a teacher's process of evaluating and improving her course, *Paradigms in Psychology*. You'll notice that the teacher tracks students' progress throughout the entire process.

Step 1: Track Students' Progress

It's week 5 of a 15-week undergraduate course, *Paradigms in Psychology*.

The teacher reflects on her students' progress. She has kept a journal to record her impressions along the way. She noted that her students actively engaged in the introduction icebreaker exercise and participated in all activities during the first two weeks. Things seemed to be going great.

Then, in the third week, the students' participation began to wane and their contributions showed less individuality. The teacher noted in her journal:

> Students' posts on the discussion board do not invite further discussion. Their answers are factually correct, but they are failing to address the interpretive parts of my questions. The closed nature of their responses makes the discussion board more of a short-answer quiz than a true discussion.

The first unit test showed that most of the students could recall the information presented in the videotaped lectures and through the other online learning resources.

Step 2: Identify Problems

The teacher was disappointed in the students' level of critical thinking and wondered what was going on; only a few students applied the concepts learned to new situations or generated original examples of the concepts covered.

Her teaching journal provided the key to target further investigation. She had noted that there was a qualitative difference in the students' online contributions as the weeks progressed; students' responses demonstrated a higher degree of critical thinking and originality in the first two weeks. Students also interacted more with each other.

The teacher checked the LMS participation reports to see if the students' patterns of online activity changed as the course progressed. It turned out that the frequency of online participation remained fairly consistent over the first four weeks of the course. Almost all students had posted responses to the discussion questions each week and had completed the required assignments. A consistent proportion of students (86%) had viewed—or at least accessed—all the required learning resources.

The statistical reports did, however, show two participation areas that had changed in weeks 3 and 4:

- The number of times students viewed the discussion board had decreased.

- The number of student-to-student exchanges had gone down significantly.

In other words, the students weren't reading or responding to each other's posts in weeks 3 and 4.

Step 3: Analyze Contributing Factors

The teacher reviewed the online discussion forum and recognized that the quality of the discussion questions and instructions declined between weeks 2 and 3. During the first two weeks, students were directed to react to interesting personal insights that sparked further online conversation. Figures 6.10 and 6.11 show the discussion prompts.

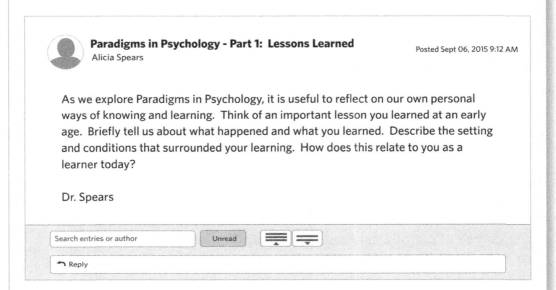

Figure 6.10 Online Discussion Prompt: Week 1

Paradigms in Psychology Course - Part II: Paradigms of Psychology
Alicia Spears   Sept 13, 2015 8:45 am

After reading Chapters 1 and 2 of our textbook and viewing the short lecture for this week, use the stories your classmates posted as "Lessons Learned" (week 1) as case studies to illustrate different learning theories.

1. Choose a student's post as a case study. Select one to which no one else has attached a response (only one response for each student's "Lesson Learned" story). Post the following as a response to that student's thread.

2. Analyze the way the "Lessons Learned" was conveyed and decide which of the 4 paradigms of psychology this anecdote best represents the author's perspective: Behaviorism, Cognitivism, Constructivism or Humanism. Obviously these little vignettes will not provide enough detail to illustrate all or most of the hallmarks of a given Paradigm. Feel free to fill in with conjecture.

3. Note specifics attributes from the text and lecture to support your response.

Part III: The Author's Response

Do you agree with how your classmate characterized your clinical perspective? Post a brief reply under your classmate's response.

Dr. Spears

| Search entries or author | | Unread | ☰ ☰ |

↩ Reply

Figure 6.11 Online Discussion Prompt: Week 2

These exercises produced thoughtful and original contributions from students. The teacher noticed that the discussion prompts for weeks 1 and 2 required students to use a variety of thinking skills (bolded below for emphasis) and to engage personally with one another. The prompts asked students to:

- **Reflect** on the course material in relationship to their personal experience.

- **Demonstrate comprehension** of the material covered in the text and lectures.

- Apply concepts learned to **critically analyze** a context.

- Use "conjecture" to **critically and creatively make their case**.

- **Evaluate** the validity of their peers' reviews of their stories.

- **Read and respond to others' comments.**

The teacher found that the discussion prompt and instructions for the third week's discussion did not require the same spectrum of thinking or interaction with others that made the previous week's discussion engaging (see Figure 6.12).

The discussion prompts for week 3 were not good starting questions because they asked students to demonstrate comprehension of the content, rather than to evaluate or apply information. Consequently, the students'

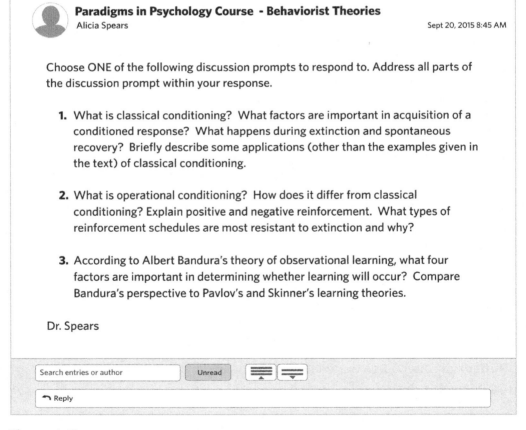

Paradigms in Psychology Course - Behaviorist Theories

Alicia Spears   Sept 20, 2015 8:45 AM

Choose ONE of the following discussion prompts to respond to. Address all parts of the discussion prompt within your response.

1. What is classical conditioning? What factors are important in acquisition of a conditioned response? What happens during extinction and spontaneous recovery? Briefly describe some applications (other than the examples given in the text) of classical conditioning.

2. What is operational conditioning? How does it differ from classical conditioning? Explain positive and negative reinforcement. What types of reinforcement schedules are most resistant to extinction and why?

3. According to Albert Bandura's theory of observational learning, what four factors are important in determining whether learning will occur? Compare Bandura's perspective to Pavlov's and Skinner's learning theories.

Dr. Spears

Search entries or author   Unread

↩ Reply

Figure 6.12 Online Discussion Prompt: Week 3

answers covered the same material and were redundant. Furthermore, students were all required to answer the teacher's questions without encouragement to respond to one another. So students' posts were self-contained short essays that did not invite online interaction.

Step 4: Make Changes

The teacher decided to revise her approach to the online discussion forum. She sent a course announcement to her students explaining the change (see Figure 6.13 below).

Announcement ▽

Paradigms in Psychology Course
Posted Sept 27, 2015 8:06 AM

Dear Class,
I'm making a few changes to our discussion forum to allow for more original input. I'm hoping that the revised structure will better prepare you for the analysis and application of concepts required of the end-of-term project and unit tests. I'd also like to reinvigorate the discussion with the kind of interaction and creativity that we enjoyed during the first couple weeks of the semester. So, to those ends...

The discussion prompts will have 3 parts to them.

Part I: Choose one of my questions and respond.
   I will post a series of questions about various topics addressed in the weekly unit. The questions are intended to examine the topic critically, comparing, contrasting and relating it to other course content and your own experience. Back up your response with information from the lectures, readings and any other relevant (and valid) resources.

Part II: Ask your own question.
   Post a question about this topic for a classmate to answer. The question might extend from your own response or address another related issue. Good questions are open ended, hone in on controversial issues, and often ask for opinions and subjective answers (so long as they are supported by information). Be creative -- think about different context to which the psychology of learning is evident-- current events, our own lives, characters and situations in movies and TV.

** I will post new discussion prompts each week by Saturday at midnight. Please select and respond to one prompt and post your question for a classmate by Wednesday at midnight.

Part II: Respond to a classmate's question.
   Read your classmates' responses and questions. Choose one student's question and answer it. Only one response per student. By Thursday, if there are no

Figure 6.13 Announcement Posted within the LMS and Emailed to All Students

students' questions open for response, you may add a second response to a student of your choice. Try not to be redundant and move your response into new territory.

** Respond to one of your classmate's questions by the following Saturday. Feel free to continue dialogue after you have completed the required exchange. I'll keep the week's discussion forum open for this purpose.

I will draw from your questions and responses for the unit tests. (So it's a good idea to use the full discussion forum for review.)

Show All Announcements

Figure 6.13 continued

Step 5: Monitor the Effects of Change

The teacher monitored the students' online interaction over the next few weeks and found that the new format raised the caliber of the students' contributions considerably. She noted in her teaching journal:

> The changes in the discussion questions are paying off. Most of the students seem to have internalized the range of thinking skills required to produce a sophisticated response. I was pleased to see the improvement in the reasoning and examples they exhibited on the last test. They justified their answers by citing specific information and were able to make connections and draw distinctions among issues raised.

Overall, the students' exchanges of questions and answers were successful. They came up with original and fun questions that enlivened the discussion board and challenged the students to think critically and creatively (see Figure 6.14). This is an example of a student's question:

 Jennifer Stevens
Posted Sept 29, 2015 9:06 PM

Maslow's Hierarchy of Needs suggests that we are motivated to achieve certain needs. When one need is fulfilled we move on to the next. Using the context of the television show Breaking Bad, describe Walter White's descent into crime as a progression through Maslow's Hierarchy of Needs.

Figure 6.14 A Student's Question for Classmates After Changes in Prompts

Some timing and coordination issues arose with the implementation of the new discussion procedures. Two students consistently lagged behind in their posts to the discussion board each week. These students' questions went unanswered because they missed the designated window for response (Wednesday to Saturday). The teacher posted an announcement to remind students about the importance of posting their questions by Wednesday to give time for classmates to respond. She also emailed the two students who were late responders to inquire about the reasons for their consistent delay. One student said that he worked during the weekends and was not able to complete the readings and watch the lectures until Thursday. The other student said she would try to respond promptly in the future. The teacher asked the late students to respond to each other's questions—better late than never.

6.6 Summary and Standards

During the middle weeks of an online course, students are busy reviewing resources, participating in discussions, and completing assignments. The teacher serves as a guide through the process. **She introduces each study unit to help students understand what is expected of them and how the activities fit within the overall course plan.** The flexible time frame of asynchronous learning can make it hard for some students to keep up with the schedule. Teachers post reminders, help students plan their work schedules, and check in with students who may be struggling to provide support.

The online environment needs a human touch to personalize learning. Teachers use a conversational tone and provide individualized feedback to establish authentic connections with their students. They promote interaction among the students by encouraging them to respond to each other's questions and comments. Personalizing online interaction helps to form a responsive and supportive class community.

Teachers have a wealth of data available to them about students' participation in online courses. They can track students' activity and progress toward the learning outcomes. As an active participant in the course, teachers also have their own experience of the online interaction to guide their interpretation of the data and evaluate the effectiveness of course design and their instruction and make modifications as necessary. It is recommended that changes made in the middle of the semester are clearly explained and are minimally disruptive to students' routines.

☐ Learning activities and course requirements are clearly defined and explained to students.

☐ Opportunities for frequent teacher-student interaction are provided.

☐ Learners are encouraged to interact with others (classmates, guest speakers, etc.) and benefit from their experience and expertise.

☐ Course evaluation and improvement is an ongoing process.

☐ A variety of information (student performance data, feedback, etc.) is used to evaluate the effectiveness of course design and instruction.

☐ The rights and privacy of students are protected in accordance with the laws and policies that govern all the institution's courses.

☐ Changes made to a course in progress are clearly communicated to students and respect the established workload and time requirements.

References and Further Reading

Garrison, D. R., & Cleveland-Innes, M. (2005). Facilitating cognitive presence in online learning: Interaction is not enough. *The American Journal of Distance Education*, *19*(3), 133–148.

Marsh, J. A., Pane, J. F., & Hamilton, L. S. (2006). *Making sense of data-driven decision making in education.* Retrieved from www.rand.org/content/dam/rand/pubs/occasional_papers/2006/RAND_OP170.pdf

Moore, M. G. (1991). Distance education theory. *The American Journal of Distance Education, 5*(3), 1–6.

Pellegrino, J. P., Chudowsky, N., & Glaser, R. (Eds.) (2001). *Knowing what students know: The science and design of educational assessment.* Washington, DC: National Academy Press.

Protheroe, N. (2011). *Improving teaching and learning with data-based decisions: Asking the right questions and acting on the answers.* Retrieved from www.rogersschools.net/common/pages/DisplayFile.aspx?itemId=3497164

U.S. Department of Education, Privacy Technical Assistance Center (2015). *Protecting student privacy while using online educational services: Model terms of service.* Retrieved from http://ptac.ed.gov/sites/default/files/TOS_Guidance_Mar2016.pdf

Vai, M., & Sosulski, K. (2016). *Essentials of online course design: A standards-based guide* (2nd ed.). New York, NY: Routledge.

Vendlinski, T. P., Niemi, D., Wand, J., & Monempour, S. (2008). *Improving formative assessment practice with educational information technology.* Retrieved from http://santacruzmonterey.edleadersforequityandexcellence.com/docs/f09/improving_teaching_and_learning_with_databased_decisions.pdf

Chapter 7 The Ending Weeks: Synthesizing and Extending Learning

Teaching an Online Course

The Beginning Weeks	The Middle Weeks	The Ending Weeks

In the ending weeks of the course, students are deeply engaged in the discussions and learning activities. They know what to do and are comfortable in the online course routine. But as deadlines for final projects and exams approach, students may be anxious about their ability to fulfill all course requirements and get a good grade.

For teachers, the closing weeks of a course present the following challenges:

1. Some students may lag behind or have questions about the end-of-term assignments. Students often need help to:
   - manage their time and complete the course requirements; and
   - understand expectations for successful final projects.

2. They hope that their students are able to integrate what they've learned into their own thinking and value it as they move beyond the course. Students may need help and encouragement to:

- recognize the key concepts learned throughout the semester;

- understand how these concepts fit together;

- apply them to new situations within the course and beyond; and

- take ownership over their learning process.

3. As the course comes to an end, they need to gauge the degree to which students have met the learning objectives for the course. They also want to know how effective the course design and instruction were in supporting learners' needs. To understand these issues, teachers:

- assess students' learning; and

- evaluate the course design and their instruction.

This chapter discusses ways online teachers handle these instructional concerns and provides standards to help guide your practice. Detailed discussion about assessment of students' learning is addressed in Chapter 9.

7.1 Helping Students to Reach the Finish Line

The end of a course is a busy time. Students have to keep up with the regular course routines (reading weekly material, watching lectures, doing assignments, and participating in discussions) while studying for exams and working on final projects. Here are some ways you can help them.

Provide a Checklist of Requirements

In the beginning weeks, teachers help students establish a work plan. During the ending weeks, they encourage students to review and adjust this plan to complete final projects. Posting an announcement that outlines what students need to accomplish can be a good way to help them prioritize their efforts to get the work done well and on time. Figure 7.1 provides an example.

Time to get going!
José Luis León   May 23 at 9:10 pm

We are rounding the bend to the end of the course – only three weeks left in the semester! The best is yet to come, but we need to be vigilant and help each other to the finish line. Review the syllabus and make sure you are on track to complete the assignments and final project. Please let me know NOW if you have any questions about the requirements or grading criteria. Post questions about the course in the Q & A forum. Feel free to send me an email if you have personal questions or concerns.

In addition to reviewing the weekly learning resources and participating in our discussions, you need to finish up your final projects and course evaluations. Here's the checklist to help guide your work:

Final Project Count Down Checklist

By this Sunday, April 26:
- Complete a draft of your final paper and submitted it for peer review (See "Peer Review Assignment" for complete instructions).
- Post any questions about end-of-term requirement to out Q & A Forum.

By next Sunday, May 3rd:
- Select a paper from the Peer Review Forum and give feedback, using the grading rubric
- and guidelines provided.
- Fill out the course evaluation survey.

NOTE: I rely on your feedback to improve the course and my teaching. I appreciate your thoughts and candor.

By Sunday, May 17th:
- Submit the course evaluation survey. (Thank you!)
- Re-work your final paper using the peer review comments and submit it to the dropbox.
- Download the portions of this course you want to save.

NOTE: The course will be left online for two weeks after the end of the semester. It will be "frozen", meaning no further contributions can be made. But you are free to access and save what you like.

Full steam ahead!

Show All Announcements

Figure 7.1 An Announcement to Help Students Manage Their Work Schedules

Reminders about the due dates for submitting assignments are posted online.

Provide Examples of Final Projects

Examples of students' past work can help your students visualize the end result of an assignment. They are usually chosen by the teacher (or course design team) to illustrate the quality of work expected. Posting a range of former students' final projects can inspire students to consider a wider realm of possibilities than they might originally think of on their own.

It is also useful to share an explanation of how the example was graded. Students can then see how the criteria are applied to a final product.

 Students are given clear expectations and criteria for assignments. Examples are included for clarification when needed.

Support Students Who Are Lagging Behind

Some learners might have trouble keeping up with the pace of the course for personal or academic reasons. By the ending weeks, they may be at risk of being unable to fulfill the course requirements. It is important that online teachers identify these learners and provide them individualized support if possible.

The online environment offers teachers a wealth of information about students' activities and progress (see Chapter 6 for more information on tracking students' performance). Teachers can use this information to identify learners who are showing difficulties keeping up with the course activity and reach out to them by email, chat, or videoconferencing. Together, the teacher and student can figure out how to get the student back on track. **A timely intervention by the teacher can help students devise a strategy to succeed.**

 Teachers track students' progress and offer them support to keep up with the course.

7.2 Promoting Self-Directed Learning

As the end of the semester approaches, teachers may shift more responsibility for learning over to the students to help them become self-directed learners. Self-directed learning promotes a healthy integration of self-management and self-monitoring that will serve students long after the semester is over. Growth in this area is a process that teachers encourage throughout the course and students learn over time. From the beginning weeks, teachers provide and reinforce a clear course schedule to help students manage their own work routines effectively. Teachers' consistent feedback helps students understand what is expected of them and how they can rise to meet the course challenges.

Teaching Dilemma

How much direction do students need?

Increasing students' responsibilities and independence is important for their growth. Yet many students also need direction and support to get their work done by the end of the semester.

Like so much of teaching, promoting self-directed learning while providing sufficient support for students to succeed is a balancing act. Many teachers find that well-defined timelines and well-established assessment provide enough structure for students to handle more responsibilities. Your instructional strategy in this area will depend upon the maturity of your students, the tasks included in the course design, and the learning goals for the students.

You also need to consider individual differences. While some students might be ready to fly on their own, others will require more direction to complete course requirements. By the ending weeks of the course, you will have gathered enough information on each learner so as to get a clear picture of his or her needs. The online environment offers you the means to provide personalized support.

As students' knowledge and confidence grow throughout the semester, teachers may loosen their reins of control and encourage students to share leadership roles in the course. This shift in responsibilities may happen informally as teachers step back and allow students to interact with one another without interceding.

Encourage Students to Lead Discussions

By the end of the course, many teachers intentionally withdraw from the leadership roles in the discussions. They are still active participants, reading along and peppering in comments to let students know that they are there. But now they participate more in a supportive role and encourage students to take the lead. Teachers become more of a resource on the side, pointing students to information, adding occasional questions to challenge or encourage students' critical thinking.

Teachers formally pass the responsibility for initiating and facilitating discussions to students. This can really help students take charge of their learning, but remember that they may need guidance and support to lead a productive conversation. Spend time describing the criteria for good discussion prompts (see Chapter 8, p. 212). Ask a couple of students to post questions that address the week's readings. This responsibility can shift to different pairs from week to week. The class can also be divided into smaller group discussions to allow for more student discussion leaders. It is important that teachers continue to participate as needed to keep the discussion moving forward.

Another way to share leadership responsibility is to assign one or two students to post a summarizing comment at the end of a week's discussion. This can be a challenging exercise that requires careful attention to all that was shared in the discussion, prioritizing of important concepts and synthesizing different people's contributions. It is often helpful to model a few discussion summaries before handing this task off to students.

Personal Reflection

Margaret Foley McCabe

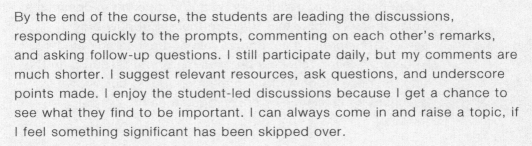

At the beginning of a course, I tend to model the kinds of comments I want my students to post. I give a personal response to a question and back it up with information from the learning resources. I may stir up some controversy and throw another question out to keep the conversation building. Students pick up this kind of discussion strategy.

By the end of the course, the students are leading the discussions, responding quickly to the prompts, commenting on each other's remarks, and asking follow-up questions. I still participate daily, but my comments are much shorter. I suggest relevant resources, ask questions, and underscore points made. I enjoy the student-led discussions because I get a chance to see what they find to be important. I can always come in and raise a topic, if I feel something significant has been skipped over.

See Chapter 8 for more about discussion facilitation strategies.

 Teachers encourage students to take responsibility for their learning.

Invite Students to Assess their Learning

By the end of the semester, teachers have spent considerable time clarifying and demonstrating the criteria used to assess students' learning. Now it's time to test students' understanding of the criteria through application. Teachers often use self-assessment and peer assessment as part of the final grading process. Feedback provided by others can encourage students to monitor and improve the quality of their work (see Chapter 9 for more about self- and peer-review exercises).

 Feedback from a variety of sources corrects, clarifies, amplifies, and extends learning.

7.3 Reviewing and Synthesizing Learning

By the last weeks of the semester, your students will have learned many things. But what will they take with them after the course is over? Meaningful learning occurs when students understand the connections among the facts and skills they have acquired. Wiggins and McTighe (2005) stress the importance of focusing on the "big ideas" that frame the course outline to help students prioritize and connect what they have learned.

Identify and Connect the Core Concepts

As the course draws to an end, it's time to look back and identify the most important concepts and skills that your students have learned. The syllabus will list the course themes, major topics, and learning outcomes, but there may be other important issues that were addressed. In our experience, every group of online students will find interest in different aspects of a given topic. They bring unique perspectives to the discussions and explore unexpected tangents. This incidental learning can be significant to the students' growth and may count as part of the "big ideas" explored. **During the last weeks of the semester, emphasize the key concepts and help students synthesize their learning by drawing connections among them.**

A concept map is a diagram that shows relationships among concepts. It helps students to understand and integrate ideas into a cohesive whole (Jonassen, Beissner, & Yacci, 1993).

Some teachers make video recordings or post written commentary explaining how the content explored during the beginning and middle weeks pertains to the larger and more complex issues addressed in the end. Tom Geary creates a conceptual map to encourage his students to think through the connections between and among the topics discussed throughout the course.

Teaching Tip

Use concept-mapping tools

There are many concept-mapping tools available on the Internet. Many are free and easy to use. For example, with Cmap Cloud, you can create maps such as the one included in Figure 3.7 on p. 71. There are online tutorials on YouTube that show the process step by step.

 Look for examples of concept-mapping tools on the book's website (www.essentialsofonlineteaching.com).

Encourage Self-Reflection

Students learn by doing, but they understand what they have learned through reflection. John Dewey (1910) describes reflection as active, persistent and careful consideration of experience. Self-reflection is an essential step for students to make sense of what they have learned in the course, yet in the hurriedness of the end of the semester, the pause required for such thought can get lost.

You can encourage students' self-reflection by having them keep a journal or blog as they develop their end-of-term projects. Ask students to respond to questions that encourage:

- **Retrospective thinking.** How does their project relate to what they have learned previously in the course?

- **Problem-solving.** What challenges have they encountered as they worked on the project and how did they solve them?

- **Self-awareness.** How does the student's project reflect his or her unique understanding of the topic and assignment? What have they learned from the work on this project?

Joyce Anderson promotes students' self-reflection in a final writing assignment she calls "progress report" (see Figure 7.2).

Announcement | ▽

Progress Report: Options

(Choose one technical writing context to develop in an appropriate professional format for an audience indicated):

1. Write a memo/progress report to your instructor reflecting on your progress as a technical writer. Explain the insights and information you gained in English 312. Organize your thoughts. Be specific.

2. Write a self-evaluation using your writing from this course. Summarize and reflect on your development as a technical writer in a narrative report. Point to specific circumstances as a student in English 312 where you recorded professional activity, as well as insights about failure or achievements in technical writing. Indicate your progress with specific examples.

3. Write a guide to a fellow English 312 student to help him/her study for an English final exam. What significant concepts, strategies, writing practices would you direct your reader to know to illustrate mastery of English 312? What technical applications indicate that a student has made progress in learning about technical writing? Provide examples from the course content and writing activities in English 312.50D.

Please post your memo (progress report) in the dropbox by Friday, December 6. Your reflection will help me to evaluate your progress and learning in technical writing: English 312.

Show All Announcements

Figure 7.2 An Example of a Self-Reflection Assignment from Joyce Anderson's *Technical Writing* Course

If the course outline does not include a reflection exercise, you can interject questions that promote self-reflection in the discussions and in your feedback to students. Figure 7.3 shows a teacher's feedback on a student's assignment. The teacher acknowledges the student's improvements and encourages him to critically reflect on his growth.

Teacher's Comment

John, great job on this policy analysis of Title IX and its application to transgender rights. I posted questions for your consideration and suggestions for improvement as side notes throughout the paper.

Think back to your first assignment, "The Penalties for Drunk Driving," and note how far your understanding of policy analysis has come. This current paper shows growth in: (1) your grasp of the problem addressed by the policy; (2) your analysis of the data cited as evidence of the problem; and (3) your attention to whom and what the policy intends to protect. Your current policy paper focuses on the specifics of the policy rather than conjecture about the topic. Well done.

Have you found occasion to use policy analysis outside of this course?

Figure 7.3 A Teacher's Feedback Promoting Student's Retrospection

Students will view your feedback when they check assignment submissions in the LMS. See Figure 7.4 for an example.

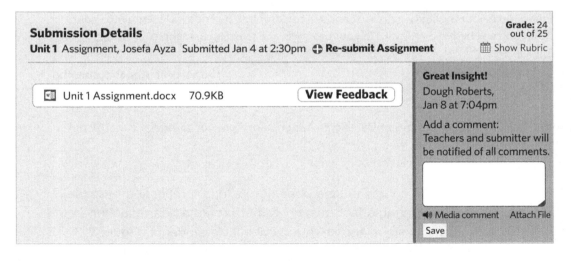

Submission Details **Grade:** 24 out of 25

Unit 1 Assignment, Josefa Ayza Submitted Jan 4 at 2:30pm ⊕ **Re-submit Assignment**   📅 Show Rubric

📄 Unit 1 Assignment.docx   70.9KB   **View Feedback**

Great Insight!
Dough Roberts,
Jan 8 at 7:04pm

Add a comment:
Teachers and submitter will be notified of all comments.

◀) Media comment   Attach File
Save

Figure 7.4 Screen Showing Where Students View Feedback in Canvas

☑ Activities include opportunities for students to review, synthesize, and reflect on their learning.

7.4 Concluding the Course

How you finish an online course is as important as how you launch it. By the end of the semester, your students are likely to have formed bonds that come from substantial time and personal investment in the shared course experience. It's important to acknowledge these relationships and create a satisfying conclusion that lets students affirm accomplishments and carry their learning forward. Many courses include activities during the ending weeks to:

- celebrate what was learned and the bonds formed among participants; and

- share feedback about the course experience.

It is also important to tell students what to do in the final days. Usually, courses are left open a few weeks after the end date so that learners can print any resources they need, find out their grades, and read the teacher's feedback and final discussion comments. Clear instructions and time frames from teachers can help students benefit from the last days of access to the online course.

Wrap-Up Discussion

In asynchronous courses, there is no one, shared moment for goodbyes. Instead, everyone logs on at different times during the final week, turns in his or her assignments, and posts a final comment. It's a good idea to designate a discussion for closing remarks. Like the icebreaker at the beginning of the course, a wrap-up discussion gives students an opportunity to speak to the group from a personal perspective.

Some teachers make the final discussion into a game, similar to the icebreaker activity. For example, a teacher invites students to post a "gift" for their classmates in the final discussion. The "gift" could be anything they felt represented their course experience in any way, such as a:

- favorite quote;

- link to a website;

- joke;

- photo;

- drawing; or

- video (could be of themselves saying goodbye).

A wrap-up discussion can simply be an open-ended invitation for students to share something they learned in the course — or to just say goodbye and thank people for their camaraderie and support. The point is to **provide a space for a satisfying closure to the course**.

Courses are usually left open for students to view a few weeks after the end of the semester. Students can log on and see this final discussion as a collective farewell to the course and each other.

Evaluate the Course

Institutions typically distribute course evaluations at the end of the semester that ask students to numerically rank different aspects of the course experience from excellent to very poor. The questions on such standardized surveys tend to be general, such as "What is your overall rating of this course?" and "What is your overall rating of the instructor's teaching effectiveness?" These surveys gather statistics about the students' general satisfaction, but don't provide much information to help teachers improve the course or their teaching.

Many online teachers distribute their own course surveys at the end of the semester, asking open-ended questions about the students' experience with various components of the course. Descriptive feedback can provide insight into the students' perspective and be very helpful in fine-tuning your course and your teaching for next semester (Gravestock & Gregor-Greenleaf, 2008).

Most LMSs have survey tools that allow you to create and distribute short-answer surveys. Or you can simply email your students a survey with a request to complete and return (see Chapter 3, p. 85).

Here are some tips to get the most out of end-of-course feedback surveys:

- **Include a clear introduction.** Let students know that you are seeking their input to understand their experience and improve the course and your teaching.

- **Limit the number of questions.** A few open-ended questions will allow for students to provide detailed and nuanced responses. For example:
  - What are the strengths of this course?
  - How could this course be improved?
  - How would you describe your interactions with the teacher?
  - How would you describe you interactions with your peers?
  - What are the strengths of the teacher and her teaching?
  - How could the teacher improve her teaching?
  - What would you tell students who are interested in taking this course?

- **Name a due date for response.** Ask students to complete and submit the survey by a given date and send a reminder a few days before the deadline.

- **Consider incentives.** Some teachers give participation points for completing and submitting end-of-course feedback surveys.

Figure 7.5 shows an example of an end-of-course survey created and distributed by a teacher.

☑ A variety of information (student performance data, feedback, etc.) is used to evaluate the effectiveness of course design and instruction.

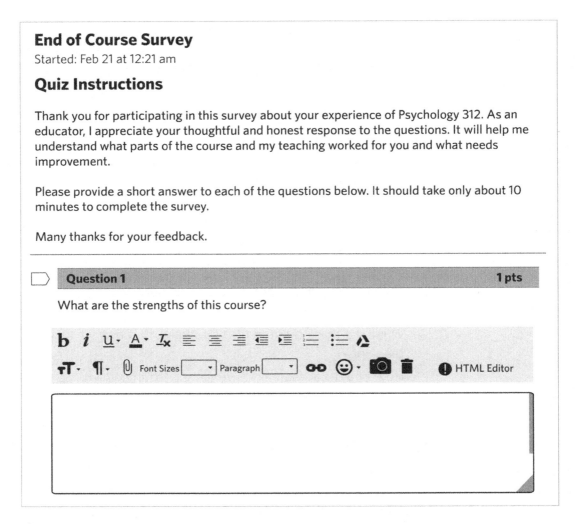

Figure 7.5 Example of Descriptive End-of-Course Survey

Post a Final Announcement

It's the last day of the semester and you have completed the course journey with your students. Post a final announcement to bring closure to the class. Figure 7.6 provides an example.

☑ Students are given clear instructions about course closure.

Announcement | ▽

Jan Merodoski
Posted May 19 22:03

Dear Students,

This brings us to the end of EDU631 Introduction to Research. A few final instructions..

- I will have your research projects graded by December 22. Please look for these along with my comments in the dropbox. I will also leave an audio recording reviewing your final paper. I hope this is helpful as you continue to develop and carry out your research.

- At midnight tonight, this space will no longer be open for posting comments. However, it will be left on the system until the start of next semester. You are free to print or download any course material you find useful.

Thank you all for sharing your thoughts and work with me over the semester. It will be strange not to check in with you daily. I have enjoyed learning with all of you and wish you the best in all your next endeavors. Please drop me a line sometime and let me know what you are doing.
Happy holidays!

My best,
Dr. Merodoski

Show All Announcements

Figure 7.6 Example of a Final Course Announcement

7.5 Summary and Standards

The ending weeks of an online course are filled with practical and instructional challenges. Teachers help students to fulfill requirements by posting reminders of upcoming due dates, clarifying criteria for final projects, and helping them prioritize their work schedules.

Teachers encourage students to take more responsibility for their learning over time. By the ending weeks, students are often active leaders in online discussions and may be given tasks such as facilitating discussions, posting summaries at the end of discussions, and providing feedback for their peers.

As a course draws to a close, the teacher initiates discussions and activities to review and synthesize the key concepts of the course and encourage students to reflect upon what they have learned and its future value to them. The teacher also asks for feedback to evaluate course design and instruction to improve future efforts.

- ☐ Reminders about the due dates for submitting assignments are posted online.

- ☐ Students are given clear expectations and criteria for assignments. Examples are included for clarification when needed.

- ☐ Teachers track students' progress and offer them support to keep up with the course.

- ☐ Teachers encourage students to take responsibility for their learning.

- ☐ Feedback from a variety of sources corrects, clarifies, amplifies, and extends learning.

- ☐ Activities include opportunities for students to review, synthesize, and reflect on their learning.

- ☐ A variety of information (student performance data, feedback, etc.) is used to evaluate the effectiveness of course design and instruction.

- ☐ Students are given clear instructions about course closure.

References and Further Reading

Chee, C. S., & Oo, P. S. (2012). Reflective thinking and teaching practices: A precursor for incorporating critical thinking into the classroom? *International Journal of Instruction*, 5(1), 167–182.

Costa, L., & Kallick, B. (2008). *Learning and leading with habits of mind: 16 essential characteristics for success*. Alexandria, VA: Association for Supervision and Curriculum Development (ASCD).

Dewey, J. (1910). *How we think*. New York, NY: D.C. Heath & Co.

Gravestock, P., & Gregor-Greenleaf, E. (2008). *Student course evaluations: Research, models and trends*. Toronto, Canada: Higher Education Quality Council of Ontario.

Hubball, H., Collins, J., & Pratt, D. (2005). Enhancing reflective teaching practices: Implications for faculty development programs. *The Canadian Journal of Higher Education, 34*(3), 57–81.

Jonassen, D. H, Beissner, K., & Yacci, M. A. (1993). *Structural knowledge: Techniques for conveying, assessing and acquiring structural knowledge*. Hillsdale, NJ: Lawrence Erlbaum Associates.

Perkins, D. (1991). The ability to think and act flexibly with what one knows: Educating for insight. *Educational Leadership, 49*(2), 4–8.

Rogers, C. (2002). Defining reflection: Another look at John Dewey and reflective thinking. *Teachers College Record, 104*(4), 842–866. Retrieved from www.tcrecord.org (ID number 10890).

Wiggins, G. & McTighe, J. (2005). *Understanding by design* (2nd ed.). Alexandria, VA: Association for Supervision and Curriculum Development.

The very essence of online learning is collaborative. It's not a solo voice or one-to-one interaction. It's about sharing ideas, building ideas, and learning from others' perspectives.

(Joyce Anderson, writing teacher)

Historical Note
The Shift Toward Online Collaborative Learning

Prior to the 1980s, most distance learning courses were solitary experiences for students. They received materials and assignments from an instructor and sent in their work for feedback. Course goals and instructional methods tended to be determined by the host institution and were transmitted to students. All this changed when online collaboration became possible through the Internet in the 1990s. The ability to interact and collaborate online allowed teachers and designers to incorporate more progressive teaching methods into online courses. A new wave of online instruction focused on "social-constructivist views of learning based on the ideas of Dewey (1897), Piaget (1959) and Vygotsky (1978)" (Siemens, Gasevic, & Dawson, 2015, p. 17). Linda Harasim (2006) summarizes some important shifts that are reflected in this new model of online teaching and learning. She describes a transformation from:

- knowledge transmission to knowledge building;

- teacher-centered to learning-centered; and

- passive to active learning.

Certainly not all online courses today reflect a social-constructivist point of view (see Chapters 1 and 2). But the ability for students and teachers to collaborate online has shifted the tide in this direction.

Many online courses today are taught as collaborative learning experiences. Students participate in weekly discussions in which they explore content and build knowledge together. They also work collaboratively in small groups to create projects or give each other feedback. All these kinds of activities tap into the potential of the online environment to include many voices in sustained conversation over time.

8.1 Weighing the Benefits and Drawbacks of Collaboration

Collaborative learning has many potential benefits, but it can also add instructional challenges. Group work and discussions can take additional time, effort, and coordination. When thinking about whether to make a particular task a collaborative challenge, ask yourself: "Can students learn more by working together on this task than they could on their own?" Meaningful collaboration serves the students and improves the learning outcomes.

If the course you are preparing to teach includes collaborative activities (group discussions, small group projects, peer reviews, etc.), its important to emphasize the benefits of the group process while managing the organizational challenges and resistance some students have toward teamwork.

Benefits of Collaboration

Collaboration can promote:

- **Active learning.** Students are required to contribute and engage with others during collaborative activities.

- **Learning from multiple perspectives.** Students consider other viewpoints and build collective knowledge.

- **Interpersonal development.** Students learn to work with peers, advance their own ideas, incorporate the ideas of others, and resolve conflicts.

- **Trust.** The rapport among students in collaborative learning activities builds personal relationships and trust.

- **Critical thinking skills.** Collaborative learning creates a situation in which students must explain, discuss, evaluate, and incorporate various perspectives.

- **Motivation.** Collaboration with others encourages students' investment because peers depend on their mutual effort and participation.

Asynchronous communication is particularly well suited for collaboration because the open time frame allows all participants the opportunity to contribute. It also gives people time to review information and reflect before commenting. So online discussions can produce thoughtful exchanges among students.

Personal Reflection

Scott Thornbury

Because students have much more time to consider their response [in online discussions], the quality of their participation is more mindful. The time factor is incredibly important here . . . I am constantly amazed at the kinds of peer teaching and incidental learning that is going on. There are often very rich, long conversations happening. I think the discussion boards are quite amazing at being able to support that.

Such in-depth, "mindful" discussions are supported by the online environment, but facilitated by an instructor who recognizes the value of collaboration.

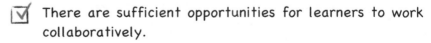

☑ There are sufficient opportunities for learners to work collaboratively.

☑ Collaborative activities are used to encourage students to learn from each other and develop interpersonal skills.

Drawbacks of Collaboration

Like all instructional strategies, collaborative learning activities have limitations to consider. Collaboration can result in:

- **More time spent on the task.** The collaborative process (exchanging ideas, problem-solving, forming consensus, formulating a work plan, etc.) can take more time than independent work.

- **Less flexibility for students' participation.** Students often choose to study online because their schedules require maximum flexibility and coordinating work with other students can be difficult.

- **Unequal participation.** Students have different commitment levels, work habits, interests, and skills. Sometimes a few students do most of the work for the group.

- **Conflict.** Students may have difficulty resolving problems and working together.

Learning preferences may also affect how students approach group work. Some people favor independent learning strategies rather than interactions with others (Kolb, 1984). While it is often good to stretch students' comfort zones and encourage new learning experiences, it is also important to weigh individuals' preferences and attitudes toward collaborative activities.

Conditions for Successful Collaboration

Let's say that you have evaluated the situation and decide that students will benefit from working together on a particular activity. Now what? The online environment has the potential to support meaningful collaboration, but it doesn't happen automatically. Teachers need to:

- set the stage for collaboration;

- support the group process; and

- help students draw meaning from the experience.

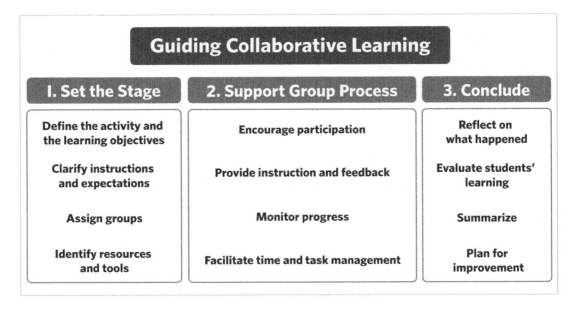

Figure 8.1 Instructional Tasks Required to Guide Collaborative Learning

This is a familiar cycle that teachers work through for most planned instruction. However, as you lead a collaborative learning activity, it's important that you make decisions that reinforce teamwork, as well as the academic learning outcome for the specific activity. Figure 8.1 illustrates the tasks involved in guiding collaborative learning.

Different collaborative activities demand different kinds of support from teachers. For this reason, we will address strategies for facilitating a collaborative discussion separately from managing small group work.

Group Size

What is the right group size for a collaborative activity? There are several factors to consider when deciding the appropriate numbers of participants in a group. Think about the kind of collaborative activity you are planning and the dynamics you envision:

- For in-depth group dialogue, 10–15 members post enough comments to keep the online interaction moving while still small enough for all participants to know each other and develop rapport and trust (Fisher, Thompson, & Silverberg, 2005).

- Larger groups of 15–25 students work well for discussions that benefit from generating lots of ideas and opinions around a topic. Large discussions often focus on comparing and evaluating multiple perspectives (Fisher et al., 2005).

- Small groups of three to five members work best for cooperative projects. Fewer can leave students stranded without anyone to work with and more can lessen members' individual responsibilities (Graham & Misanchuk, 2004).

- Pairs work well to provide students with immediate feedback (peer reviews) and for short-term, sideline exercises that complement whole-class activities (i.e. sharing reactions to a video, comparing stories about a topic, practicing skills).

☑ Students are grouped deliberately for different kinds of learning activities.

Teaching Tip

Divide large classes into small groups

Classes with more than 30 students can be divided in half (or more) to create group sizes that work better for collaborative activities. Small groups and pairs can also be used in conjunction with large group discussions to combine benefits of both groupings.

8.2   What Makes a Good Collaborative Discussion?

You log on to your course and see that your students are engaged in a great discussion. They share informed views about issues related to the week's readings and lecture, ask each other questions, and bring new information to the conversation. Their comments reflect a growing understanding about the topic and enthusiasm for the group exploration.

Discussions such as the one described above are common in online classes. They thrive because they are launched with a clear purpose and a compelling question. The students are provided with resources to inform their contributions and they know what is expected of them and how they will be evaluated. The teacher is an active participant in collaborative discussions, providing support and guidance as needed (see Chapter 3, pp. 64–68, for an example of a discussion with student comments and a description of the LMS discussion tool).

To set the stage for a great discussion, consider the following components.

A Clear Purpose

As you open a discussion forum, include a brief statement about its purpose and how students are expected to participate in it.

Online discussion forums are flexible workspaces that can be used for many different purposes. Figure 8.2 describes some common uses for online discussion forums and provides examples of teachers' introductions about their use.

 Discussions are set up with a clear purpose and guidelines for participation.

Common Instructional Uses of Online Discussion Forums

1. **Class Discussion.** Students and teachers explore course content together.

   Teacher's introduction:

   > This discussion forum provides a space for us to dig into the issues raised in our weekly readings, lectures, and assignments. I'll start the discussion off with a discussion prompt, and you respond—supporting your comments with references from the learning resources or your experience. Participate frequently, put yourself into it, and let us know what you think. Ask questions and respond to one another's contributions too (please check the participation rubric found under ASSESSMENT as a guide to posting here).

2. **Q&A Forum.** Students post questions that are answered by the teacher or other classmates.

   Teacher's introduction:

   > If you have any questions about the course, please post them here. This includes (but is not limited to) questions about procedures, assignments, technical issues, and due dates. There's a good chance others may be wondering the same thing, so check the issues posted before sending yours. This Q&A forum provides a place for all of us to help each other. Please feel free to answer each other's questions and I will check in at least four times a week to make sure we are all in sync.

3. **Shared Repository of Information.** Students share information about designated topics.

   Teacher's introduction:

   Several of you have asked about different presentation tools that can be used for your final projects. I would like to use this discussion forum as a place to share information and experience in this area. If you have used and would like to recommend a presentation tool, please post a link in this forum. Give us a brief description and what you like about it.

4. **Social Forum.** Students get to know each other personally. Some teachers use this space for the initial icebreaker activity and keep it open as an ongoing social forum.

   Teacher's introduction:

   Welcome to our virtual coffee shop. Pull up a stool, order a latte or a chai, and let us know what's on your mind. This is just for fun—so relax and enjoy.

Figure 8.2 Six Instructional Options for Using Discussion Forums

211

5. **Small Group Work.** Teachers open a discussion forum for each small group (or individual student) to interact while they develop a group project or discuss a topic. This group can be closed so that only the members of the group can enter (see Chapter 3, pp. 67–68, for more information on configuring small group discussions).

Teacher's introduction:

Pam, Hector, Sonya, and Tim, this forum is for your group interactions while you prepare your final project. Remember it is due on Monday, April 11.

6. **Student Presentations.** Teachers open a discussion forum for students to present their projects to the class.

Teacher's introduction:

This forum will be used for Pam, Hector, Sonya, and Tim to present their final project (by Monday, April 11). For the next four days (until Friday, April 15), each of you is to view the project and post a question to the group. All group members are expected to answer your classmates' questions and add follow-up information.

Figure 8.2 continued

A Good Discussion Prompt

Think of an online discussion as the students' response to an interesting challenge. The students have to do something—review information, collect data, reflect on their past experience—to meet this challenge. A good discussion prompt invites a range of responses from students so they are interested in reading what their peers have to say. If collaboration is important to the purpose of the discussion, a good prompt invites students to compare their answers and engage with people with different ideas. Interesting discussion prompts often provide context followed by a question or series of questions. Here are some guidelines and suggestions to consider when crafting discussion prompts:

- Avoid asking yes/no questions. This generates thin and redundant responses.

- Avoid questions that have a single factual answer. The first student to answer correctly ends the discussion.

- Ask questions that require critical thinking. You can target different levels of thinking:

  - Analysis: Why do you think . . . ? What is the meaning of . . . ? What are the causes . . . ?

  - Comparison: What are the similarities and differences between . . . ?

  - Synthesis: Given [some combination of factors], how would you characterize . . . ?

  - Evaluation: Which solution better addresses the problem and why . . . ?

  - Application: Where else have you seen . . . ? How could this apply to . . . ?

- Begin prompts with a problem statement. Discussion prompts often include a scenario that gives everyone a shared context for response. A problem or ethical dilemma is often described, followed by questions that require critical thinking to answer. For example:

  > The Wisconsin State Supreme Court is considering the constitutionality of Milwaukee's school choice program. The program allows underprivileged children to use a voucher system to bring public funding to pay for private education. Advocates believe that the program is social justice for the poor who have few or no options for education for their children. Critics believe that school choice will ensure the total demise of public education because it drains funding from public schools. Another opposition group fears that public funding brought to private education will give government too much control over religious schools.

  > What do you think? Imagine that you lived in a neighborhood with failing schools and could not afford private education for your child. How would you feel about school choice? What if you were a teacher in a struggling inner-city public school? What are the short- and long-term effects of school choice programs?

- Ask questions that require students to apply information from earlier lessons. For example:

  > Recalling last week's exploration of micro and macroeconomic perspectives, who wins and who loses with school vouchers for private education? Post a response from each perspective.

- Ask questions that relate to the learning resources. Students may be asked to compare and contrast information offered by different sources and use the lectures and other resources to support their positions. For example:

  > Consider the main female characters in *Great Expectations* and *Of Human Bondage*. How does gender influence the choices that are available to Estella and Mildred Rogers and the decisions that they make? In light of this week's lecture about cultural acquisition of gender, how might these characters face similar decisions today?

- Ask questions that invite students to draw from personal experience. One of the best ways to get students involved in discussions is to relate the course content to their lives. For example:

  > Cognitive dissonance theory predicts that when a person's behavior conflicts with his or her belief or attitude, they will experience unpleasant emotional arousal and change their attitude to fit their behavior. In this theory, the dissonance between behavior and belief exerts a punishing effect that motivates attitude change.
  >
  > Have you ever experienced cognitive dissonance? How did you change or resolve the tension?

Many teachers launch a discussion with a compelling prompt and then weave follow-up questions into the discussion to encourage students to think more deeply and more critically about an issue.

 Discussions begin with a compelling prompt that invites a range of responses.

Clear Participation Criteria

Tell and show students how you want them to participate in the discussions. Set the tone and style for participation in the initial icebreaker discussion and emphasize the importance of contributing frequently and responding to one another (see Chapter 5, pp. 134–138, for further suggestions).

Assessment criteria can serve as a guide for students' process as well. Define standards of quality to let students know what is expected of them, specifying:

- how often they are expected to participate;

- the characteristics of a good discussion post; and

- how students are expected to respond to one another.

Rubrics work well to describe how students' participation will be assessed.

Many teachers define participation criteria in relation to grades. They assign an overall grade to students' participation on a weekly or monthly basis that reflects a combination of attributes to define quality. Table 8.1 provides an example of a more generalized rubric.

Table 8.1 A Rubric for Assessing Participation in a Discussion Forum

Rubric for Participation in Weekly Discussions			
Excellent 100%	Good 85%	Average 75%	Poor Failing Grade
Posted three or more times. Participation was distributed throughout the week. Answered the discussion prompt with well-developed position, supported by information from the learning resources. Offered personal insight and new information to the discussion. Responded to others' comments thoughtfully and asked follow-up questions.	Posted three or more times. Answered the questions in the discussion prompts with thoughtful comments that were not well supported. Responded adequately to others' comments.	Posted two comments that answered the discussion questions, but were not well developed or supported. Did not respond or responded to classmates' comments with superficial replies.	Did not post or posted one comment that was off-topic or did not address the issues raised in the discussion prompt. Did not respond to others.

The rubric shown in Table 8.2 assigns points for frequency and quality of students' responses. The quality of students' contribution is evaluated on students' initial posting, follow-up, content, support, and clarity. What makes "excellent" participation is clearly defined.

Table 8.2 Rubric for Assessing Weekly Participation in Discussions

Criteria	Excellent 3 points	Good 2 points	Acceptable 1 point	Poor 0 points
Frequency	Posts four to six times throughout the week.	Posts three or four times on different days.	Posts one or two times on the same day.	Does not participate.
Initial Response to the Discussion Prompt	Posts well-developed comments that address all aspects of the task and extends concepts.	Posts comments that respond to all aspects of the task, but lacks development of ideas.	Responds with trivial comments that do not address all aspects of the task.	Posts no initial response.
Follow-Up Postings	Responds to and builds on others' contributions and asks meaningful questions.	Makes meaningful comments on other's posts but does not add new ideas.	Posts superficial responses to others (agrees/disagrees).	Posts no follow-up comments to others.
Content of Postings	Posts are factually accurate, relevant, and thoughtful, and bring new insights to the discussion.	Posts add factually accurate and relevant information to the discussion, but report rather than extend concepts.	Posts do not add new perspectives or information to the discussion.	Posts include information that is incorrect, irrelevant, or inappropriate to the discussion.
References and Support	Supports posts with references to the course readings, independent resources, and personal experience.	Cites some references from readings and personal experience.	Supports comments with personal experience, but does not reference course material or independent sources.	Does not support comments.
Clarity of Posts	Ideas are communicated clearly and logically in a style that is easy to read, conversational, and free of distracting errors.	Posts are well presented and easy to read with some distracting writing conventions or errors.	Contributions are understandable, but writing style, organization of ideas, or errors distract from the message.	Ideas are presented in a disorganized way with conventional errors that make it difficult to understand.

> ☑ Criteria/rubrics clearly inform learners about how they will be assessed on specific assignments and online participation.

Teacher's Active Participation

Teachers support collaborative learning in different ways that reflect their instructional style, the needs of the students, and the goals of a particular activity (see Chapter 2 for a discussion about factors that may influence teachers' decisions). At times, they may act as leaders, guiding their students toward desired ends, and other times as facilitators, managing from the sidelines.

Personal Reflection

Margaret Foley McCabe

As a teacher, my participation in the discussions is a delicate balancing act. It requires being assertive when the group requires direction and disciplined enough to pull back and let conversation and group decisions flow organically. It means using my status as the teacher to motivate participation while giving enough time and opportunity for students to jump in on their own. It's important for me to keep both the academic and process-oriented learning outcomes in mind. I try to steer the discussion toward the lesson's topics, while encouraging students to bring their own ideas to the table and to value all perspectives offered.

When the class is debating an issue, I am careful not to make a case for one side of an argument because I recognize that students may misinterpret my opinion as the "right" answer. I ask a lot of questions and I sometimes play devil's advocate to open a realm of possible positions on a topic. In this way, I hope to encourage students to take risks and offer their own views, backed up by the facts as they understand them.

Teachers reinforce collaborative learning goals by:

- **Modeling participation** that values multiple perspectives.

  Ian raises a really interesting point that I'd not considered before . . .

- **Asking follow-up questions** that make students think a problem through for themselves or with the help of their peers.

  Several people have made a case for "net metering," which requires utility companies to credit customers for solar energy. Yet there's been a recent pushback by utility companies about this practice. Can anyone summarize the electric companies' position?

- **Encouraging participation** by sending emails to underperforming students or posting announcements or a comment that encourages all students to contribute regularly.

- **Encouraging student-to-student interaction.** Teachers do not take every other turn in the discussion. They allow students time to respond to one another and may add feedback praising student-to-student interaction.

- **Weaving discussion.** Sometimes online discussion can splinter off into different tangents and be hard to follow. Teachers can begin a new thread in a discussion that brings the group back together.

  I've been following three really interesting conversations that have sprung from our initial question about renewable energy sources.

  - A few of you are talking about how to harness tidal power and its problems as an intermittent energy source.
  - Another group is focused on the "not in my backyard" challenge to wind farming.
  - And there's a discussion about government incentives and commercialization of renewable energy sources.

  Considering the points you have been discussing, what do you think is the biggest obstacle preventing solar, hydroelectric, and wind power from being a main energy source of the future?

- **Directing the discussion toward the task.** If students' comments stray too far from the intended topic, the teacher may reiterate the central question or dilemma.

- **Monitoring the discussion regularly.** Online discussions build in a unique way over time. A student posts a comment, another student responds. Perhaps a new thread is opened with more comments and responses. You have to keep up with these emerging conversations to have a clear sense of what is happening.

- **Adding or pointing to relevant information.** When students raise questions or express opinions about issues that call for more information, the teacher may provide information or suggest resources.

> George brings up a relevant issue. Teachers in community programs face the challenge of helping students become independent learners. I suggest that you look into Mezirow's theory on self-directed learning.

☑ The teacher monitors discussions and facilitates the learning process.

Personal Reflection

Tisha Bender

I don't like to interject too much information within the discussion. I prefer for the students to talk among themselves. When I see that students' responses show a lack of understanding about something or could benefit from further information, I may put together a "mini-lecture" and post it as a learning resource. My mini-lectures are just a few paragraphs explaining some concept. I would then go into the discussion and suggest that students read the new mini-lecture. This keeps my instruction from interrupting the flow of conversation.

Purposeful Closure

Teachers can configure discussions to have a start and end date (see Chapter 3, Figure 3.6).

Most online discussions are active for a week or two and then the group moves on to address new questions in the next discussion. The syllabus usually outlines a schedule for weekly discussions to keep the group moving forward together. You can use several strategies to conclude a discussion in a satisfying way that brings closure and attention to what has been learned:

- **Discussion summaries**. The focus of online discussions is fluid; topics can splinter off into interesting tangents that trigger new conversation. This is the lively and meandering way online discussions build. It can be challenging to understand how it all fits together and to reflect on what was learned. So it is helpful for teachers to post summaries of major points raised at the end of the discussion (see Chapter 7, p. 191, for suggested strategies). The summary can be posted as a comment or uploaded to the learning resources. Teachers can also share this responsibility with students. They may assign pairs of students to summarize the weekly discussions, shifting the responsibility to different students each week.

- **Reflection and application**. Encourage students to reflect on what they have learned in the discussion and apply it to their assignments. Many teachers include information explored within discussion as the basis for some test questions.

- **Student evaluation**. Teachers use the assessment criteria described on the syllabus and explained through rubrics to evaluate students' participation. It is important to let students know how they are doing in a timely manner— especially if their participation does not meet expectations (see Chapter 9, pp. 254–262, for suggestions on feedback). When needed, contact students individually to discuss ways to improve their participation.

Teaching Tip

Take notes to track your experience

It's helpful to keep track of your thoughts as your students finish a discussion. These notes will help you recognize patterns in students' participation, address issues that need improvement, and carry forward aspects that are working well. Jot down your thoughts about:

- students' participation level;
- students' responses to the discussion prompt; and
- follow-up questions and topics raised.

These notes will also be helpful when you teach this course again and prepare to facilitate this discussion (see Chapter 6, p. 170, for more about the use of teachers' journals).

8.3 What Makes Successful Group Work?

Effective group work is challenging and interesting. It uses the talents and diversity of the participants and requires active learning. The small group context allows students to get to know each other as people and build relationships. The social aspects of group learning can also be a lot of fun—which should never be underestimated as a significant part of learning.

Group work requires careful setup to be successful. It also requires students' investment in the process—an open and enthusiastic attitude toward working with others can help a lot. Figure 8.3 provides an example of a collaborative project conducted over several weeks. Notice how the teacher sets the activity up by explaining the purpose and procedures.

Introduction to Policy Analysis
Small Group Project: Policy Presentation

Activity
For the next two weeks, you will work in groups to create a presentation of a policy solution to a controversial social issue.

Teams
I have divided our class into six teams with four students in each. Each team is assigned a "hot topic" to research. Your team will narrow the topic by defining a central "problem" that a policy can address.

Teams	Topic
Carole, Justine, Patricia, Francis	Minimum wage
Peter, Kim, Sean, Therese	Cost of higher education
Laura, Carl, Fiona, Alex	Animal testing
Mauricio, Jennifer, Ian, Serge	Medical marijuana
Saul, Ernestine, Aina, Pekka	Standardized tests
Michael, Victor, Brigid, Marjorie	Gun control

Preparation
I have assigned each team a discussion forum to use as a workspace to prepare your presentation (your name is on your forum). Only your team and I have access to this discussion board. So feel free to talk among yourselves.

I've outlined steps that need to be accomplished in the time frame given. How you work out the roles and responsibilities is up to you. I encourage you to take time at the beginning to discuss your group process and plan strategically. Note that this is a collaborative activity and your grade will reflect your participation in the team process, as well as your team's presentation. I have posted a rubric for this assignment in our course resources.

Presentations
On May 16, I will open a discussion forum called "Policy Presentations". Your group will upload your presentations to this forum and lead a discussion about your proposed policy.

Figure 8.3 Instructions Shared with Students for Small Group Presentations

Timeline

Sunday, May 8–Sunday, May 15

1. Prepare your team's policy position on the issue.

   - Discuss the topic and define the central problem.
   - Identify issues that require research and carry out the research.
   - Draft a policy proposal to address the problem.
   - Justify your proposal.
   - Decide on the format in which you want to present your policy.
   - Be prepared to lead a discussion, answer questions and defend your policy initiative.

2. Create a multimedia presentation that is between 8–10 minutes in length. You can use images, voiceover, text, video clips, graphs, etc.

3. Upload your group's presentation to the Presentation Forum by May 16.

Monday, May 16–Sunday, May 22

1. Each group posts leads a discussion about its policy initiative.

2. All students view the 6 presentations and participate in the discussions surrounding the proposed policies.

Figure 8.3 continued

If you are preparing to teach a course that has been designed to include group work, the lesson plan will likely include purpose (or objective), procedures, learning outcomes, and means of assessment. However, some course designs may just suggest small group work as an alternative option to independent students assignments. In these cases, the purpose for collaboration and process may not be defined. Whatever your situation, it is good to think through the whole process from beginning to end. Similar to good discussions, successful group work requires that teachers tend to several components.

Personal Reflection

Margaret Foley McCabe and Patricia González-Flores

In today's connected world, professionals from all disciplines reach across organizations and the world to share information and work together at a distance. Students need to know how to work effectively in online groups to participate in this realm of the workforce.

The writing of this book offers a case in point to demonstrate the power of online collaborative tools. We wrote this book together over two years from our homes in Atlanta, Georgia and Mexico City. We were never in the same place, but worked together daily, sharing links to research, exchanging documents through email, editing our text together on Google Docs and talking for hours using video conferencing. We also held online conferences with our editor and many teachers throughout the process. Online tools allowed us to work seamlessly from different time zones and with conflicting schedules. The following collaborative strategies worked for us. We:

- mapped out goals on a timeline;
- made weekly "To Do" lists, indicating who was responsible for what and when it would be done;
- talked frequently in real-time. Personal connection matters.
- played to our strengths. Each of us is better at different tasks and we learned to divide jobs accordingly;
- defined a system to name shared files;
- used the subject line in emails to identify attachments; and
- found a method and style to edit each other's work that was supportive and efficient.

Incorporating online group work into your course helps students develop their own collaborative strategies that will serve them in their careers.

Clear Expectations

Share a thorough description of a group activity to let students know what is expected of them. This information can be posted as a document in the LMS learning resources, and reinforced through announcements, emails, and in discussions.

The project description should include enough detail that students will be able to carry out the work together asynchronously at a distance.

Group work requires careful planning and management. Here's what students need to know about collaborative activities:

- **The purpose of collaborating.** Tell students why they will work in teams and what you hope they will learn through the task, both academically and as a result of teamwork. Describe how the activity leads to the learning outcomes identified on the syllabus.

- **The end product.** What is the group expected to produce as a result of the activity? This is the tangible learning outcome for the assignment. Define all the requirements and criteria for success. Providing a range of examples of former students' projects helps to clarify your expectations while keeping creative possibilities open.

- **The procedures.** Students need to understand how the group will communicate online and the steps involved in the group project. It's important to provide enough structure to help the group coordinate efforts. You can open discussions for each small group. Most LMSs have a tool to create groups and assign students to them (see Figures 8.4 and 8.5).

Add Group   X

Group Name   Policy 1 - Negative

Limit groups to   4   members (Leave blank to use group set max)

Cancel   Save

Figure 8.4 Creating a Group in Canvas

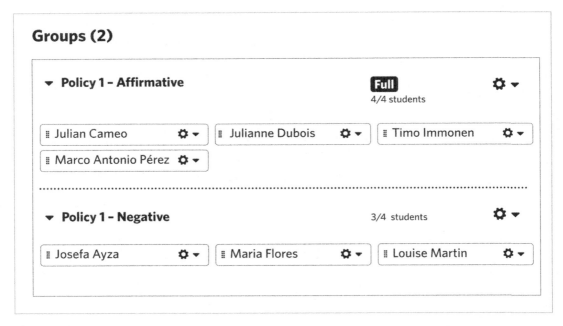

Figure 8.5 Adding Students to a Group in Canvas

- **The project timeline.** Include a start and due date in the course syllabus and send weekly reminders about the project timeline. Remember that asynchronous interaction takes time. Allow a sufficient number of days for the group to discuss issues and arrive at conclusions. For long-term projects (three or more weeks), try breaking the assignment down into steps and giving interim deadlines for teams to submit portions of work or progress reports for feedback. This will help coordinate the team's effort and motivate them to keep on track.

- **The resources and tools.** Let your students know what kinds of resources and tools they will need for a group project. Point to appropriate websites and journals for research and consider including information on strategies for effective teamwork. Suggest that students use simple collaborative editing tools such as wikis or Google Docs to write or edit a document together (see Chapter 3, pp. 88–92, for a description of these tools). They can also use free videoconferencing tools such as Skype or Google Hangouts to talk internationally while recording audio and video if they choose. Collaborative tools and applications are plentiful and evolving. It is impractical to address specifics in this guide. As you consider the possibilities, remember to keep it simple.

 See the book's website for examples of tools that can be used for small group collaboration online: www.essentials ofonlineteaching.com.

- **The assessment strategy.** Assessing collaborative work can be tricky. You want to encourage students to work cooperatively and productively as a team, while grading individual students' efforts fairly. Consider assessing collaborative work in terms of the:
  - team's process; and
  - final product.

Teachers often use a combination of assessment strategies to grade each of these areas. They may include self, peer, and teacher assessment to come up with the final grade. Determine an appropriate weight for each kind of evaluation:

Self-evaluation of contribution toward team project	10 points
Peer evaluation of student's contribution toward team project	10 points
Teacher evaluation of team's project	30 points
Total project	50 points

See Chapter 9 for more information on self- and team evaluations.

☑ The purpose and procedures for collaborative activities are clearly explained.

☑ Group work is designed to allow sufficient and flexible time for students to collaborate asynchronously.

Teaching Dilemma

Should a teacher assign students' roles in group projects?

Many group projects require students to fulfill different roles or perform different tasks to make the project come together on time. Assigning roles to students is one way to make collaborative work easier to coordinate. The specific roles will depend on the type of group project. Some common project roles include:

- leader;

- researcher;

- writer;

- designer;

- IT manager/multimedia producer; and

- presenter.

Other times, it's best to list the suggested roles or required tasks and let students sort out their group's internal dynamics. Assigning roles is more efficient, but giving students greater control over the group process offers opportunity for students to learn project management skills.

Whether you decide to assign roles or allow students to plan their team's process will depend on the:

- **Learning objectives for the project.** If decision-making and project management are part of the goals, you may consider building in time to allow students to decide how to divide the labor.

- **Project time frame.** More flexibility requires more time.

- **Maturity and experience of students.** Older students and students who are used to working together in teams will require less guidance by the teacher.

- **Openness of the task.** Creative projects are often intentionally ill defined. In such cases, assigning specific roles may be impractical.

Group Assignment

The method of choosing the group can make a difference. You can allow students to self-select or assign them to groups. Both ways have advantages and disadvantages.

Self-Selected Groups

There is an inherent motivation in working with people you choose or who choose you. Self-selection may lead to more homogeneous grouping because people tend to pick partners with similar interests, personalities, and work habits. There is also the risk that some students will not be chosen and will feel left out.

To avoid procedural problems, include detailed instructions about how students are to form groups. Figure 8.6 provides an example of instructions for a self-selected peer review activity (more information is provided about peer review in Chapter 9).

Peer Review Assignment #1

Critique a classmate's essays using the Peer Review Sheet (attached). Students' essays are posted as links in this week's discussion forum.

- By Tuesday, Feb. 2, choose one student's work to review and post a comment in the discussion letting everyone know whose work you will be critiquing. (Note: Each essay must be critiqued only once.)

- On Wednesday at 8 A.M., I will give a participation point to everyone who has completed step 1. I will assign a student's work to anyone who has not self-selected an essay to review (without awarding a point).

- Submit your reviews as a comment in the discussion by Saturday, Feb. 6, at midnight (EST). You will be graded on the quality of your review.

- Read the peer review of your work and respond to the criticism.

Figure 8.6 An Example of Self-Selected Peer Review Assignment

Teacher-Assigned Groups

When creating groups, think about interpersonal issues as well as task requirements. You want to match the students to the groups (so that they work well together) and the groups to the task (so that they are able to successfully complete the challenge). Here are some choices to consider:

Homogeneous vs. Diverse Groups

When homogeneous grouping is used, students are placed in learning teams with others who are similar to them with respect to some characteristic that is meaningful to the project. For instance, students may share an academic interest or express shared views about an issue raised in the course. They may have similar experiences or some other trait that will make consensus building easier. Grouping people with similarities can promote bonding and enthusiasm for the work (Kagan, 1995). However, homogeneous grouping may limit the range of perspectives, knowledge, and skills of the group as a whole.

When group work involves open-ended tasks, mixed grouping will give greater variety of views, interests, skills, thinking styles, and backgrounds that can widen the creative possibilities for the project. Heterogeneous groups also provide opportunity for students to develop communication and negotiation skills—important to real-world situations and project management. However, sometimes students dislike working in mixed groups because stronger students tend to assume more responsibility than weaker students and resentments can arise on both sides of the spectrum.
To capitalize on the benefits and circumvent problems:

- Make sure the groups have a balanced range of strong to weaker students.

- Outline specific tasks/roles so that every person has a job and is held accountable.

- Require documentation of all students' contributions that will be considered as part of the project grade.

- Encourage the groups to begin with a discussion to plan their process and problem-solving strategies.

- Monitor group progress and offer support as appropriate.

Consistent vs. Fluid Work Groups

Some teachers assign small groups or partners to work together throughout the course. Consistent groups allow students get to know each other and develop a work routine that carries over from one activity to the next. Here is a quotation that illustrates a student's preference for consistent work groups:

> I like working with the same three people. After we get an assignment, we begin our work with a group chat—texting about the assignment and figuring out the plan of attack. Lori usually takes charge and sends us all an email that outlines what was decided and divides up jobs. We're all good at different things. Ben does most of the research and I usually do the write-up. Andrew is our techie and figures out how to present it. We all edit the final product. We've gotten really good at working together and I wouldn't want to have to figure this out again and again.

Consistent groups are also used for semester-long projects. This provides continuity for students to do in-depth work.

There are also good reasons to shift groups throughout the semester. Changing students' work groups widens opportunities for them to get to know and learn from more people. This builds rapport among the class and can enhance whole-group discussions. Fluid grouping also allows students to be grouped differently for different tasks. Some assignments may require a balance of skills while others may be better served by shared interests. For example, a teacher may group students who have different skill sets to work collaboratively on a multimedia presentation. That same teacher may group students who share a particular academic or career interest to work together on a long-term research project. Changing groups from one activity to the next can also alleviate interpersonal problems that can arise as students negotiate group work.

Option to Work Independently

Some students simply don't want to work in groups. Depending on the course, the students, and the particular activity, it is sometimes best to give students a choice to work in groups or independently. Tom Geary, who teaches a composition course online, gave this as an example of such a case:

> I have a student who is in the military and he signed up for an online course to give him maximum flexibility. He just wants to read the material, watch the videos, do his work, and be done with it. While I feel that he is missing out on a lot of extra knowledge that is being offered by the group, I let him do his own thing. He's told me that he's getting a lot out of the class and he produces acceptable work on his own. Sometimes you have to be flexible to students' preferences and situations — especially for adult learners.

If a collaborative activity is essential to your course design, this needs to be explained and justified to students. For instance, many courses require active participation in discussions because the negotiation of ideas among the students is critical to the learning outcomes. While a student may feel that he or she learns best by reading along and working independently on the assignments, this is probably not an appropriate option for a discussion-based course.

However, some course activities may still work effectively, whether as a collaborative or individual effort. In such cases, teachers can give assignments that have options for group or individual work. The criteria for assessing both options may need to be adjusted.

Note: LMSs usually offer several options for assigning students to groups: self-enrollment, random group creation, manual assignment.

Teacher Support

Once students are working in groups, the teacher's role shifts to the sidelines. As the facilitator, you watch and assist as needed. Keep an eye on:

- **Timing.** Post reminders to help the teams to countdown to the finish line.

- **Group conflict.** Sometimes group members don't get along or their participation detracts from the group's effectiveness. Dealing with this is part of the collaborative learning process. However, the teacher can help by introducing conflict resolution strategies:

  - Ask students to express their issue with a team member in terms of the project goals and team process (avoid personal criticism).

  - Ask students to propose solutions.

  - Give students an opportunity (and incentive) to find consensus.

  - If conflict cannot be resolved, the teacher will need to work out an acceptable alternative plan.

  - If group work is a major part of your course design, it may be worthwhile to spend time on team process skills—including conflict resolution—before and during the collaborative work. The group project discussion forum described above could be used for such purposes.

- **Quality of work.** It's important for teachers to direct the team to the criteria for assessing the group activity. Groups may misunderstand the task of the assignment or the list of project requirements. Interim checkups can circumvent major problems at the end. Or distribute self-evaluation questions that help the team to determine if its work is headed in the right direction.

☑ Teachers monitor and assist students in collaborative work as needed.

Opportunity for Reflection

At the end of a group activity, it's important for the students to review what happened, what they learned, and how it can be applied to future situations. This can be accomplished as a whole-class discussion, a follow-up assignment for the groups, or as an individual reflection activity.

Use the learning outcomes defined for the activity as the basis for your questions.

For example, as a follow-up to the policy presentation activity described in Figure 8.3, the teacher may ask questions about:

- Policy analysis, e.g:

  Based on your team's presentation, what are the central problems that the policy addresses? Can you think of other public policies that address this issue?

- Teamwork, e.g:

  How did your team decide on the best argument to put forth? What did you learn from this decision-making process?

- The discussion, e.g:

  Considering the policy discussion, did your opinion of the policy change? Identify how the discussion influenced your perspective.

Student participation in self-assessment and team assessment are also opportunities for reflection (see Chapter 9 for discussion and examples of students' participation in evaluation).

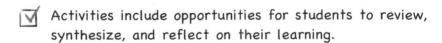 Activities include opportunities for students to review, synthesize, and reflect on their learning.

8.4   Summary and Standards

Collaboration is at the heart of many online courses. Asynchronous discussions allow students to participate in rich and sustained conversation. Teachers support this by setting up discussions with a clear purpose and interesting questions that encourage critical thinking and invite multiple perspectives to the table. Students are provided with clear guidelines about effective participation in discussions and understand their responsibilities to the process. Teachers act as guides and facilitators in discussions, adding information and assistance as needed.

The online environment can also support a range of other kinds of group learning activities. Small group and paired activities can provide an interesting diversion from whole-class discussions. They allow students to get to know one another on a more personal level and encourage interdependency and team problem-solving. Small group activities require clear expectations, purposeful grouping, opportunities for reflection, and teacher support to succeed online.

- [ ] There are sufficient opportunities for learners to work collaboratively.

- [ ] Collaborative activities are used to encourage students to learn from each other and develop interpersonal skills.

- [ ] Students are grouped deliberately for different kinds of learning activities.

- [ ] Discussions are set up with a clear purpose and guidelines for participation.

- [ ] Discussions begin with a compelling prompt that invites a range of responses.

- [ ] Criteria/rubrics clearly inform learners about how they will be assessed on specific assignments and online participation.

- [ ] The teacher monitors discussions and facilitates the learning process.

- [ ] The purpose and procedures for collaborative activities are clearly explained.

- [ ] Group work is designed to allow sufficient and flexible time for students to collaborate asynchronously.

☐ Teachers monitor and assist students in collaborative work as needed.

☐ Activities include opportunities for students to review, synthesize, and reflect on their learning.

References and Further Reading

Bender, T. (2012). *Discussion-based online teaching to enhance student learning* (2nd ed.). Sterling, VA: Stylist.

Carabajal, K., LaPointe, D., & Gunawardena, C. N. (2007). Group development in online distance learning groups. In M. G. Moore (Ed.). *Handbook of distance education* (pp. 137–148). Mahwah, NJ: Lawrence Erlbaum Associates.

Davidson, N. (1990). *Cooperative learning in mathematics: A handbook for teachers*, Menlo Park, CA: Addison-Wesley.

Eberly Center for Teaching Excellence, Carnegie Mellon (2015). *Design and teach a course: Instructional strategies*. Retrieved from www.cmu.edu/teaching/designteach/design/instructionalstrategies/discussions.html

Fisher, M., Thompson, G. S., & Silverberg, D. A. (2005). Effective group dynamics in e-learning: Case study. *Journal of Educational Technology Systems*, *33*(3), 205–222.

Garrison, R. D., Anderson, T., & Archer, W. (2004). *Critical thinking, cognitive presence, and computer conferencing in distance education*. Retrieved from http://cde.athabascau.ca/coi_site/documents/Garrison_Anderson_Archer_CogPres_Final

Garrison, R. D., & Baynton, M. (1987). Beyond independence in distance education: The concept of control. *American Journal of Distance Education*, *1*(3), 3–15.

Graham, C. R., & Misanchuk, M. (2004). Computer-mediated learning groups: Benefits and challenges to using groupwork. In T. Roberts (Ed.). *Online Learning Environments*. Retrieved from www.ifets.info/journals/10_4/22.pdf

Harasim, L. (March 13, 2006). *Online collaborative learning (OCL): The next generation for elearning*. Public presentation, Sao Paulo, Brasil. Retrieved from www.slideshare.net/aquifolium/linda-harasim-on-online-collaborative-learning

Johnson, D. W., & Johnson, R. T. (1994). *An overview of cooperative learning*. Baltimore, MD: Brookes Press.

Kagan, S. (1995, February). *The structural approach to cooperative learning*. Paper presented at the Midwest Regional ASCD Conference: Creating New Realities. Omaha, NE.

Kolb, D. A. (1984). *Experiential learning: Experience as the source of learning and development* (Vol. 1). Englewood Cliffs, NJ: Prentice Hall.

Palmer, G., Peters, R., & Streetman, R. (2003). Cooperative learning. In M. Orey (Ed.). *Emerging perspectives on learning, teaching, and technology*. Retrieved from http://epltt.coe,uga.edu

Roberts, S. T. (2004). *Online collaborative learning: Theory and practice*. Hershey, PA: Information Science.

Rohrbeck, C. A. (2003). Peer-assisted learning interventions with elementary school students: A meta-analytic review. *Journal of Educational Psychology, 94*(2), 240–257.

Siemens, G., Gasevic, D., & Dawson, S. (2015). *Preparing for the digital university: A review of the history and current state of distance, blended and online learning*. Athabasca University, Canada. Creative Commons Attribution-ShareAlike 4.0 International License.

Slavin, R. E. (2009). Cooperative learning. In G. McCulloch & D. Crook (Eds.). *International encyclopedia of education*. Abingdon, UK: Routledge.

Vygotsky, L. (1978). *Mind in society: The development of higher psychological process* (M. Cole, Trans.). Cambridge, MA: Harvard University Press.

Walsh, J. A., & Sattes, B. D (2015). *Questioning for classroom discussion*. Alexandria, VA: Association for Supervision and Curriculum Development.

Chapter 9 Online Assessment

> Learning is a process, not a product. However, because this process takes place in the mind, we can only infer that it has occurred from students' products or performances.
>
> (Ambrose, Bridges, Lovett, DiPietro, & Norman, 2010)

Assessment is an important part of the learning process. It lets everyone—teachers, students, administrators, parents, and other stakeholders—know about students' progress toward academic goals. Trends in course grade and other marks of achievement tell teachers how well the course design and their instruction is serving the students, individually and collectively. They will then have information to make adjustments to target student needs.

Assessment also provides information to motivate student growth. For this to happen, assessment needs to include feedback that helps students understand the connection between their work and the target outcomes. It needs to be supportive, focusing on student efforts and offering strategies for improvement. It needs to be timely so students are able to put the suggestions to use. And assessment should help students recognize their progress and achievements over time and encourage them to aim higher.

The online environment offers a gold mine of information to assess student learning. Nearly all online course interaction is posted and stored on an LMS and is easily reviewed at any time. While all this data may provide rich opportunities for researchers, they can present a daunting challenge for teachers. How do you get a handle on all this information, evaluate student progress, and provide useful feedback? The key is to have a good assessment plan from the beginning of the course that is woven into the students' learning process.

The assessment plan is usually defined during the course design phase. Designers identify the learning outcomes for the course and decide what students will do to gain knowledge, explore ideas, practice skills, and demonstrate learning. They identify student products and performance that will serve as the basis for assessment and the criteria used for evaluation.

Once the course begins, it's up to the teacher to implement the assessment plan as part of his or her instruction. Teachers:

- communicate the assessment plan to students;

- gather information about students' performance from different kinds of activities;

- provide ongoing feedback;

- use fair grading practices; and

- guard against cheating and plagiarism.

This chapter explains how online teachers accomplish each of these instructional tasks to help their students reach the course goals.

9.1 Communicating a Clear Assessment Plan

When students understand the assessment process, they are more likely to do well in a course (Huba & Freed, 2000). They are able to see the connections between the course goals and the coursework. This improves their investment in the learning activities and helps them organize their time and efforts. They understand the criteria used to evaluate their work and why these standards are important. When they receive feedback based on the established criteria, they see it as helpful, rather than as criticism. This is the kind of growth-oriented culture most teachers want to encourage in their courses.

Help your students develop a clear understanding of the course assessment plan by explaining to them:

- what they are expected to learn;

- how they can demonstrate their learning;

- how the coursework will be evaluated and graded;

- how and when they will receive feedback on their work;

- the consequences of cheating and plagiarism; and

- how and where they can get support.

Present the assessment plan at the beginning of the course and reinforce it frequently throughout the semester. There are several ways to communicate this information in the online environment.

Share the Assessment Plan Through the Syllabus

The course syllabus is the most complete representation of how the whole course fits together. It presents the learning outcomes and describes what students will do to reach them. It also includes the assessment plan. Here, students learn what assignments and projects they will turn in, when they are due, and how to submit them. The grading policies and criteria for assessment are also explained in most course syllabi.

Figure 9.1 shows part of Rosario Freixas' syllabus for her course, *Research in Social Work I* (the complete document is several pages long and provides: a course overview statement; contact information; a list of course goals; learning outcomes; resources; assignments; a course timeline; and the assessment information shown here). In the excerpt below, you can see that Rosario gives a breakdown of how students' final grades are calculated. This lets students know that the assessment of their learning will be based on their participation in the discussions and completion of unit activities and final assignment. Rosario posts specific instructions for the five unit activities, the final project, and participation on the LMS, along with criteria used to grade each.

Universidad Nacional Autónoma de México
Escuela Nacional de Trabajo Social

(Excerpt from Course Syllabus for Introduction to Scientific Research)

Professor: Rosario Freixas

Weighted Assessment

Participation in the discussion forums	20%
5 unit activities	40%
Final assignment	40%

Please note:

- All quotations should be clearly indicated using APA style citation standards.

- Copying information from other sources without quoting them is considered plagiarism, which is a serious breach of academic integrity and will result in a failing grade.

Figure 9.1 An Excerpt of Rosario Freixa's Assessment

In addition to the course syllabus, some teachers post further explanations about the assessment process. For example, Scott Thornbury distributes a document called "How this Course Works" that spells out what students are expected to do and what they can expect from him. Figure 9.2 shows an excerpt from this document that focuses on the assessment process within the course, *English in the World*.

☑ All graded activities are listed at the beginning of the course.

☑ The relationship between graded elements and the final grade is clear.

☑ The consequences of missed deadlines are stated and fair.

Scott Thornbury: English in the World
Document: How This Course Works

Course Assessment

1. You are assessed on your coursework (70%) and on your participation in the discussions (30%). Please read carefully the information about assessment in the course description (see Modules). Written work can be sent to me either as an email attachment or (preferably) using the upload function in the Assignments menu. Please submit all written work in the form of a Word document (unless asked otherwise)—not as a PDF, Pages document, etc. Written work will be graded and returned, with comments inserted using the Speedgrader tool. The grades are recorded in the Gradebook and can be consulted by clicking on Grades. Normally, I don't allow extensions on course assignments, as this creates a backlog both for you and for me, and also means that everyone starts to get out of sync. Moreover, granting extensions to some seems unfair to those others who ARE prepared to meet deadlines. That being said, I will, of course, always be sensitive to appeals based on exceptional, individual circumstances. Also (obviously), if you miss out on participating in a discussion, you don't get a second chance.

Figure 9.2 An Excerpt from a Course Document Explaining the Assessment Process for Scott Thornbury's Course, *English in the World*

Clarify the Assessment Process as You Introduce a New Unit Online

Most online courses are organized to explore a new unit each week of the semester. Teachers often begin the week with an announcement to let students know what's coming up. Assessment is a very important part of the week's plan. Tell students which activities will be graded and review the due dates and procedures for submitting assignments. Let them know where to find the criteria for assessing the week's assignments and how they will receive feedback. Encourage students to post questions or send you an email if they have concerns. It's important to go through all this information each time you introduce a new type of activity or assignment.

Instructions for Week 2
Posted March 14, 2016

Hello Human Centered Designers!

This week we will dive into the principles and philosophy of Human Centered Design (HCD) and you will begin to work on your final project. By next Sunday, you should be able to:

- **describe the HCD mindset;**
- **explain the three phases in HCD; and**
- **define a problem that could be improved by incorporating a HCD mindset.**

Our week's learning resources include 2 videos explaining aspects of the HCD mindset and 2 research studies examining the impact of applying this approach to solve a problem.

We will explore the HCD mindset and generate examples of its use in the discussion forum. Remember that your participation in the discussion counts for 30% of your overall course grade. Please review the Participation Rubric under the Assessments menu to make sure you are meeting (or exceeding) expectations. If you have concerns about your discussion participation, please email me or ask a general question in the Q&A forum.

We will also begin work towards the final course project. The research studies included in the week's readings serve as examples for your final project.

You have two assignments to submit to the dropbox this week. (Complete instructions are found under the Assignments menu.)

1. Due Thursday, March 17 at midnight: Sample Study Evaluation Practice.
Pick one of the two sample studies included in our resources this week. Apply the grading criteria we will use to assess your final project (find the rubric under the Assessment menu) to evaluate the sample study. This will help you with your final project and let me know that you understand the criteria.

2. Due Sunday, March 20th at midnight: Problem Statement.
Define a problem you want to solve with HDC mindset and turn in a one-page description to the dropbox. I will provide feedback on your Problem Statements by Wednesday, March 23rd for you to incorporate into your work.

Good luck!
Eric Wright

Show All announcements

Figure 9.3 An Announcement Presenting the Fourth Unit of an *Introduction to Human-Centered Design* Course

Figure 9.3 on page 243 shows an example of a teacher's announcement to launch a new week in an *Introduction to Human-Centered Design* course. Notice how the teacher explains assessment as part of the week's learning process. He draws connections between the learning outcomes and the week's discussion and assignments. He also tells students where to find the pertinent grading rubrics, when to submit assignments, and how they will receive feedback.

Teaching Tip

Plan how to handle technical problems

Establish a contingency plan to handle technical problems that may interfere with students' completion of assessment tasks (participation in online discussions or completion of assignments, quizzes, or tests). Course policies and procedures describe what students should do in case they are unable to complete assessments for technical reasons. Usually, students are responsible for contacting the teacher within 24 hours of a missed deadline. It's a good idea to outline this contingency plan and the course policies explaining students' responsibilities in the syllabus. Post a reminder about the procedures to follow in case of technical problems before major assignments are due or tests are given (see Chapter 4, p. 122, for an example of a contingency plan for technical problems).

☑ The relationship between learning outcomes and assessments is evident.

☑ Due dates for submission of assignments are clear.

☑ The manner of submission for graded assignments is clear.

☑ Students are informed about procedures to follow in the event of technical difficulties.

Present the Grading Criteria as Rubrics

Rubrics are often used to explain the criteria for assessing students' products and performance. They provide a scoring guide that pinpoints all the attributes of successful work and defines a range of quality from excellent to poor. Not all online course designs include rubrics to assess students' work and performance. If you choose to use them in your teaching, here is a list of steps by Kenneth Wolf and Ellen Stevens (2007) for developing effective rubrics:

- **Step 1: Identify performance criteria.** List the features of the assignment that will be assessed in the first column.

- **Step 2: Set the performance levels in the first row.** These can be numerical points, letter grades, or some percentage.

- **Step 3: Create performance descriptions for each feature in the remaining cells.** Write a brief statement that describes the different levels of performance expected in each of the remaining cells.

Table 9.1 illustrates the process of creating a rubric to assess students' essays. The criteria listed in step 1 are shown in the first column. The performance levels are presented in the first row. The performance description for each level appears in the remaining cells.

Personal Reflection

Patricia González-Flores

It is challenging to help students understand how to use assessment as a tool for improvement—not just a measure of achievement. To do this, teachers need to describe the rationale for and function of the assessment process. You are trying to help students to internalize performance criteria to be able to self-assess and improve their work in the future.

Table 9.1 The Process of Creating a Rubric

Criteria	Superior (3 points)	Good (2 points)	Satisfactory (1 point)	Unsatisfactory (0 points)
Ideas presented	Ideas are relevant, original, and well developed.	Ideas are relevant and well developed, but lack originality.	Ideas are relevant, but lack originality and development.	Ideas are not relevant, original, or well developed.
Text organization	The text is organized logically, with a beginning, middle, and end. Ideas flow conveying meaning.	The text has a beginning, middle, and end. One or two transitions between ideas are not smooth.	The text lacks a beginning, middle, or end. The flow of ideas is lost in three or more transitions.	The text is not structured logically. There is not a clear beginning, middle, and end.
Spelling and grammar	There are no spelling or grammar mistakes.	There are no more than three spelling or grammar mistakes.	There are between four and seven spelling or grammar mistakes.	There are more than eight grammar mistakes.

Share examples of coursework that illustrate different levels of performance to help students understand assessment criteria.

☑ **The means and criteria for assessment are clearly explained to students.**

☑ **Criteria/rubrics clearly inform learners about how they will be assessed on specific assignments and online participation.**

9.2 Gathering a Variety of Information About Students' Learning

Effective assessment captures snapshots of students' learning throughout a variety of course activities. It looks at different kinds of products that students create, as well as performance-based tasks to consider a full range of students' achievements. This allows teachers to get to know students' personalities, identify their learning styles, and understand their strengths and weaknesses. The online environment offers useful tools for tracking students' progress, evaluating their work and providing constructive feedback as students work through different types of course activities.

Assignments

Students generate a variety of products as they move through the learning activities and complete assignments. Teachers use these products—papers, worksheets, multimedia presentations, and other coursework—as a basis for assessment:

- LMS grading tools (such as SpeedGrader or Crocodoc) let you view a student's assignment and write comments in the margins. This makes it easy to keep track of your evaluation as you read and provide instructive feedback that targets specific points. Figure 9.4 shows an example of a teacher's feedback using a grading tool.

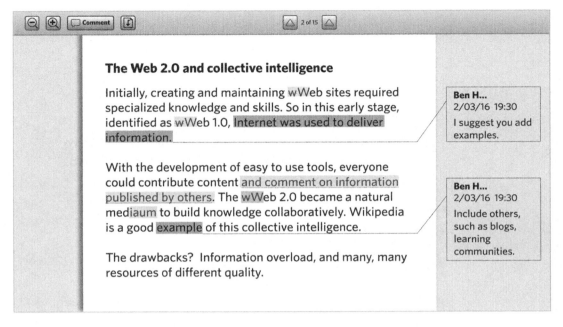

Figure 9.4 A Screen Showing Crocodoc, the Grading Tool in the Free LMS Edmodo. The teacher's suggested edits appear within the texts and comments in the right margin.

- Digital rubrics are available in many LMSs. You can use them to assign points for each feature established on the grading criteria and the system will calculate the grade. Figure 9.5 shows a rubric used in a course taught in Moodle LMS. To grade a paper, the teacher clicks on the level that best describes the learner's performance and can add a comment within the right-hand column. The student in this example received three points for the "ideas presented."

Rubrics are helpful to both teachers and students because they:

1. provide a clear and easy way for teachers to evaluate students' work; and

2. give students targeted feedback to make improvements.

Grade:

This rubric will be used to grade your essay in the Economy I course.

Ideas presented	Ideas are relevant, original and well developed. 3 points	Ideas are relevant and well developed, but lack originality. 2 points	Ideas are relevant, but lack originality and development. 1 points	Ideas are not relevant, original or well developed. 0 points	Excellent job! You lay out a thoughtful insight about the growth of GDP.

Figure 9.5 The Digital Rubric Used for Grading in Moodle

Participation in Discussions

Academic discussions provide many opportunities for students to practice with new ideas, ask questions, and collaborate with their peers and teacher to develop more informed positions on course topics. This is why assessment of discussions looks at students' participation over time, rather than evaluating individual contributions.

- Grading students' participation in online discussions promotes accountability and increases students' contributions (students tend to participate more when their grades depend on it). Participation, usually in the form of online discussions, commonly accounts for 15–30% of the students' course grade.

- Grading rubrics for discussion participation describe the frequency, quality, and characteristics of students' comments (see Chapter 8, pp. 215 and 216, for examples of participation rubrics). This helps to clarify expectations for participation and raises the quality of students' contributions.

- Weekly academic discussions can add up to more than 100 messages. After reading the whole discussion, teachers can use the gradebook tool to display each student's comments. This makes it easier to track and grade individual learners' contributions.

Quizzes and Tests

Quizzes and exams are often used online as an efficient way to test students' comprehension and recall of material. Closed-question quizzes (i.e. true and false, multiple-choice) are graded automatically and offer immediate feedback to students and teachers about students' learning. In the example below (see Figure 9.6), the teacher can see who has completed the test and how many attempts each student made to get the score shown on the right. This information is useful for instruction because teachers can identify what students know and where clarification may be needed.

Moderate Quiz

	Student	Attempt	Time	Attempts Left	Score	↻
☐	Ayza, Josefa	2	finished in 3 minutes	0	7	✏
☐	Cameo, Julián	—		2		✏
☐	Margain, Adrienne	1	finished in less than a minute	1	7	✏
☐	Martin, Louise	3	finished in 2 minutes	0	10	✏
☐	Immonen, Timo	1	finished in 1 minute	1	9	✏
☐	Sanders, July	1	finished in less than a minute	1	7	✏
☐	Flynn, Morton	3	finished in 3 minutes	0	10	✏

Figure 9.6 Students' Results in a Quiz as Presented in Canvas LMS

Many teachers are concerned about the possibility of students cheating on un-proctored exams. While this is an inherent challenge online, there are some strategies to help you minimize the impact of cheating on assessments:

- **Open-ended questions (rather than closed ones) provide opportunities for students to demonstrate original thought.** Teachers may consider asking students to support their responses to test questions with evidence raised in the discussions, within the course resources, and/or from personal experience. This makes it harder to download ready-made answers from the Internet. When they grade, teachers can compare a student's answers to the writing style and reasoning he or she has shared in the discussions and other online interactions.

- **Graded tests can be timed.** Teachers often designate a 24-hour time period in which students must complete an exam. Once the student begins the exam, he or she has an hour (or whatever time frame is appropriate) to finish it. The time limit creates a situation similar to an open-book test in a classroom. The student is free to use resources, but dependence on references will take time away from completing the test.

Personal Reflection

Sepi Yalda

Sometimes my online students become overly reliant on access to resources and do not bother really learning the information covered in them. For example, in one of my courses, a student had difficulty on an open-book online exam. She had "looked over" all the material, but didn't think she needed to memorize any of it because she could always go back and review the videos or access the websites later. While taking the online exam (with time limit), she ran out of time and couldn't finish several questions. Also, her essay response suggested that she hadn't integrated the ideas discussed. I suggested that she study the material as she would for a closed-book test—to watch and read the resources in their entirety and study them for understanding. I advised her to make a study guide for herself that prioritized the information covered and think about how her study guide related to the questions and comments on the online discussion board. She ended up getting an A on the next test.

Teaching Tip

Make the most of the LMS gradebook

An LMS's gradebook shows accumulated course grades for each student and can be accessed at any time by teachers and learners (see Figure 9.7). It calculates grades automatically, factoring in the weight assigned to each activity. This is a great time-saving feature for teachers.

To take advantage of this tool, you need to make sure that the gradebook is set up before the course starts:

- Check that all graded activities are included.

	Paradigms of Psychology						
	Individual analytical work					Collaborative work	
Surname First Name	Behavioral Case Study Analysis (30 pts)	Group discussion (5 pts)	Cognitive Case Study Analysis (30 pts)	Group discussion (5 pts)	Category total (70 pts)	Group project (30 pts)	Category total (30 pts)
Barn, Eric	28	4	-	5	37	26	26
Doe, July	20	3	-	5	28	26	26
Jinkens, Matt	30	3	-	4	37	29	29
Ryn, Jack	15	2	-	4	21	-	-

Joyce Smithers ▼

Figure 9.7 The Gradebook in an Online Course. In this example, students have received grades on four activities. The gradebook automatically adds the students' grades for category designated by the teacher—in this case, individual and collaborative work.

- Verify that the weight assigned to discussions, assignments, and tests is correct. This usually appears in the column heading.

Most LMSs allow teachers to include activities in the gradebook that do not require a student submission (i.e. students taking part in webinars or live events). The teacher would assign credit or a grade when he or she receives confirmation that the student participated in the event.

Time spent confirming and making adjustments within the gradebook before the course starts will save you time during the semester (see Chapter 3, p. 87, for an explanation of how to use gradebook). You will simply have to review and mark student assignments as they come in. The gradebook program does the averaging. No more burdensome calculations!

Personal Reflection

Dan Eastmond

Assessment is a vital component in competency-based learning at Western Governors University, because WGU measures learning rather than time spent on a course. When a student and his or her mentor determine that the student has learned the competencies for a course, the student demonstrates his or her mastery of those competencies by completing an assessment.

Depending on the course, students may take objective examinations, analyze case studies, demonstrate problem-solving, develop plans, budgets, and/or write reports to demonstrate learning. Students may complete objective exams using secure online proctoring provided by WGU. For these exams, the results are available almost immediately. Performance objectives are reviewed by faculty evaluators and are returned to students within 72 hours.

Once students pass required assessments for each course, they receive credit and move on to the next course in their degree program. Students who do not pass the tasks or exams are directed back to the learning modules associated with the competencies and the course mentors to further develop the knowledge and skills required for credit. Then they resubmit or retake the evaluation when they are ready. In this way, assessment is woven into the learning process by allowing students to implement a study strategy for mastering the competencies.

☑ The course includes ongoing and frequent assessment.

☑ A variety of information (student performance data, feedback, etc.) is used to evaluate the effectiveness of course design and instruction.

☑ Teachers and students can easily track learners' progress.

9.3 Providing Ongoing Feedback

Feedback is an essential part of effective assessment. It helps students understand how their efforts relate to the learning outcomes and gives them guidance on how to improve their learning. Research by Bellon, Bellon, and Blank (1991) suggests that "Academic feedback is more strongly and consistently related to achievement than any other teaching behavior." It can also boost a student's confidence, self-awareness, and enthusiasm for learning (Black, Harrison, Lee, Marshall, & William, 2003; Gibbs & Simpson, 2005; Hattie & Timperley, 2007).

There are many opportunities for students to receive feedback in an online course. Teachers, peers, and the automated responses in learning activities all provide useful information about students' progress. Let's look at some of the qualities that make feedback effective.

Effective Feedback Is Frequent and Timely

As we have said many times throughout this book, online students need frequent feedback to know that their contributions have been seen and that they are on track. It's important to provide timely feedback on assignments so that their work is still fresh in their minds and they can use the suggestions to improve future efforts. As Gibbs and Simpson (2005, p. 19) explain, "If students do not receive feedback fast enough then they will have moved on to new content and the feedback is irrelevant to their ongoing studies and is extremely unlikely to result in additional appropriate learning activity, directed by the feedback."

Teachers' timely feedback is also important in discussions. Teachers' evaluative comments can show students how the criteria used for assessing student participation relates to the discussion posts. This helps them understand how to apply the criteria and improve their contributions. Here's an example:

> **Teacher:** Paul, thanks for the summary of the research findings. You've hit on all the salient points. However, I'd like you to relate this research to your own experience or outside readings. Please make sure that you (and I'm talking to everyone now) respond to all parts of the discussion prompts.

Feedback in discussions can also serve as a timely instruction, seizing an opportunity to correct a mistaken assumption or clarify a concept. The following comment provides an example:

> **Teacher:** Yes, the rapid progress made in eradicating the Ebola virus certainly is encouraging. I want to draw your attention to a common misconception that is sneaking into our discussion. Several people have made reference to "killing the Ebola virus." Scientifically speaking, you can't kill a virus. Can anyone explain this further?

Students also require feedback on their work in progress. Once students turn in an essay, it might be too late to tell them that the work was off-topic or ill structured. A teacher's feedback on drafts or work plans helps students focus and target their efforts productively. As we suggested in Chapter 7 (page 188), consider breaking projects into phases with deliverables at each stage that the teacher or peers can review and comment upon.

Some online teachers have found it useful to organize the assessment process for assignments in two stages:

1. A first draft is submitted to the teacher for feedback (not graded at this stage).

2. The corrected paper is submitted again, receives feedback, and is graded.

In the next chapter, Scott Thornbury describes how well this strategy has worked for his students. He reports that "This feedback policy is so popular with students, I can't NOT do it" (see page 270 for a description of how Scott implements this feedback loop).

Effective Feedback Is Specific

Generalizations or broad comments are often used to describe an overall impression of students' work. However, vague statements such as "Good work" or "Needs improvement" provide very little useful information for students. Effective feedback points to specifics within the student's work and explains how these particular features are on target or need improvement.

Vague feedback:

Mary, your writing style is not appropriate for this assignment.

Specific feedback:

Mary, you are using colloquial expressions that are not appropriate for a scientific research paper. Formal language is required. Avoid using contractions (don't, isn't, needn't) and slang. I suggest you review the two examples of research studies in our readings this week and focus on the tone and precision of the language used. I have marked specific paragraphs, sentences, and phrases that need revision. Please let me know if you have questions.

Effective Feedback Offers Personalized Support

Feedback serves a motivational as well as instructional purpose. Be attentive to students' feelings and use a positive emotional tone as you assess their work:

> Elise, nice start to your research project. You have made good progress on your analysis of discrimination in TV ads. Your comments about the use of images to show women's submission are very clear.
>
> The section in which you describe the use of symbols (pages 4–7) in advertising is difficult to follow. Think through your main ideas and organize the paper's sections accordingly. What about inserting screens to illustrate your points?
>
> I'm looking forward to seeing this work develop. You are on your way to creating a powerful project.

Effective Feedback Invites Action

Effective feedback causes students to reflect on their work and take actions to improve it. As you write feedback, suggest specific actions that the learners can implement to achieve the learning outcomes.

> Excellent work, John! You have presented a relevant research problem. I found your description of epidemic patterns in the last decade very detailed and well supported with data and authors' contributions (scary stuff!).
>
> Your hypothesis needs revision. Globalization is a broad concept. What particular aspects of the global world affect epidemics? Think of the specific variables that are related to your problem. Is it international travel? Or changes of cultural practices promoted by mass media?

☑ Ongoing feedback about students' progress toward learning outcomes is provided.

☑ Teacher feedback is provided in a timely fashion.

☑ Feedback is personalized, specific, and action-oriented.

9.4　Sharing Responsibilities for Providing Feedback

It's not necessary or beneficial for the teacher to provide all the feedback students need. On a practical level, asynchronous learning means that students are often waiting for responses to questions and for feedback on their work. The more people giving feedback, the less time students have to wait. And there is significant educational value in student feedback too. Student feedback:

* increases student responsibility for their learning;

* encourages critical reflection; and

* promotes a deeper understanding of the assessment process.

Peer Review

In peer review, a student's assignment is reviewed by one or two classmates, ideally using a rubric. Students make comments on each other's work and can even assign a grade.

> The real value [of self- and peer assessment] may lie in students internalizing the standards expected so that they can supervise themselves and improve the quality of their own assignments.
>
> (Gibbs & Simpson, 2005, p. 20)

Peer review is often used as an effective means for students to get timely feedback. It also provides the student reviewer an opportunity to develop a working knowledge of the criteria used to evaluate successful work. The process teaches both the reviewer and the author to assess and edit their own work. This is an important skill involved in self-directed learning and serves online students well. Experience has shown that the feedback provided by a peer might be easier to understand because it is phrased in more familiar terms (Black et al., 2003).

Teaching Tip

Be prepared with alternative management solutions

Sometimes students are late in submitting an assignment for peer review. This disrupts the timing and distribution for the peer review process. Teachers need to be ready to make accommodations for such circumstances. The following steps can help facilitate the peer review process:

1. Give clear instructions about how students' work is distributed for peer review. Include the date by which all students' work must be submitted for review and the date all reviews must be completed.

2. Identify any student who is left out of the peer review exchange process (his or her work has not been selected for review and/or doesn't have a peer's work to review).

3. Adjust the strategy to make sure that everyone reviews and is reviewed by peers. For example, if a student is left without a peer-review partner (or group), the teacher can:
   * invite other students to review a second work for extra credit;
   * add the student to another group; or
   * review the student's work him or herself.

Personal Reflection

Patricia González-Flores

Giving and receiving feedback is a skill that students need to learn. I find that laying some ground rules helps. I emphasize that feedback needs to be supportive and constructive. Simply saying "I like how you say that . . . " or "That's not right!" does not offer enough information. I give a rubric to guide students' reviews and tell them to consider each criteria as they look at their classmate's assignment. They must identify the level of performance attained and justify their evaluation. They also have to point out specific suggestions for revisions.

At the same time, I mention that it's important to be receptive to constructive comments about their own work. I stress that a thoughtful critique is a gift that benefits both the giver and receiver.

Self-Assessment

Self-assessment requires students to reflect on their own work and evaluate how well they are performing. In a sense, self-assessment challenges students to be their own teacher — gathering information about their own learning and evaluating it against a given criteria. As in peer review exercises, the focus of self-assessment is on providing opportunities for students to be able to identify what constitutes good (and poor) work and apply this understanding to make improvements. Self-assessment deepens students' understanding of their own learning process and promotes self-directed learning (Brown, 2004–2005).

Self-assessment takes many forms:

- Reflective activities such as journal writing and wrap-up discussions can include self-assessment if the guiding prompts for these activities include evaluative questions (see Figure 9.8).

Follow-up to Job Application Assignment  Published | Edit | ⚙ ▾

> As a follow-up to the Job Application Assignment, post a self-assessment of your performance on your blog addressing the questions below. Note that the goal of this assignment is not to grade yourself; it is intended to help you recognize how your performance compares to the criteria established for this exercise. Full credit will be awarded for honest and thorough responses that clearly apply the criteria for this assignment (see rubric) to support your assessment.
>
> 1. Assess the quality of your resume using the criteria described on the rubric.
> 2. How successful do you think you were in explaining the connection between your resume and the job description in your cover letter? What could be improved?

Points 10
Submitting a file upload

Figure 9.8 An Example of a Self-Assessment Exercise

Teaching Tip

Track students' self-assessment

The gradebook tool can be set up to record student responses to self-assessment surveys and quizzes so teachers can see how they are progressing. Promote the use of self-assessment opportunities by awarding points for completion of these exercises. They are not usually graded because the focus of the quiz or survey is on self-monitoring rather than demonstration of mastery (see Chapter 3, p. 85, for an example of an automated self-assessment quiz).

- Easy feedback surveys or automated self-assessment quizzes can help students evaluate the effectiveness of their study habits. Many online courses include self-check exercises that students do after they have reviewed the learning resources each week. These activities are intended to help them monitor their comprehension of the material and give them guidance in prioritizing the content covered.

- Self-assessment may be used in conjunction with peer-review assignments. Ask students to follow the same procedure to review their own work.

☑ Feedback from a variety of sources corrects, clarifies, amplifies, and extends learning.

☑ Teachers encourage students to take responsibility for their learning.

☑ Self-assessment and peer-review activities are included to help learners improve their study habits and the quality of their work.

9.5 Guarding Against Cheating and Plagiarism

Teachers everywhere (online and in classrooms) worry about cheating and plagiarism. Search engines on the Internet make it easier for students to locate information through the click of a mouse rather than reading assigned learning resources. They can easily download essays and blogs that address questions posed in course assignments rather than writing original work. Cheating and plagiarism are certainly not unique to online students. Yet the lack of physical contact between teachers and students and the lack of boundaries between an online course and the Internet heightens many teachers' concerns.

How can teachers know that student work is original? Here are some suggestions for preventing cheating and plagiarism:

- **Assess learning frequently and through varied means.** If a final grade is determined by several assessments, the pressure on students is reduced and teachers get to know their students' personality and skills (Reed, n.d.).

- **Gather evidence about students' learning progress as well as their final products.** Seeing how students perform the different steps in a project helps teachers confirm that they produced it. Request that students keep a personal journal in a blog and look at it when you have doubts.

- **Modify assignments slightly from one semester to the next.** You will be able to identify papers created by previous groups.

- **Use quizzes or exams for self-assessment purposes.** If grading an online test is required by the course design, consider taking steps to minimize cheating:
  - Use open-ended test questions that require personalized responses.
  - Make the test available online at a specific day and time. This will prevent students from sharing test questions and answers (choose a time that is practical for all students and respects time zone differences).
  - Limit the time students have to complete the test so that it does not allow extra time to research answers.
  - Randomize the order of questions so that students cannot easily collaborate or share answers.

- **Advise students about the consequences of cheating and plagiarism.** Explain the guidelines for using other writers' ideas and quoting. Specify unacceptable actions and their impact on student grades and institutional standing. This is especially important if you are teaching international students because policies and cultural practices vary from country to country.

- **Ask students to scan their papers with a plagiarism-checking software** (such as Turn-It-In) before submitting them. Make it a habit to check students' work for plagiarism yourself.

☑ Assessment takes into account the fact that online students have access to resources on the Internet and lack supervision while completing assignments and exams.

☑ The consequences of cheating and plagiarism are clearly explained to students.

263

Personal Reflection

Carmen Coronado

It is fairly easy to know when a paper is not original. My students' work is based on personal situations, so no two students will have identical projects. Occasionally, students copy projects from previous groups. That is harder to identify because we have more than 200 students taking this course in different sections. I cannot know which products are turned in for other groups. So we change the instructions for the assignment slightly from one semester to the other. We can then know when a product from a previous semester has been copied.

I use multiple-choice quizzes in my undergraduate courses as ungraded opportunities for my students to gage their understanding. I invite students to answer the quiz, read the text again if they made mistakes, and answer again. The goal is to use the resource to help students learn—they can respond as many times as it takes to get it right and feel confident that they understand the basic concepts.

9.6   Summary and Standards

Effective assessment is an integral part of online teaching and learning. Online discussions, activities, and assignments create a large amount of data about students' progress through the course that serve as evidence of learning. A well-designed and implemented assessment strategy helps teachers sort through and analyze this information in meaningful ways to support student growth.

The means of assessing student performance is clearly communicated upfront. Effective assessment considers a variety of information about students' learning. It includes ongoing feedback that is timely, targeted, personalized, and encourages students to improve their work and learning habits.

Teachers and students all participate in assessing learning. Peer reviews and self-assessment are often used to provide students with immediate feedback on their work. These activities challenge students to internalize and apply the assessment criteria and develop self-directed learning skills. Effective assessment also takes measures to guard against cheating and plagiarism.

☐ All graded activities are listed at the beginning of the course.

☐ The relationship between graded elements and the final grade is clear.

☐ The consequences of missed deadlines are stated and fair.

☐ The relationship between learning outcomes and assessments is evident.

☐ Due dates for submission of assignments are clear.

☐ The manner of submission for graded assignments is clear.

☐ Students are informed about procedures to follow in the event of technical difficulties.

☐ The means and criteria for assessment are clearly explained to students.

☐ Criteria/rubrics clearly inform learners about how they will be assessed on specific assignments and online participation.

☐ The course includes ongoing and frequent assessment.

☐ A variety of information (student performance data, feedback, etc.) is used to evaluate the effectiveness of course design and instruction.

☐ Teachers and students can easily track learners' progress.

☐ Ongoing feedback about students' progress toward learning outcomes is provided.

☐ Teacher feedback is provided in a timely fashion.

☐ Feedback is personalized, specific, and action-oriented.

☐ Feedback from a variety of sources corrects, clarifies, amplifies, and extends learning.

☐ Teachers encourage students to take responsibility for their learning.

☐ Self-assessment and peer-review activities are included to help learners improve their study habits and the quality of their work.

☐ Assessment takes into account the fact that online students have access to resources on the Internet and lack supervision while completing assignments and exams.

☐ The consequences of cheating and plagiarism are clearly explained to students.

References and Further Reading

Ambrose, S. A., Bridges, M. W., Lovett, M. C., DiPietro, M., & Norman, M. K. (2010). *How learning works: Seven research-based principles for smart teaching*. San Francisco, CA: Jossey-Bass.

Bellon, J. J., Bellon, E. C., & Blank, M. A. (1991). *Teaching from a research knowledge base: A development and renewal process*. Facsimile edition. Englewood Cliffs, NJ: Prentice Hall.

Black, P., Harrison, C., Lee, C., Marshall, B., & William, D. (2003). *Assessment for learning: Putting it into practice*. Berkshire, UK: Open University Press.

Brown, S. (2004–2005). Assessment for learning. *Learning and Teaching in Higher Education*, 1, 81–89.

Cooper, N. J. (2000). Facilitating learning from formative feedback in level 3 assessment. *Assessment and Evaluation in Higher Education*, 25(3), 279–291.

Gibbs, G., & Simpson, C. (2005). Conditions under which assessment supports students' learning. *Learning and Teaching in Higher Education*, 1. Retrieved from www.open.ac.uk/fast/pdfs/Gibbs%20 and%20Simpson%202004-05.pdf

Hattie, J. (2012). *Visible learning for teachers: Maximizing impact on learning*. New York, NY: Routledge.

Hattie, J. & Timperley, H. (2007). The power of feedback. *Review of Educational Research, 77*(1), 81–112.

Huba, M. E., & Freed, J. E. (2000). *Learner-centered assessment on college campuses: Shifting the focus from teaching to learning.* Boston, MA: Allyn & Bacon.

Reed, E. (n.d.). Assessing student learning online: It's more than multiple choice. In *Assessing online learning strategies, challenges and opportunities.* Retrieved from www.facultyfocus.com/wp-content/uploads/images/AssessingOnlineLearning-OC.pdf

Shank, P. (2016). *Avoiding assessment mistakes that compromise competence and quality.* Retrieved from www.facultyfocus.com/wp-content/uploads/images/AssessingOnlineLearning-OC.pdf

Suskie, L. (May, 2002). *Fair assessment practices: Giving students equitable opportunities to demonstrate learning.* Retrieved from www.elcamino.edu/beta/administration/vpsca/docs/assessment/FairAssessmentPractices_Suskie.pdf

Wildflower, L. (2010). Teaching professionals to be effective online facilitators and instructors: Lessons from hard-won experience. In K. E. Rudestam & J. Schoenholtz-Read (Eds.). *Handbook of online learning* (2nd ed.) (pp. 387–403). Thousand Oaks, CA: Sage.

Wolf, K., & Stevens, E. (2007). The role of rubrics in advancing and assessing student learning. *The Journal of Effective Teaching, 7*(1), 3–14.

Chapter 10 Pulling It All Together: An Online Teacher in Action

Successful online teachers make informed decisions about how to support learning and respond to student needs as they arise. Throughout this guide, we have discussed factors that influence teaching decisions. We've highlighted issues that teachers need to address as they launch an online course, help their students to progress through the planned activities, and reach the learning objectives. The standards of good practice offered throughout serve as a checklist to help you make and evaluate your instructional decisions along the way.

Now it's time to pull it all together. We will look at how an experienced online teacher applies the standards of good practice as he teaches a course. To do this, we talked with veteran online teacher Scott Thornbury about his most recent course, *English in the World*. Focusing on one course allows us to move beyond generalities and consider instructional choices a teacher makes in a particular context. While your teaching situation may not match the specifics of this course, it's helpful to consider Scott's thinking behind his instructional decisions. As you read, notice how Scott:

1. organizes his time to carry out various teaching tasks;

2. gets the students involved;

3. scaffolds instruction to meet students' changing needs;

4. assesses students' progress;

5. provides feedback; and

6. evaluates and improves the course in progress.

We have organized this case study to address the central issues we explored in the previous chapters of this guide. It's our hope that this example will provide insights that are applicable to your situation.

10.1 The Teacher and the Course

This course is a good example of people connecting globally through technology. Scott Thornbury is from New Zealand, lives in Barcelona, and spends most of his summer teaching in New York City. He teaches *English in the World* as an online course for The New School for Social Research. The 12 students in this class participate from places around the world.

English in the World is a graduate course "that brings together topics related to the global spread of English and its political, cultural, ethical, and economic ramifications." It is organized around a core text that serves as the basis for online discussion and assignments. The course is taught over a 15-week semester. A new discussion forum is opened every week and Scott and his students contribute actively to it. At the end of each week, there are over 150 comments posted on the discussion board.

Scott spends about one and a half hours three days a week tending the discussion boards and checks in at least once a day the rest of the week (for a total of about five hours a week online):

ST: *Many of my students work during the week, so the most active days are over the weekend. [Living in Barcelona] I have about a six-hour advantage on most of my students. I get up and deal with the discussion board first thing in the morning and clear the deck. When I log in, there are usually about 15–20 postings that will have come overnight. So there is quite a lot to read, process, and comment on.*

Scott believes that online discussions provide a tremendous opportunity for learning:

ST: *I would say that the quality of learning and instruction in online discussion is better than in face-to-face discussion. Classroom discussion is so concentrated and happens so fast. All you can hope for is to be a catalyst to further learning outside of class. Whereas online, there is time for everyone to contribute, to think deeply about the subject before responding, review the conversation over days and develop ideas collaboratively. Online, you get a sense that students were very different individuals when they started the course than they will become 15 weeks later.*

In this course, students submit five assignments over the semester. The assignments range from case studies and literature reviews to ethnographic research and personal reflections. At the end of the semester, students are asked to synthesize their reflections about their learning into a final paper.

Scott gives all students the opportunity to receive feedback on a draft of the assignment a week before the graded paper is due. Providing feedback on the first draft of students' assignments takes substantial focus and time. Scott spends about 10 hours over two or three days reviewing and commenting on the first drafts. In most cases, the students' final submissions take considerably less time to grade because of improvements through the revision process. Scott recognizes the intense time commitment this feedback loop requires, but reminds himself that there are only five assignments to grade throughout the semester. Spread out over 15 weeks, providing feedback on students' work requires about four hours a week.

The rest of his teaching time is distributed among tracking students' progress, handling "housekeeping issues," and improving the course in progress. Scott estimates that he spends a total of about 9–10 hours a week teaching his online course. He suggests that this is equivalent to on-site teaching time:

ST: *This is roughly the same amount of time as I spend on my face-to-face course, taking into consideration preparation, class sessions, and grading. Teaching time is just spent* *differently online. Because the course content, discussion tasks, and assignments are uploaded ahead of time, I focus much more of my time on interacting with students online than I do in the classroom.*

Table 10.1 Scott's Weekly Teaching Schedule

Teaching Task	Weekly Hours
Facilitating discussions	5
Reviewing assignments and providing feedback	4
Housekeeping and course improvement	1

Scott is an active participant in his online course. As the students are engaged in the learning activities, he asks himself, "What can I do to help?" Scott's advice to teachers who are new to online teaching is: "Be present. **You can't overestimate the importance of being present online.** Students want and expect individualized and consistent instructive presence."

☑ Teachers and students are active participants in the learning process.

☑ Teacher feedback is provided in a timely fashion.

10.2 Factors That Influence Online Teaching

Scott created the course *English in the World*, so it reflects his beliefs about how people learn and the best ways to explore the particular course content. His instruction is also informed by his experience teaching international graduate students, teaching online, and teaching within the culture and policies of The New School's TESOL program. Let's look at how each of these influences plays a part in Scott's teaching.

Teacher's Beliefs

Scott believes that "people learn by doing things:"

ST: *I subscribe to a belief that learning is a social-cognitive process. It's one that is mediated through collaboration and through well-placed interventions by the instructor. So the instructor's knowledge is not the starting point, but it is there to help scaffold the collaborative discovery process. And I think that online discussion boards are quite amazing at being able to facilitate that.*

Scott's beliefs about teaching and learning are evident in his instruction. He initiates discussions with a "task" and explains the significance of this term:

ST: *A task for me implies active decision-making with some kind of outcome. It may not be a written product; it may mean thinking through something and coming up with a decision about it in your own head.*

Scott gives students tasks to challenge them to reflect on the information presented through readings, lectures, and discussions, and to come to terms with it from their own points of view. Figure 10.1 shows an excerpt from an online discussion in *English in the World*. Notice how the discussion task requires students to take a stance and support their views with evidence from the learning resources. Scott's follow-up questions encourage the student to dig deeper into the issues nested within her response.

The whole course is set up as a collaborative learning experience. Students explore issues, share their views, compare experiences, and reshape their understandings to accommodate broader awareness. The instructional model is clearly driven by Scott's beliefs about the social nature of learning.

The subject matter and content of *English in the World* also influence the way the course is designed and taught. Scott explains:

ST: *If you ask any of the instructors in our program, you'd get quite a diversity of opinions about the best way to use the technology for their particular subject matter. Some of the subjects are very practical—such as classroom methodology*

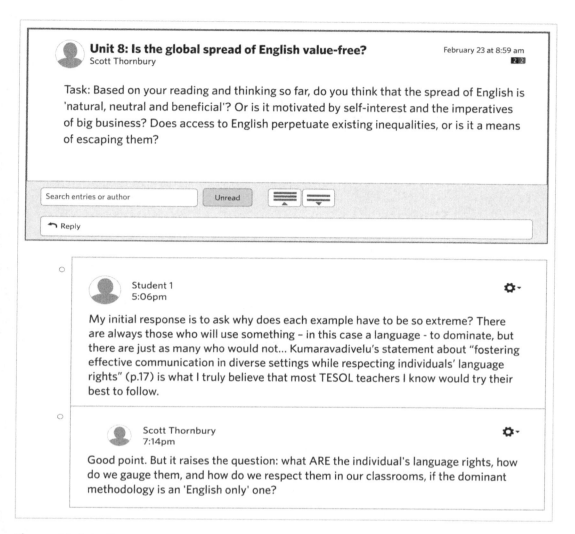

Unit 8: Is the global spread of English value-free? February 23 at 8:59 am
Scott Thornbury

Task: Based on your reading and thinking so far, do you think that the spread of English is 'natural, neutral and beneficial'? Or is it motivated by self-interest and the imperatives of big business? Does access to English perpetuate existing inequalities, or is it a means of escaping them?

Search entries or author | Unread

Reply

Student 1
5:06pm

My initial response is to ask why does each example have to be so extreme? There are always those who will use something – in this case a language - to dominate, but there are just as many who would not... Kumaravadivelu's statement about "fostering effective communication in diverse settings while respecting individuals' language rights" (p.17) is what I truly believe that most TESOL teachers I know would try their best to follow.

Scott Thornbury
7:14pm

Good point. But it raises the question: what ARE the individual's language rights, how do we gauge them, and how do we respect them in our classrooms, if the dominant methodology is an 'English only' one?

Figure 10.1 An Excerpt from a Discussion in Which a Student Responds to a Task and Scott Asks a Follow-Up Question

and classroom management. In these courses, the students need to see demonstrations and demonstrate themselves. So we have an online practicum in which the students videotape themselves in the classroom and upload it for review, instruction, and discussion.

The course I'm teaching is very discursive and quite controversial because we are dealing with issues such as identity, gender, religion, culture, and development. A lot of issues are being fed into the pot and students are asked to form opinions based on their readings. So it's potentially quite sensitive. My role is to help students think through and be better informed about these issues. There are no right or wrong positions, but students need to be able to argue their point with more precision.

My role is to open questions. People tend to take a safe line of argument on controversial issues and my job is to play the devil's advocate, to push students' thinking to the limits of their competence, to say, "Hold on, think this through." So that's a very different task than asking, "What's the difference between a noun and a verb?"

Students

Scott's students are working professionals who teach English in various capacities around the world. They are master's students in The New School's Teaching English to Speakers of Other Languages (TESOL) program. Scott recognizes the breadth of personal and work experience that his students bring to the class and draws this into the discussions and assignments. The course tasks and Scott's interventions encourage students to use their own situations as a focus for study, to share what they know, and to learn from each other.

The geographical location of the students also plays a role in Scott's teaching decisions. Scott's students are scattered around different time zones with different levels of connectivity to the Internet. His instruction respects these conditions:

ST: *I don't do synchronous communication [for group interaction]. I really can't because of the time zones. And I don't use technology that requires a lot of bandwidth. Internet connections for some students are not dependable. I have a student in Nicaragua, for example, who has enough trouble just keeping the discussion board contributions going with her limited connectivity.*

The small class size of *English in the World* allows Scott to interact individually with his students. He is able to give extensive feedback on all their work and keep track of their progress throughout the course.

 Online teaching is tailored to meet the needs of the particular student population served.

The Online Environment

With a minimal emphasis on technology, Scott has found ways to use the tools of the LMS to serve his instructional purposes:

ST: *I use the most basic features of the system. I share content as videos or documents uploaded to the LMS. We collaborate on the discussion board. Students submit assignments and I review the work and give students comments using a feedback feature. That's really all it is.*

A few years ago, we made the transition from one LMS to another one. I thought, "What is this going to involve? What am I going to have to learn? How much help will I need? I just dreaded it!" And it made me realize what it must be like for new online teachers—it's like a jungle . . . You just see all these different functionalities and systems. But what you quickly discover, of course, is the new system is just like the old one. It's just a discussion board. You can strip the whole thing down to about two essential components: (1) how to put content up; and (2) how to manage discussions. You can add things as you go along, but just get that right and you're away.

Scott worries that online discussions can be somewhat impersonal because you can't see or feel others' presence in the room. He also recognizes that students like to feel connected to their teacher. To address these issues, Scott creates videos of himself introducing some of the week's lessons. This is popular with his students:

ST: *When I ask students if the videos make a difference, they always say "Yes, yes . . . we really love the videos and we'd like to see more." One of the things that students feel is lacking in online learning is that they don't have enough contact with their instructor. The videos allow a semblance of face to face.*

He also includes audio feedback on students' assignments so they can hear his voice and get a sense of his personal inflections and style.

 Learning activities and ease of use determine the best technologies to use.

☑ Courses include a variety of relevant multimedia to support learning and appeal to individual preferences.

Priorities of the Host Institution

Scott is conscious of how his course and his teaching fit within the host institutions' priorities. The New School for Social Research is a progressive university that names "academic freedom" and "intellectual inquiry" as its founding principles and a dedication to global peace and justice in its mission. The New School was among the first universities in the United States to bring its regular academic programs online, using the same faculty as the campus-based programs and capping the online courses at 16 students. *English in the World* exemplifies many of the hallmarks of the university's graduate offerings:

- *English in the World* deals with global issues affecting personal communication and international relations and seeks to promote culturally sensitive and responsible pedagogy. The course goals support the university's mission.

- The seminar format of the course is typical of New School classes.

- The university promotes the kind of intensive student-teacher interaction that Scott encourages in his teaching.

- Course requirements, rigor, and grading policies of *English in the World* are equivalent to campus-based courses.

☑ Online teaching is aligned with the priorities and practices of the host institution.

10.3 Digital Tools and Resources

Scott intentionally keeps his course technologically simple. He communicates with his students using:

- **Announcements.** He posts a few brief statements at the beginning of each week highlighting the main theme for the week's readings and discussion. He may alert students about an upcoming due date or let them know that he will have their assignments returned to them with comments by a certain day.

- **Discussion forum.** This is where the heart of the course interactions takes place:

  ST: *I think online discussions are quite amazing at facilitating collaboration. Well-placed interventions by the so-called "better-other" or whatever you want to call the instructor helps to scaffold the discovery process. I am always amazed at how the right question or comment can provoke students to make a leap forward in their thinking. And I'm amazed by the kind of peer teaching that is going on in the discussions. There is a lot of incidental learning happening through rich, long conversations online.*

  Scott always staggers the start date of each new discussion forum so that there aren't two conversations happening at the same time.

- **Email.** He sends students emails if he is concerned about their lack of participation. Students are encouraged to email him if they have any issues that fall outside of general course discussions.

- **An early alert system.** The New School implements a campus-wide system called Starfish that notifies students who have not logged on, participated, or fulfilled course requirements. Scott explains how it's used:

  ST: *I fill out a progress report periodically on all my students. If there is a problem, the system sends out an automatic alert to the student, the administration, and me.*

  The system also allows him to check off a box for exceptionally good work or participation:

  ST: *I also send kudos to students who are really participating well. They love this. Many of them email to thank me for this notice and mention that it's important for them that they know they are doing well. This kind of small feedback is really important at the beginning.*

- **Live sessions.** Scott conducts mid-semester individual videoconferences using Skype with all his students. This two-way synchronous communication provides a personalized and immediate connection.

- **Learning resources.** The course content for *English in the World* is presented through:
  - two textbooks;
  - an e-book that students can download for free;
  - supplementary articles available online through the university's library;
  - short videos in which Scott introduces the weekly units; and
  - selected videos available on the Internet that Scott links to weekly activities.

Over the years, Scott has increased his use of video and multimedia presentations in the course:

ST: *Instead of posting a lot of text, I now present a lecture with slides and video. Not more than 10 minutes in length. I also post the written lecture so the students have the option of reading it and they can approach the material from two modalities. It can be useful to different kinds of learners.*

I create more videos as the course is in progress. Instead of writing out a summary of each discussion (as I used to do), I make a video feedback about the discussion. This satisfies the students' desire to see their instructor, and it saves me a lot of time.

Students also share resources on the discussion board. They post links within their comments. For example, a student found a video of an instructor teaching a lesson on pronunciation. Scott felt it was relevant and useful:

ST: *So I thanked him for posting it and said that I would incorporate the link in the course next semester. My students do this kind of thing regularly.*

Scott clearly values students' contributions to the course's knowledge base.

☑ Weekly announcements call students' attention to important and timely course information.

☑ Discussion forums are used to support online course interaction.

☑ Email facilitates private conversations between teachers and students, or among students.

10.4 Preparing to Teach Online

Scott taught his first online course for The New School in 2002. Prior to this, he participated in a three-week faculty development program offered by the university to:

1. familiarize instructors with the online environment and its tools; and

2. provide guidance about online course design.

The workshop was taught online, so teachers got a chance to understand the challenge of online learning from a student's point of view and practice with LMS tools. Scott is appreciative of the university's ongoing technical support:

ST: *We have a very supportive IT team who has been there since the inception. They are great at providing one-on-one support when needed and have a very effective induction program for new teachers. It's really fantastic.*

After the workshop, Scott spent several months adapting a course he had taught previously in the classroom for the online environment. Scott created *English in the World* so that it could also be taught by other teachers:

ST: *I wasn't sure when I created it that I would be the one to teach it. So it all needed to be self-contained—all the reading, lectures, and assignments were ready to go ahead of time. For me as the teacher, this is great because I can concentrate on the interaction with students and not on presenting the content during the course.*

Before the semester begins, Scott loads the course onto the LMS with all the material students need to get started. He posts:

- a complete syllabus that provides information about the course content, objectives, assignments, schedule, grading, and how to get support;

- a document called "How This Course Works," which explains course procedures and assessment policies;

- a screencast showing students how to access the university's library and locate resources;

- an announcement welcoming students to the course; and

- video lectures, documents, and links to course content for each week.

Scott also uploads all the assignments and readies the 15 weeks of discussions by posting a starting task in each. The icebreaker is the only discussion he makes visible to students as they first enter the course. He will make the other discussion forums visible to students each Monday night throughout the rest of the semester. He explains:

ST: *This gives students the whole week to read, prepare, and participate in a new discussion. But when the discussion is over at the end of the week, I close it. It's finished. This keeps everyone moving along together.*

He thinks through the whole course process from beginning to end and tries to prepare as much as he can before the semester begins:

ST: *I double-check each module before we get to it to make sure everything is up to date—there are no broken links, there are no connections to YouTube videos that no longer exist—that kind of thing. I make sure that it is all running smoothly.*

Ultimately, this level of preparation makes him more responsive to students because he can focus on the interaction rather than the course materials.

☑ Teachers are competent in the use of the digital tools and resources necessary to teach the online course.

☑ A syllabus including contact information, a course outline, requirements, and expectations for student participation is accessible from the start of the course and throughout.

☑ Correct, working links are provided to course materials and resources.

10.5   The Beginning Weeks

Scott finds that most students understand what to do after reading the introductory material. But in case they have questions, he creates a discussion board for students to ask about the course. He explains the use of this forum in the document "How This Course Works":

ST: *There is a discussion board called* **Your Questions** *that is simply a site for posting questions and problems relating to a particular unit, or to the course as a whole. I will deal with these questions promptly. I tell my students, "Unless you have a question of a private nature, please use this forum to ask general questions about the course, since the answers to these questions are likely to be of interest to everyone."*

Students begin to interact with each other in the **icebreaker** discussion (see Chapter 4, p. 117, for an excerpt from Scott's icebreaker prompt and initial posting):

ST: *The icebreaker is always fun. The one we did in this course was fabulous. Because the course starts off with a review of some basic principles of sociolinguistics and emphasizes sensitivity to context, I wanted to come at it from a personal perspective. So the opening task was for students to make a list responding to these kinds of questions:*

- *What do people call you?*
- *What do people call you at work?*
- *Do they address you by your first name?*
- *Are you called Mr., Miss, Ms., or Mam?*

- *What do your friends call you? Do you have nicknames?*
- *What are you called at home?*

This task really got them going. Everyone immediately joined in and had lots to share. It got us involved and connected in a personal way to each other and the subject matter.

It was interesting that when I said that I preferred for my students to call me Scott—not Prof. Thornbury—some of them had a hard time with this, particularly the younger students. Some continued to call me Prof. when they asked questions.

In addition to initiating and facilitating discussion, Scott's **teaching responsibilities include keeping students on task**. He recognizes that students sometimes need a bit of prodding and herding to engage in the online activities. Scott refers to this as "pastoral sheepdog work:"

ST: *One of the roles of an online instructor is what I call a "sheepdog role," where you sort of yap at the students' heels, trying to round them up and get them on task.*

When Scott notices that certain students are not participating as expected, he contacts them:

ST: *It's a problem when people don't post [to the discussion] or post at the very last minute. Or when people's comments on other people's posts are kind of trivial, to say the least. I have two methods to deal with this:*

- *I email straight to the student saying, "Come on, shape up and get in there." And I remind them of the rules. **They are graded on participation**, which makes it easier to be vigilant about it. All you have to do is remind them that they won't get a good grade if they're not there. Also, I remind them that when the discussion is over [at the end of the week], it's over. It's not something that you can recoup. So they really need to be in there at the right time.*
- *As I have mentioned, I fill out a progress survey in Starfish. It seems to work pretty well because the alert gives the student a bit of a shock, which is sometimes the push they need to shape up.*

The Starfish Alert System's survey is shown in Figure 10.2. Scott initiates an alert by checking off a student's name and chooses an automated comment that summarizes a problem. A message is then sent to the student and an academic advisor alerting them to the issue. In the example below, the student is at "risk of a low or failing grade."

	Student	Item Name	Status	Created ▼
◯	👤 Jane Doe	⚑ Risk of Low or Failing Grade	Active	03-09-2016 by Thornbury, Scott via Survey

Figure 10.2 Example of Starfish Alert System Activation Survey

After an alert has been sent to the student and administration, Scott receives an automated confirmation (e.g. Figure 10.3). Notice the official language of the notification and the mention of referral to academic advisement.

Recent Tracking Item Summary: Friday, February 26, 2016

1 flag included in this summary.

• Academic Concern in Language Analysis: Grammar

Subject: Academic Concern in Language Analysis: Grammar

Thank you for the information regarding the academic concern for [Student's name] in Language Analysis: Grammar.

The information will be reviewed by advisors to follow up about the concern. Where relevant, referrals for support services will be provided to the student (study, skills, academic writing skills, etc.).

After the appropriate advisor or staff member has met with [Student's name], a resolution will be noted in Starfish. To view comments related to this flag, please log into Starfish, select the folder for this student, and click on Notes link for the update.

Figure 10.3 Confirmation Sent to Scott from the Starfish System

After the first week or so of the semester, students settle into a routine. In Scott's class, his students tend to spend the first days of the week reading and viewing the core material:

ST: *Then on Wednesday or Thursday evenings they begin to post in the discussions and by Friday, Saturday, and Sunday things are full on. It can be hard for me because I'm doing all my work during the weekend. But it's a nice rhythm because I can time my participation to coincide with the students. That's important.*

At the end of the second week, students write their first assignment, a 1,000-word case study. They submit a first draft of the paper to Scott, who returns it with suggestions for revision. He uses the Canvas Speedgrader tool to mark up students' papers and interject comments (see Figure 10.4). Students then rework the assignment and turn it in again for a final grade. The grades are recorded in the Canvas gradebook and can be consulted by clicking on Grades.

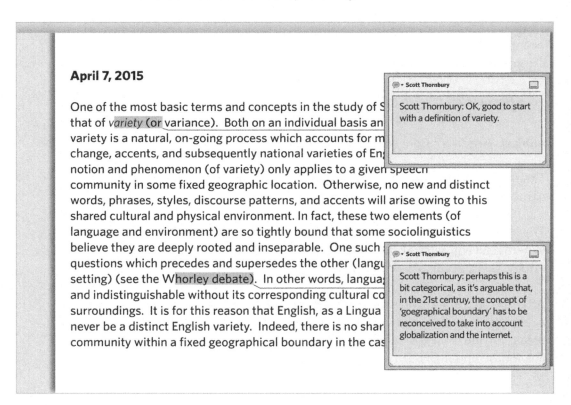

Figure 10.4 A Student's Assignment with Feedback from Scott

By the end of the third week, the students have completed a full cycle of all the different kinds of tasks they will perform throughout the course. They have reviewed the learning resources, participated in discussions, and turned in an assignment. Scott is then confident that the procedures are in place for the rest of the semester.

- ☑ Information on the syllabus and introductory course material is reviewed with students at the beginning of the course.

- ☑ Initial course activities provide an opportunity for students to interact with their teacher and peers.

- ☑ Students are provided with several options to receive support for procedural, technical, and content-related issues.

- ☑ Learners are encouraged to interact with others (classmates, guest speakers, etc.) and benefit from their experience and expertise.

- ☑ Teachers and students can easily track learners' progress.

- ☑ Discussions are set up with a clear purpose and guidelines for participation.

10.6 The Middle Weeks

During the middle weeks, the course discussion picks up pace and intensity:

ST: *By the sixth week, it's all systems go! They are a fantastic group. They are really talkative and I'm able to sit back a bit and do my instructional intervention, saying things such as "Hmm, not quite sure what you mean . . ." or I may add whatever I think is vaguely interesting or relevant. I don't feel the need to be as active in the discussions, but students need to know that I am there in the background. By this point, they are running with it. And I hope the momentum keeps up the rest of the semester.*

At the midpoint in the course, Scott knows quite a bit about his students and their learning. They have participated actively in discussions about sensitive and controversial issues. They have also written and revised three assignments. So Scott knows the quality of their work and their work habits. He schedules a videoconference session with each student to talk about how the course is going and to offer his advice and support (see Figure 10.5):

ST: *Most of the time, it's just a nice way to meet face to face and have a synchronous conversation. We get a better sense of each other. These calls usually last about 10 minutes. When students are having difficulties, we may spend a little more time—maybe 20 minutes—sorting out the problem.*

Figure 10.5 A Screen from a Live Session with Scott

The Skype sessions allow Scott to connect personally with his students. He recognizes that this is something students need because online communication lacks the energy of live physical presence:

ST: *There is nothing like the physical immediacy of living and breathing people in the room. You try to replace it [online] with videos and one-to-one Skype sessions, etc. It's really important to give space to the interpersonal stuff . . . the chitchat and connections that form relationships.*

He suggests "lowering the bar" of writing standards on the discussion board to encourage personal dialogue. He tries to keep the discussions informal and free-flowing and reserves the academic side for the assignments.

Scott relies on feedback from students to improve his instruction. For example, he tried to initiate a new activity this semester that didn't work well. So he asked his students for feedback and advice. Scott explains:

ST: *I tried to set up a buddy system where two or three students could discuss their reflections about their learning as we went along in the course. This was offered as a voluntary, ungraded opportunity for students to work with their peers. At the end of the course, they could use their discussions as the basis for their final reflection assignment.*

It was kind of dispiriting that few students took advantage of this opportunity. So I put it to the students, and asked them in an email why this isn't working. They were very forthcoming in terms of how we could make it work better. They suggested that if the groups were bigger, it might be more dynamic. And attaching some kind of credit or grade to it would make them more likely to do it.

Scott plans to try the activity again next semester with the changes the students suggested. He sees the two-way feedback as part of the learning process for both teachers and students:

ST: *As a teacher, it's important to demonstrate an open willingness to change. This is how we all learn. Sometimes*

instructors are rather defensive when things go wrong . . .
you just can't be. You just have to admit it and say, "Look, I
goofed, or this isn't working . . . " And if possible, bring
students alongside and ask them for their cooperation to solve
whatever the problem is.

The online environment gives teachers and students an opportunity to rethink how we teach and learn. As Scott points out: "It's still early days in online education in many ways. So it evolves and develops and we are all figuring it out together."

☑ Teachers use a variety of means to communicate with students throughout the course.

☑ A supportive conversational tone is used throughout the course.

☑ Course evaluation and improvement is an ongoing process.

10.7 The Ending Weeks

Discussions continue "at a relentless pace" throughout *English in the World*. Scott has found that once students are engaged and form connections with each other, they get hooked. Over the semester, his role in the discussions shifts:

ST: *I tend to withdraw a bit over time. I'm very proactive in the beginning weeks. I'm in there participating in the discussions constantly. I do a lot of modeling. I offer information and share what I think about issues. In the middle, I do a little less of that. By the end, I challenge and provoke the students. Rather than saying, "That's great," I might say, "Well, that's interesting, but have you thought about . . . ?" I will press them, especially if students are not showing much original thought. Or they are ready to be pushed further.*

During the ending weeks of the course, Scott helps students stay on track to complete the requirements. He posts reminders of upcoming deadlines and makes himself available to help. Sometimes students have problems fulfilling requirements. For example, at the end of this course, a student asked for an "Incomplete" in the course (an "Incomplete" allows the student extended time after the semester ends to fulfill course requirements and receive a grade).

ST: *This student wrote to me to say how busy she was and asked for an "Incomplete." This drives me crazy! I tried to dissuade her, saying it is not in her best interest or mine to have this going on beyond the end of the course. I asked what she needed to get the job done and she said, "a couple weeks." So I suggested she focus on completing the assignment rather than participating in the discussion for two weeks. I explained that she would lose the participation points toward her grade, but would accomplish a more important goal by completing the assignment on time.*

This student prioritized her time and finished the assignment. Sometimes students just need a little help organizing their time and committing themselves to the task.

Scott asks his students to keep a journal throughout the semester to record their reflections about the readings, lectures, and discussions. At the end of the course, the students write a 1,500-word summary of their thoughts, responding to these questions:

- What ideas or arguments will I take with me from this course?

- What areas, if any, do I feel I still need to explore? How?

- How do I situate myself in relation to the main themes of the course?

- How can I expect to apply what I have learned?

The students' answers to these questions revealed significant growth in understanding of language, culture, identity, and pedagogy. One student remarked that she was surprised by her own evolution:

> **Student:** As I read one of my past discussion board posts, I was surprised to find out that I was against code mixing in class. My reason back then was because I believed students had to fully immerse in the target language environment for them to effectively learn in the least time possible. However, my attitude toward code mixing in class has subtly shifted and reformed. Now I don't see code mixing as a threat in the classroom anymore. Instead, I think it can be used wisely by a teacher to clarify misunderstandings. The value of students' LI is something I use to overlook . . .

Scott sees this kind of growth frequently in his online students. The end-of-course surveys distributed by the university suggest that Scott's students are also satisfied with the course: 91% of them agreed or strongly agreed with the statement "Overall, my learning experience in this course was positive."

- ☑ Reminders about the due dates for submitting assignments are posted online.

- ☑ Teachers encourage students to take responsibility for their learning.

- ☑ Activities include opportunities for students to review, synthesize, and reflect on their learning.

- ☑ Teachers track students' progress and offer them support to keep up with the course.

- ☑ The teacher monitors discussions and facilitates the learning process.

- ☑ A variety of information (student performance data, feedback, etc.) is used to evaluate the effectiveness of course design and instruction.

- ☑ Reflection on teaching provides information for course improvement.

10.8 The Essentials of Online Teaching

Throughout this guide, we have presented different kinds of online courses that range in subject matter, student populations, and instructional approaches. We have shared many teachers' strategies for teaching effectively online. While their courses vary in significant ways, these teachers—such as like Scott—share an informed perspective about their online teaching. They:

- understand their students' needs and the context in which they teach;

- have explored the tools and features of their online environment;

- have a thorough understanding of their course design;

- understand their role in supporting students' learning;

- know how to encourage students to participate and motivate them to do their best;

- know when to lead, when to facilitate, when to watch, and when to reach out to help students learn;

- assess students' progress and adjust their teaching strategies as needed; and

- reflect on their practice and continually seek to improve the course and become better teachers.

If you are new to online teaching and learning, the thought of instructing through technology can be daunting. It's really not as complicated as it may seem. With an open mind and playful attitude, you can explore the tools and dynamics of the online environment and get a feel for how it works. You can learn the basic technologies that allow you to communicate with students and carry out instructional tasks. The real challenge is noticing the decisions that require your attention as you set up and teach the course. This is where the standards offered throughout this guide can help.

Each standard highlights a different aspect of instruction that requires a decision. Simply recognizing the instructional choice informs your practice. For example, in Chapter 8, we include the standard:

☐ **Discussions begin with a compelling prompt that invites a range of responses.**

Checking your discussion prompts brings awareness to their instructional importance. Likewise, all the standards in this guide point to teaching decisions that have a significant impact on students' online experience. The standards do not provide a recipe for success, but they name the ingredients to consider as you make teaching decisions and provide guidance that will help you achieve your instructional goals.

10.9 Summary and Standards

Scott Thornbury's online course *English in the World* provides an example of the standards of good practice in action. This course was used as a case study to demonstrate how the instructional issues described throughout this guide can be handled online. Scott has thought through his course with his students in mind. He has a clear idea about his role as their teacher and his teaching reflects this awareness.

Scott's teaching of *English in the World* illustrates the use of many of the standards included throughout this guide. Instead of listing the standards here, we have included a complete list in Appendix A.

References and Further Reading

Greene, M. (1989). The question of standards. *Teachers College Record*, *91*(1), 9–14. Retrieved from www.tcrecord.org

Using the Standards Checklist

A.1 Pedagogical and Management Strategies

☐ Online teaching is aligned with the priorities and practices of the host institution. (C2, p. 46) (C10, p. 276)

☐ A syllabus including contact information, a course outline, requirements, and expectations for student participation is accessible from the start of the course and throughout. (C4, p. 104) (C10, p. 281)

☐ Information on the syllabus and introductory course material is reviewed with students at the beginning of the course. (C5, p. 130) (C10, p. 285)

☐ Learning activities and course requirements are clearly defined and explained to students. (C5, p.152) (C6, p. 158)

☐ All graded activities are listed at the beginning of the course. (C9, p. 241)

☐ Due dates for submission of assignments are clear. (C4, p. 112) (C9, p. 244)

☐ The manner of submission for graded assignments is clear. (C9, p. 244)

☐ Teachers use a variety of means to communicate with students throughout the course. (C3, p. 70) (C5, p. 132) (C10, p. 288)

☐ Email facilitates private conversations between teachers and students, or among students. (C3, p. 69) (C10, p. 279)

☐ Students are provided with several options to receive support for procedural, technical, and content-related issues. (C5, p. 133) (C10, p. 285)

☐ Instructions direct students to initial course activities. (C4, p. 115)

☐ A consistent routine of weekly course activities is established to help online learners organize their schedules. (C4, p. 110) (C5, p. 152)

☐ Sufficient time is allotted for students to complete the learning activities. (C4, p. 112)

☐ Enrolled students who have not participated in the course during the first weeks are contacted. (C5, p. 134)

☐ Weekly announcements call students' attention to important and timely course information. (C3, p. 63) (C10, p. 279)

☐ Teachers provide students with guidelines for using resources. (C3, p. 80)

☐ Reminders about the due dates for submitting assignments are posted online. (C7, p. 189) (C10, p. 290)

☐ Teachers and students can easily track learners' progress. (C3, p. 88) (C9, p. 254) (C10, p. 285)

☐ The rights and privacy of students are protected in accordance with the laws and policies that govern all the institution's courses. (C6, p. 172)

☐ Students are given clear instructions about course closure. (C7, p. 200)

A.2 Engaged Teaching and Learning

☐ Teachers and students are active participants in the learning process. (C1, p. 26) (C10, p. 271)

☐ Online teaching is tailored to meet the needs of the particular student population served. (C2, p. 40) (C10, 274)

☐ Teachers encourage students to take responsibility for their learning. (C7, p. 192) (C9, p. 262) (C10, p. 290)

☐ A teacher's introduction within a course personalizes his or her online interaction with students. (C4, p. 120)

☐ A supportive conversational tone is used throughout the course. (C5, p. 145) (C10, p. 288)

☐ Opportunities for frequent teacher-student interaction are provided. (C6, p. 163)

☐ Discussion forums are used to support online course interaction. (C3, p. 67) (C10, p. 279)

☐ Discussions are set up with a clear purpose and guidelines for participation. (C8, p. 214) (C10, p. 292)

☐ Discussions begin with a compelling prompt that invites a range of responses. (C8, p. 214) (C10, p. 292)

☐ The teacher monitors discussions and facilitates the learning process. (C8, p. 219) (C10, p. 290)

☐ Activities and instruction engage students in a range of thinking skills, including critical and creative thinking, analysis, and problem-solving. (C2, p. 42)

☐ Learning resources include authentic materials and relate to real-life applications. (C3, p. 78)

☐ Activities include opportunities for students to review, synthesize, and reflect on their learning. (C7, p. 196) (C8, p. 234) (C10, p. 290)

A.3 Selection and Use of Technology

☐ Learning activities and ease of use determine the best technologies to use. (C2, p. 45) (C3, p. 60) (C10, p. 275)

☐ Teachers are competent in the use of the digital tools and resources necessary to teach the online course. (C3, p. 92) (C10, p. 281)

☐ Introductory activities help students master technical competencies required to participate in the course. (C5, p. 129)

☐ Courses include a variety of relevant multimedia to support learning and appeal to individual preferences. (C3, p. 78) (C10, p. 276)

☐ Learning resources are shared in formats that are accessible to all students. (C3, p. 78)

☐ Correct, working links are provided to course materials and resources. (C4, p. 122) (C10, p. 281)

☐ Students are informed about procedures to follow in the event of technical difficulties. (C4, p. 123) (C9, p. 244)

A.4 Collaboration

☐ Learners are encouraged to interact with others (classmates, guest speakers, etc.) and benefit from their experience and expertise. (C3, p. 79) (C5, p. 148) (C6, p. 165) (C10, p. 285)

☐ Initial course activities provide an opportunity for students to interact with their teacher and peers. (C4, p. 117) (C5, p. 138) (C10, p. 285)

☐ Collaborative activities are used to encourage students to learn from each other and develop interpersonal skills. (C8, p. 206)

☐ The purpose and procedures for collaborative activities are clearly explained. (C8, p. 227)

☐ There are sufficient opportunities for learners to work collaboratively. (C8, p. 206)

☐ Students are grouped deliberately for different kinds of learning activities. (C8, p. 209)

☐ Group work is designed to allow sufficient and flexible time for students to collaborate asynchronously. (C8, p. 227)

☐ Teachers monitor and assist students in collaborative work as needed. (C8, p. 233)

A.5 Assessment

☐ The course includes ongoing and frequent assessment. (C3, p. 81) (C9, p. 254)

☐ The means and criteria for assessment are clearly explained to students. (C9, p. 247)

☐ The relationship between learning outcomes and assessments is evident. (C9, p. 244)

☐ The relationship between graded elements and the final grade is clear. (C9, p. 241)

☐ The consequences of missed deadlines are stated and fair. (C9, p. 241)

☐ The consequences of cheating and plagiarism are clearly explained to students. (C9, p. 263)

☐ Students are given clear expectations and criteria for assignments. Examples are included for clarification when needed. (C7, p. 189)

☐ Criteria/rubrics clearly inform learners about how they will be assessed on specific assignments and online participation. (C3, p. 84) (C8, p. 217) (C9, p. 247)

☐ Self-assessment and peer-review activities are included to help learners improve their study habits and the quality of their work. (C9, p. 262)

☐ Assessment takes into account the fact that online students have access to resources on the Internet and lack supervision while completing assignments and exams. (C9, p. 263)

A.6   Feedback

- ☐ Ongoing feedback about students' progress toward learning outcomes is provided. (C9, p. 258)

- ☐ Feedback from a variety of sources corrects, clarifies, amplifies, and extends learning. (C7, p. 192) (C9, p. 262)

- ☐ Feedback is personalized, specific, and action-oriented. (C9, p. 258)

- ☐ Teacher feedback is provided in a timely fashion. (C5, p. 138) (C9, p. 258) (C10, p. 271)

- ☐ Teachers track students' progress and offer them support to keep up with the course. (C7, p. 189) (C10, p. 290)

A.7   Course Evaluation and Improvement

- ☐ Course evaluation and improvement is an ongoing process. (C5, p. 153) (C6, p. 172) (C10, p. 288)

- ☐ A variety of information (student performance data, feedback, etc.) is used to evaluate the effectiveness of course design and instruction. (C6, p. 172) (C7, p. 199) (C9, p. 254) (C10, p. 290)

- ☐ Reflection on teaching provides information for course improvement. (C5, p. 153) (C10, p. 290)

- ☐ Changes made to a course in progress are clearly communicated to students and respect the established workload and time requirements. (C6, p. 176)

Index

accountability 26, 249

Anderson, Joyce xi, 46, 48, 49, 141, 159,160, 166, 194,195, 204

announcements
  definition 21, 62
  examples 61, 63, 80, 130, 159, 160, 181, 188, 195, 201, 243
  uses of 30, 50, 60, 63, 97, 128, 130, 158,159, 218, 224, 276, 279, 294
  writing conventions of 145

Anspacher, Stephen v

Archibald, William xi, 161

assessment 238–266
  curriculum alignment 101, 169, 265
  evaluating competencies 14, 16
  feedback 11, 17, 19, 25, 220, 239, 254–258, 266, 270
  gathering data 239, 247–252, 262, 265
  grading 239, 265
  group work 227, 232–234,
  participation in discussions 211, 214–217, 249
  peer review 15, 43, 50, 87, 169, 173, 192, 205, 209, 229, 258–260, 262, 265, 266, 297
  purposes of 238
  rubrics 82, 84, 97, 98, 214–217, 235, 246–247, 265
  self-assessment 82, 107, 148, 192, 234, 261–262, 263, 266
  student progress 7, 9, 11, 81–88, 97, 187

tests and quizzes 21, 58, 250–251, 264
time spent on 31

assessment of course *see* course improvement

assessment plan 103, 190, 214–217, 239–244, 265, 280

assessment tools
  assignments 81, 255, 263, 265
  gradebook 87, 132, 252
  LMS quiz and exam editor 86

assignments
  assessment of 81, 255, 263, 265
  due dates 265, 290
  examples 58, 74, 108
  LMS tool 81–82
  feedback on 275
  submission of 265, 275

asynchronous communication
  collaboration 206, 235, 296
  definition and explanation 19, 23, 30, 32
  flexibility 60, 108, 183
  individualized instruction 162, 270
  self-directed learning 36, 148, 183
  time management 110, 141, 146, 175, 259
  wait time 258

beginning weeks 126–154, 281
Bender, Tisha xi, 77, 219, 236
blogs 15, 21, 91, 92, 122, 128, 139, 142, 152, 169, 194, 262, 263
Bloom's Taxonomy of Learning 41

cheating 238, 262–264, 266

class size 14, 19, 39, 45, 52, 121, 274

collaboration
  benefits 205, 224
  conditions for success 207, 224
  drawbacks 207
  group size 208–209
  managing 90, 208
  using asynchronous
    communication 206, 224
  see also group work; online
    discussion

collaborative tools 88–90, 224

collaborative resources 88–90

Competency-Based Online Course
  assessment of 253
  definition 15

concept mapping tool 194

Coronado, Carmen xi, 37, 40, 264

course see online course

course calendar 109

course design
  assessment of 171–173, 184, 187, 199, 202, 238, 290
  course calendar 109
  distinction from teaching 2, 25, 70,
  influence on teaching 31, 45, 47, 112, 166, 190, 223, 232, 233
  learning outcomes 169
  learning resources 70–86, 189
  phase 2, 11, 126
  review of 99, 101, 116, 123, 127, 153, 158, 279, 291
  student assessment 238, 245, 263
  terminology 8

course designer
  terminology 8

course improvement 51, 143, 153, 154, 157, 170–184, 198–200, 221, 268, 270, 287, 288, 290

course outline see syllabus

databases 70, 71, 73, 97

data collection
  purpose of 171–172

stored 57
tracking students' progress 171, 183–184, 199, 264

digital tools 56–96

Dunn, Robert xi, 15

Eastmond, Daniel xi, 6, 253

email
  assignment submission 242
  automated 18
  examples 158, 181–182
  external and internal email
    addresses 69, 102, 120, 123
  feedback through 144, 158, 163, 198, 218, 277, 282
  group communication 121, 131–133, 189, 224
  individual communication 16, 26–28, 31, 69, 97, 129, 131, 163, 167, 277, 279
  LMS tool 21, 50, 60, 68, 128
  time spent on 47
  writing conventions 145

end-of-course survey 198–200

ending weeks 186–202, 288–290

exams see quizzes; tests

faculty development xii, 4, 51, 52, 279

feedback 239, 254–258
  action oriented 257, 258
  automated 19, 250, 261
  evaluative 37, 51, 114, 128, 160, 204, 238, 248, 255, 270
  instructional 11, 14, 190, 195, 196, 226, 247, 255
  ongoing 239, 254, 258
  peer-to-peer 15, 192, 202, 205, 209, 258–260
  personalized 17, 25, 31, 32, 47, 135, 162–165, 183, 248, 257, 258, 275
  positive 148, 277
  specific 256, 258
  student 176, 198, 199, 220, 261, 287
  time spent on 31, 113, 166, 271

timely 138, 147, 154, 240, 242, 255, 258, 271
tools used for 43, 64, 65, 86, 87, 132, 247, 275
whole group 19, 197, 278
Freixas, Rosario xi, 38, 240, 241

Geary, Thomas M. xi, 37, 93, 95, 128, 141, 193, 232
González-Flores, Patricia i, iii, iv, xiii, 59, 245, 260
gradebook 81, 82, 87–89, 91, 132, 169, 170, 242, 249, 252–253, 261, 284
group work
  assignments 229, 234
  benefits of 205
  drawbacks of 207
  grouping students 209, 225, 229–231, 235
  management of 23, 25, 208–209, 221,
  process 233
  purpose 221, 225, 227
  roles within 228
  size 208–209
  teacher support 233
  timeline 227
  see also collaboration
guest speaker 23, 78–79, 97

host institution
  Learning Management System 20, 43, 57, 58, 92
  online program 12, 25
  policies of 172, 94, 103, 104, 172, 184, 198, 204, 263,
  priorities of 35, 45–46, 51, 53, 276,
  support 51, 52, 57, 92, 128, 133, 279

icebreaker activities
  benefits of 48, 116
  example 117, 119
  introductory activity 106, 119, 131, 280, 281
  suggestions 116, 138, 211, 214

institution see host institution
institutional support
  faculty training 51, 92, 3
  technical 3,128, 133, 128, 133, 103, 279
instruction
  distinction from course design 1
  evaluating learner progress see assessment
  facilitating 25, 42, 121, 131, 156, 164, 217, 218, 235, 271, 282
  guiding 25, 135, 157–161, 189–190, 208, 217, 219, 235
  influences on 35–46
  managing 25, 38, 90, 205, 217, 225, 259, 275
  modeling 25, 37, 38, 46, 47, 50, 52, 140–144, 191–192, 218, 288
  monitoring activity 113, 156, 166–184, 189, 219
  motivating 32, 39, 47, 62, 78, 105, 121, 127, 217–218, 226, 257, 291
  presenting content 14, 25, 32, 36, 38, 41, 62, 65, 113, 139, 177, 192, 219, 235, 242, 272, 288
  questioning 14, 27, 31, 42, 79, 134, 138, 139, 144, 192, 214, 218, 221, 272, 273
  responding/answering 1, 11, 15, 25, 27, 29, 31, 37, 47, 65, 106, 110, 135–138, 140, 147, 157, 268
  see also feedback
instructor see teacher roles

learners
  characteristics of 39–40, 274
  self-directed 36, 148–152, 190–192, 259, 260, 265, 266
  terminology 9
Learning Management System (LMS)
  benefits 43, 57

beyond the LMS 92
common features 21, 43
description of 20, 32, 42
terminology 9
learning objectives *see* learning
  outcomes
learning outcomes
  assessing progress toward 9,
    81,169, 173, 175, 184, 244,
    254, 265
  equivalent to onsite 14,15,
    51
  identifying 1, 9, 11, 49, 101,
    169, 239
    in lesson plan 223
    in syllabus 102, 193, 217,
      240
  influence on instruction 40, 41,
    59, 96, 105, 106, 157, 232,
    234, 244, 257
  writing 169, 171
learning resources
  adding and adapting 56, 70–71,
    101, 121
  audio podcasts 71, 92
  databases 70, 73–74, 97
  distributing
    accessible formats 78
    identified in syllabus 50
    links to Internet 24, 70, 72–73,
      128, 280
    uploaded to Learning
      Management System (LMS)
      50, 72–73, 121, 275
  experts 70, 79, 97
  guiding use of 58, 74, 79–80,
    106, 108, 128, 177
  media selection 71–72, 75–77
  multimedia presentations 11, 70,
    76–77
  text (documents/books/articles)
    18, 47, 50, 71, 75, 77, 275
  types of 1, 58, 71, 75
  video (including lectures) 13, 18,
    21, 26, 44, 62, 71, 76, 92, 100,
    119, 139, 161, 223, 275, 278,
    280, 287
León González, María xii, 56

McCabe, Margaret Foley i, iii, iv,
  xiii, 32, 36, 55, 113, 138, 162,
  192, 217
Mansell, Damien xii, 18, 19, 38
Mayer Foulkes, Benjamín xi, 38,
  109
Massive Open Online Courses
  (MOOCs) 13, 14, 18–19, 32,
  38
middle weeks 156–184, 285–287
multimedia presentations 76–77

networked learning 24

online course
  asynchronous communication
    23
  definition 9, 12
  delivery modes 13
  instructional models 12–20
  phases-continuum 2
  timeframe 102, 108
  typical week (*example*) 26–29
online discussion
  facilitating 25, 42, 121, 131,
    156, 164, 217, 218, 235, 271,
    282
  participation criteria 214–216
  prompts 117, 178–180, 191,
    212–214, 292,
  tone 25, 50, 119, 144
  types of forums 211–212
online education
  evolution of 11–12, 204
  rationale 45
online environment
  asynchronous communication
    19, 23, 30, 32
  Learning Management System
    20–21, 32, 42–43, 57, 92
  networked learning 24
  remote access 23
online seminar 14
online workshop 15
onsite course 9

peer review 15, 192, 258, 260,
  262, 266

personal reflections
  assessment 245
  asynchronous communication
    206
  cheating 264
  competency-based learning
    assessment 253
  facilitating discussion 217
  feedback 162
  icebreakers 138
  learning routine 108
  mini-lectures 77
  modeling participation 192
  new technologies 59
  online collaboration 224
  online contributions 32
  online presence 143
  pacing 109
  peer-reviews 260
  student-led discussions 219
  teacher's notes 40
  teacher's roles 140
  test preparation 251
  time requirement 113
  videoconferencing 163
  videotaped contribution 161
Pescina, Marína xii, 16
podcasts 71, 92
preparing to teach online 99–123

quizzes 21, 121, 244, 250–253
  see also tests

reflective teaching 152–153
remote access 23
resources *see* learning
    resources
rubrics 82, 84, 97, 98, 214–217,
    235, 246–247, 265

self-assessment 37, 263
self-directed learning 36, 148–152,
    190–192, 259, 260, 265, 266
self-reflection 36, 91, 170,
    194–195
social networks 94–96
standards
  index of standards 293

standards-based approach i, 4
  underlying principles of 5
Stairs, Allen xii, 14, 38, 140
students *see* learners
syllabus
  components of 101–104
  course plan 1, 8, 11, 21, 111,
    126, 193, 220, 240, 244, 280,
    281, 285
  examples 49, 104, 241
  institutional policies regarding
    104
  posted in the LMS 50, 99, 114,
    280
  review of 101, 106, 114, 129,
    130, 133, 285
synchronous communication
  definition 19, 60
  uses of (chat, telephone,
    videoconferencing, webinars)
    16, 19, 61, 78–79, 274, 278,
    286

teacher beliefs 35, 36, 46,
    272–274
teacher roles 37–38
teaching assistants 121
teaching dilemmas
  facilitating discussions 147
  group projects 228
  instructional tools 44
  pacing course work 112
  social networks 94
  student-directed learning
    190
teaching responsibilities 24–25
Teaching Tips
  concept-mapping tools 194
  contacting students 129
  course plan revision 105
  follow-up questions 42
  gradebook 252
  institutional policies 104
  live sessions 79
  management solutions 259
  online environment 92
  personal email addresses 69
  real data 73

self-directed learning 149
small groups 209
student assessment 261
synchronous communication
   61
teaching assistants and
   facilitators 121
teacher journal 221
technical problems 244
technical support 3, 103, 122,
   124, 128, 133, 128, 133, 103,
   244, 279
tests 21, 121, 244, 250–253
   see also quizzes
text-based interaction 44
Thornbury, Scott xii, 38, 93, 95,
   116, 117, 119, 143, 163, 206,
   241, 242, 256, 268–292
time expectation for students
   learning the environment and
      tools 128
   maintaining consistent
      expectations 174–176, 184
   online participation 103, 108,
      128, 133, 141, 143, 284
   sample schedule 151
   time management 148–151,
      159–160, 186, 233, 235, 259,
      289
   timed tests 251
time expectation for teachers
   assessing student progress
      31

asynchronous communication
   management 19, 110, 141,
   226, 227
course management 31
interacting online 31, 136, 211,
   270, 271
planning and design 31, 105,
   124, 279
preparing materials 77, 271
providing feedback 30–31,
   270
tracking student progress 47,
   160, 165–167, 252, 270
weekly routine 26–32, 268,
   270–271
time management 30–32,
   112–114, 148–150, 159–160
tracking students' activity
   166–168, 171, 177
tracking students' progress 171,
   183–184, 199, 264

Vai, Marjorie ii, xii, 21, 34, 102,
   125, 169, 174, 185
video conferencing 16, 78, 93,
   189, 224, 226, 286
video lectures see learning
   resources

Webinar course 16–17
Wheeler, Adrienne xii

Yalda, Sepi xii, 61, 74, 108, 251